THE
OIL MAN
AND
THE SEA

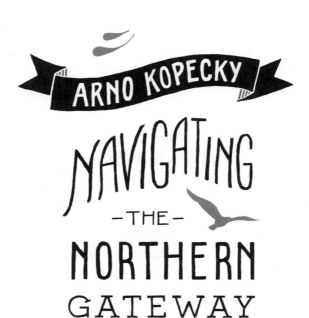

ARNO KOPECKY

NAVIGATING

-THE-

NORTHERN

GATEWAY

The OIL MAN and the SEA

DOUGLAS & McINTYRE

Douglas and McIntyre (2013) Ltd.
P.O. Box 219, Madeira Park, BC VON 2H0
www.douglas-mcintyre.com

Cataloguing data available from Library and Archives Canada
ISBN: 978-1-77100-107-6 (paper)
ISBN: 978-1-77100-108-3 (ebook)

Edited by Trena White
Copy edit by Elaine Park
Indexed by Morgan Davies
Cover and interior design by Jessica Sullivan
Cover spot illustrations by Michael Nicoll Yahgulanaas
Map by Roger Handling
Additional photo credits: Arno Kopecky pages 60, 68,
122, 218, and photo insert pages 1 (bottom), 8.
Printed in Canada

Douglas and McIntyre (2013) Ltd. would like to acknowledge
the financial support from the Government of Canada through the
Canada Book Fund and the Canada Council for the Arts, and from
the Province of British Columbia through the BC Arts Council and the
Book Publishing Tax Credit.

CONTENTS

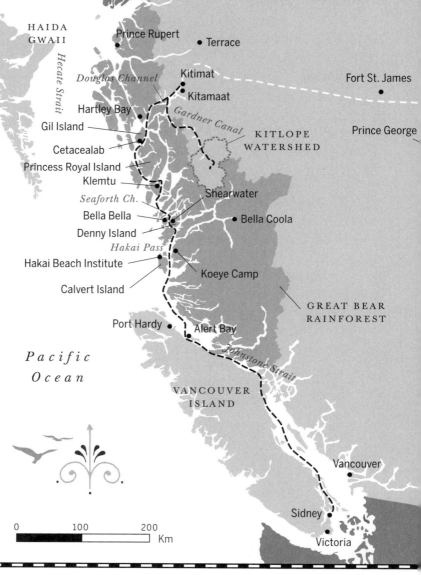

ALASKA

BRITISH COLUMBIA

HAIDA GWAII

Hecate Strait

Prince Rupert

Terrace

Douglas Channel

Kitimat

Kitamaat

Hartley Bay

Fort St. James

Gardner Canal

KITLOPE WATERSHED

Prince George

Gil Island

Cetacealab

Princess Royal Island

Klemtu

Seaforth Ch.

Shearwater

Bella Bella

Bella Coola

Denny Island

Hakai Pass

Hakai Beach Institute

Koeye Camp

Calvert Island

GREAT BEAR RAINFOREST

Port Hardy

Alert Bay

Pacific Ocean

Johnstone Strait

VANCOUVER ISLAND

Vancouver

Sidney

Victoria

0   100   200
Km

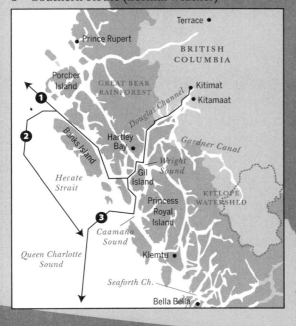

Foxy's route from
Sidney to Kitimat

Proposed Northern
Gateway route

Kitlope Watershed

Fort St. John

Dawson Creek

Tumbler Ridge

A L B E R T A

Oil Tanker Routes (inset map)
1 – Northern Route (normal weather)
2 – Southern Route (heavy weather)
3 – Southern Route (normal weather)

Bruderheim

Edmonton

Terrace

Prince Rupert

BRITISH
COLUMBIA

Porcher
Island

GREAT BEAR
RAINFOREST

Kitimat

Kitamaat

Douglas Channel

Banks Island

Hartley
Bay

Gardner Canal

Hecate
Strait

Wright
Sound

Gil
Island

KITLOPE
WATERSHED

Princess
Royal
Island

Caamaño
Sound

Klemtu

Queen Charlotte
Sound

Seaforth Ch.

Bella Bella

U S A

Foxy *making way*.

CONTENTS

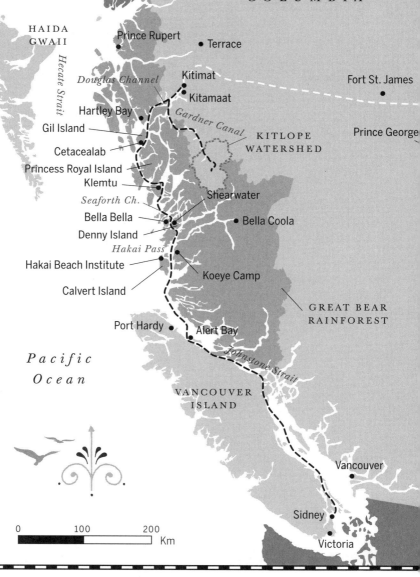

ALASKA

BRITISH
COLUMBIA

HAIDA
GWAII

Hecate Strait

Prince Rupert

Terrace

Douglas Channel

Kitimat

Kitamaat

Hartley Bay

Gardner Canal

KITLOPE
WATERSHED

Fort St. James

Prince George

Gil Island

Cetacealab

Princess Royal Island

Klemtu

Seaforth Ch.

Shearwater

Bella Bella

Bella Coola

Denny Island

Hakai Pass

Hakai Beach Institute

Koeye Camp

Calvert Island

GREAT BEAR
RAINFOREST

Port Hardy

Alert Bay

Johnstone Strait

*Pacific
Ocean*

VANCOUVER
ISLAND

Vancouver

Sidney

Victoria

0   100   200
Km

1

BY ANY
❧ OTHER NAME ❧

THE FIRST time I ever got stranded at sea, I was hunting spirit bears in the Great Bear Rainforest.

The people who rescued me were citizens of the Kitasoo Nation (and Canada, too) from a very small town called Klemtu. Like many reserves on British Columbia's central coast, Klemtu had a dark past with a brightening future, all resting on the shoulders of some three hundred survivors of the trials of the past two centuries. Buried in a vast marine labyrinth at the western edge of Canada's public transport infrastructure, the Kitasoo capital wasn't the easiest place in the world to reach, but it wasn't the hardest either. To get there I'd hitchhiked from Victoria to the top of Vancouver Island, caught a north-bound ferry across Queen Charlotte Strait, transferred to a twenty-foot water taxi in the middle of the night, and less than twenty-four hours after setting out to sea I was stepping on to Klemtu's weathered dock in the watery light of dawn.

It was April of 1999 and I was travelling with two university friends who were on spring break, like me. We'd read all about the Great Bear Rainforest, which back then was but an unofficial name dreamed up by environmentalists who hoped an emotive title would improve the region's odds of surviving the twenty-first century. Among their inspirational appeals was a coffee table book called *The Great Bear Rainforest: Canada's Forgotten Coast*, that happened to be co-written by my first journalism professor, Cameron Young, along with Ian and Karen McAllister, a young conservationist couple whose photography laid bare a hyper-lush wilderness few Canadians knew existed in their country. The trio recruited Robert F. Kennedy Jr. to write the book's cautionary foreword: "If we ever had country like that in the United States," he warned, "we've long since destroyed it."

At that time, the greatest perceived threat to the region came from Canadian chainsaws and American softwood lumber markets. Over 80 per cent of Vancouver Island's old growth forest had been logged, but here, just to the north, lay the world's largest remaining tract of coastal temperate rainforest, spread across 70,000 square kilometres of fjords and evergreen islands. While not exactly a stranger to industry, the Great Bear Rainforest was isolated and rugged enough to have been spared the worst excesses of the twentieth century, hosting enormous stands of untouched old growth. Combined, the Great Bear Rainforest's woods and ocean shelter more biomass per hectare than any other ecosystem in the world. The Kitasoo are just one of eight First Nations who have called the Great Bear Rainforest home since the end of the last ice age, making this one of the oldest continually inhabited regions on the planet. There isn't much science can say about their homeland that its residents don't already know.

Having read and written about the area, my friends and I wound up wanting to see it, too. In particular we hoped to see a kermode, or "spirit," bear. The ivory-coated Ursidae, in fact a black bear with recessive genes, lives in greater concentrations here than anywhere else on the planet, making it a darling of the ecotourist press and thus the Great Bear Rainforest's unofficial mascot.

Spirit bears don't hang around Klemtu much, but nearby Princess Royal Island was reportedly teeming with them. The only problem was that no ferry would take us there; we'd hoped instead we could find a fisherman who might take us to Princess Royal Island for a fee and pick us up one week later. Seven days of camping, we figured, would give us a fair chance at capturing our own spirit bear on film.

Nice plan, but at this hour none of the half-dozen boats tied to the dock's rusted cleats appeared to have any surviving owners. Above us, Klemtu's single paved road was deserted, and beyond that the town's weathered collection of wooden houses looked as inhabited as an archaeology site. Meanwhile the clouds that had been spitting on and off throughout the night were starting to gush in earnest, forcing us to put garbage bags on over Gore-Tex raincoats that had seemed impermeable two days earlier.

We were wondering how long to wait before we started knocking on doors when a bearded face appeared in the window of a houseboat at the end of the dock. It belonged to a treeplanting foreman from Vancouver Island; he was the only non-Kitasoo in Klemtu aside from us, we discovered when he invited us in for tea. After listening bemusedly to our story, he agreed to give us the ride we needed in his company boat.

It was a fifteen-kilometre ride from Klemtu to the southeastern tip of Princess Royal, which lies roughly eighty kilometres long and half as wide and is perforated by a number of deep inlets. It is the biggest island in the Great Bear Rainforest, and we had no idea where on it to go. Our benefactor, no kermode whisperer, understandably took us to the closest approachable bay—however soft the moss-coated forests looked, the islands from which they sprouted were made of solid granite and didn't offer a plenitude of safe landings. The bay we eventually entered had a narrow mouth that protected it from prevailing winds and currents, with still green water and a narrow gravel beach crowded by cedar, spruce and hemlock. Underneath the needled canopy a dense profusion of ferns and devil's club and thorny berry bushes crowded the forest floor. It felt like stepping into an Emily Carr painting.

It didn't take long for the thrill of our arrival to fade into a week-long state of humbled disappointment. The combination of dense bush and jagged terrain made bear-questing a physical impossibility; there was no corridor bigger than a mouse trail. Aside from an impressive diversity of bird, rodent, and insect life, the only animal we would see throughout our sojourn was the single adolescent rockfish we managed to hook from shore. Most of that rain-soaked week was spent bundled up and reading in our tents.

It wasn't the worst place to finish *Moby Dick*, but we were happy to see our ride show up when the appointed hour came. Less exciting was the moment, halfway back to Klemtu, when we heard his engine belch and die. Just like that, we were adrift, floating between green daggers, pushed gently but inexorably towards them by the inching current of a dropping tide.

And that was when the Kitasoo came to save us. One distress call over the VHF and Klemtu dispatched a trawler to pick us up. It chugged into sight within half an hour, and packed behind the gunwales we saw some twenty Kitasoo crowded on deck, all swathed in excellent rain gear and unabashedly relishing the spectacle of four white folks in need of rescue. Their amusement was affectionate, even collegial (it wasn't like they wanted to be paid, or had never been stranded themselves), and their laughter as they tossed us our tow-lines was contagious. But those smiles also contained a wink of historical irony. Who, they said without saying, is depending on whom now?

Without their intervention we'd eventually have drifted into an island, probably wrecked the boat, and possibly gone for a quick, frigid swim before clambering onto shore; but drowning was never more than a distant possibility, so it may be hyperbolic to say our lives were saved. Still, this was not a great place to be shipwrecked. Our week on Princess Royal had, if nothing else, driven home the deceptive nature of the surrounding abundance. What looked verdantly inviting from a distance turned out to be prickly, cold, and, at least for the ignorant outsider, inedible. Life may thrive here from treetop to ocean bottom, but for humans to carve their own niche into it requires a great deal of knowledge and preparation.

But we weren't shipwrecked. We were saved. After many profuse thank-yous and self-ribbings, we walked into Klemtu's sole café and drank a few pots of coffee. Later that day we caught a water taxi out of Klemtu, then a ferry back to Vancouver Island, and went back to summer classes in Victoria. I never saw Klemtu again.

In the summer of 2012, however, I did go back to the Great Bear Rainforest.

THE NAME WAS official by then. In 2006 the federal government had signed the Great Bear Rainforest Agreement, protecting one third of the region from logging and placing the rest under joint management of First Nations, industry groups, and British Columbia's provincial government—a celebratory moment in certain circles, but one that quickly passed. No sooner had the Great Bear Rainforest been baptized than Canadians started hearing it called the Northern Gateway, and a fresh battle began.

"Northern Gateway" would have made a nice allusion to local history, this being the gate through which humanity first entered the Americas, but of course that wasn't the idea. Enbridge Inc., the Calgary-based oil and gas pipeline conglomerate that coined the new name, was thinking of the future, not the past: from now on, this gate would swing into Asia rather than out of it, and it wouldn't be people who passed through but oil, or something very like it.

Not huge by global standards, but pretty big by Canada's, Enbridge is the country's third largest energy corporation, with about 6,000 employees and annual profits approaching $1 billion. More significantly, it is Canada's largest transporter of crude oil, moving over 2 million barrels a day through 25,000 kilometres of pipeline. This network represents the largest single conduit of oil flowing into the United States, with Enbridge pipelines accommodating 13 per cent of American oil imports.

Even so, the company didn't attract much media attention until 2010, when, following a decade or so of political and logistical reconnaissance, Enbridge filed its Northern Gateway Project application with the National Energy Board. From that moment forward, at least in western Canada, Enbridge became a household name.

That also happened to be the year I moved back to Canada after several years of living abroad. I settled in a coastal town near Vancouver, and as the weeks in my new home turned to months and years, the subject of the Northern Gateway proposal mushroomed around me. It was the kind of thing you heard discussed mostly in superlatives, on TV and in the paper and at the pub. Depending who was talking, Enbridge was either going to save the country or destroy it.

The media hammered home the details: an 1,177-kilometre pipeline linking Alberta's tar sands to British Columbia's central coast; more than half a million barrels of bitumen per day being piped across the Rocky Mountains and crossing a thousand waterways, more than half of which bear salmon; a projected construction cost of $5 billion, then $5.5 billion, then $6 billion. But the most fraught portion of the bitumen's journey didn't even start till the pipeline ended, in the deepwater port of Kitimat. There, at the head of an 80-kilometre-long inlet called Douglas Channel, the bitumen would be loaded onto oil tankers destined principally for China. Approximately 225 tankers a year would be hauling their 2-million-barrel payloads not just through Douglas Channel, but also through the 200 kilometres beyond it of inlets, sounds, channels and straits separating Kitimat from the open ocean. This prospective route wound directly through the turbulent heart of the Great Bear Rainforest, henceforth to be thought of as the Northern Gateway.

From the moment it was announced, the federal government embraced the proposal as its own. It wasn't hard to see why. The project, according to Enbridge's estimates (which the government also adopted), would create nearly four thousand jobs during three years of construction and was expected to raise Canada's GDP by $270 billion over the following three decades. Royalties and tax revenue would pour $86 million a year into Canada's public purse, to be divvied up between federal, provincial and municipal governments.

In a time of American decline, Northern Gateway offered the additional prize of access to Asia's awakening energy markets, where our unconventional crude stood to fetch up to thirty dollars more per barrel than refineries in the U.S. midwest were offering. Selling oil to Asia, Prime Minister Stephen Harper said, was now a "national priority" central to his vision of making Canada an "energy superpower." We may have already been the world's sixth largest oil producer at just over three million barrels a day, but 95 per cent of our exports were going to the United States. That was no way for a superpower to do business.

Perhaps most importantly, Alberta's bitumen production was expected to double in the coming decade, to almost four million barrels a day (a figure that didn't include conventional oil). Yet the province was already producing more petroleum than its pipelines could handle, with some companies resorting to trains—a much more expensive and spill-prone transport option—to get their product to market.

The pressure for new pipelines and new markets was therefore immense. And of all the proposals under the National Energy Board's consideration, Northern Gateway was the only one that offered both.

Those against the project had their own numbers, of course. The most frequently cited was 03/24, 1989. It wasn't so far north of Kitimat that the *Exxon Valdez* struck Bligh Reef, and although the spill happened a generation ago, the images still seemed fresh: that dirty rainbow of a quarter of a million barrels oozing into Prince William Sound, promptly carried off by currents and ultimately contaminating almost two thousand kilometres of Alaskan shoreline. More than eleven thousand people were recruited for cleanup operations that lasted three years and cost approximately $2 billion U.S. That figure was but a fraction of the disaster's total price tag. According to the *Exxon Valdez* Oil Spill Trustee Council, established by the state of Alaska, the state lost another $2.8 billion in foregone tourism revenue over the following decade. The tourists may have come back eventually, but a quarter-century later, the herring fishery in Prince William Sound is still closed, salmon and shellfisheries remain stunted, and you can still scoop up oil with your bare hands on beaches more than seven hundred kilometres from where the tanker ran aground.

Fears of a similar catastrophe befouling British Columbian waters weren't based on the *Exxon Valdez* alone. British Columbia's central coast marks the northern edge of a zone early European mariners dubbed the Graveyard of the Pacific, and it continues to sink boats every year. In the first decade of the twenty-first century, five major vessels—one of them a BC ferry—sank, ran aground, or collided with another vessel at various points along the Northern Gateway tanker route itself. The largest of these ships was barely half the size of the smallest class of oil tanker Enbridge proposed to bring into Kitimat, and it stretched the imagination to suppose that such behemoths could transit this treacherous route almost every day for fifty years without a similar mishap.

Because of the project's scale, Northern Gateway was subject to a public review process in which everyone from citizens, scientists, and industry leaders (including Enbridge executives and engineers) to the government of British Columbia could express their opinions, expert or otherwise. The public hearings were headed by a three-member Joint Review Panel, who would spend two years travelling throughout the communities sprinkled along the pipeline and tanker routes, as well as a handful of nearby western cities between Edmonton and Victoria. The Joint Review Panel then had until the end of 2013 to submit its formal recommendation to the National Energy Board, which would have the final say. Their decision was expected at some point in 2014.

On paper, this all looked more or less like how a democracy should work. But on January 4, 2012, four days before the Joint Review Panel kicked off the hearings in Kitimat, Canada's prime minister snuck in a troubling preamble. Speaking during a visit to Edmonton, Stephen Harper told journalists, "Growing concern has been expressed to me about the use of foreign money to really overload the public-consultation phase." The whole review process, Harper said, was in danger of being "hijacked" by foreign-funded NGOs.

Some felt that the true hijackers were to be found in the Prime Minister's Office, since one condition of a fair and impartial public hearing is that it be free from political intervention. Sure enough, just seventy-two hours later—now the day before the public hearings began—Natural Resources Minister Joe Oliver expanded on Harper's concerns with an open letter to Canadians that instantly became a national sensation. In it, Oliver accused Northern Gateway opponents of belonging to "environmental and other radical groups that would seek to block this opportunity to diversify our trade. Their goal is to stop any major project no matter what the cost to Canadian families in lost jobs and economic growth."

If you are a writer who is interested in issues of environment and globalization, this kind of talk is strangely irresistible. Journalists (myself among them) and environmental groups were quick to respond with the obvious objections: why was foreign money okay for companies like Enbridge (whose Northern Gateway investors included China's Sinopec, among others) but not for NGOs? Since when were environmentalists against jobs? What was so radical about signing up for a public hearing to express an opinion? We were still writing our op-eds when it came out that the Canada Revenue Agency had been directed to investigate the political exertions of certain registered charities, and within months of Oliver's open letter pretty much every NGO in Canada that ever said anything about Enbridge found itself hamstrung by an audit. Of particular interest to the Canada Revenue Agency was a large non-profit called Tides Canada, which operates as a clearing house to funnel money towards smaller environmental organizations. In 2006, Tides Canada pitched in half the $120-million fund that made the Great Bear Rainforest Agreement possible, drawing emphatic praise at the time from Canada's then-minister of environment, John Baird. "I hope this is a beginning, not an end," said Baird, who didn't mind that much of the money had been raised in the United States. Six years later, Tides Canada was the one group explicitly named by Joe Oliver when journalists asked him for examples of radical environmental organizations; Tides and each of the groups it funded were all subsequently audited, though not a single case of malfeasance was unearthed (perhaps the most significant outcome of the audit threat was David Suzuki's pre-emptive resignation from the board of his own foundation). This measure was defended by none other than the new environment minister, Peter Kent, who declared on national television without a trace of irony that many of Canada's most prominent environmental groups were being used "to launder offshore foreign funds for inappropriate use against Canadian interest."

When your environment minister starts attacking environmental NGOs in order to defend Big Oil, writing an article or two from your bedroom table starts to feel like a pretty lame response. Truth was, it felt lame from the start. One of the frustrating aspects of the Northern Gateway debate was how few of its protagonists had spent any time in the Great Bear Rainforest itself. The prognostications pinging through the media were for the most part lobbed from distant urban centres, based on emotional appeal or economic theory or computer simulation rather than experience; as they fell like acid rain on millions of Canadians, these arguments did little to illuminate what life and marine conditions were like in the place whose fate we were trying to decide. My own ill-fated week on Princess Royal Island all those years ago hardly made me an authority, but thinking back on it in the light of present circumstances made me want to go back; to stay longer, explore more widely, speak with the people who lived there.

And then, an opportunity arose. Around the same time my prime minister started musing about foreign interventions, my old friend Ilja Herb decided to fulfill a childhood dream and bought himself a 41-foot sailboat. Her name was *Foxy*, and she was docked in Sidney, near Victoria at the bottom of Vancouver Island. Built in the backyard of some Vancouverite in the 1980s, *Foxy* was designed for heavy seas, with a thick fibreglass hull, a deep keel, and a short mast. She did need some repairs and refurbishings—a new genoa sail, a fresh coat of hull paint, a couple of through valves, and ten or twenty other things—but if we could patch her up, her potential was limitless. She was the kind of boat you sailed around the world. If your goal was to explore an amphibious maze the size of Switzerland, with no roads and no lodgings outside a dozen landlocked towns, *Foxy* was the mothership you needed.

As for Ilja, pronounced *Il-ya,* he was a photographer by trade, an adventurer by inclination. He'd spent most of his twenties guiding rafts down some of the world's most remote rivers and, though he wasn't big on small talk, he could tell you a great story about descending Ethiopia's Omo that involved hippos and alligators and naked locals with menacingly large penises. We shared an appreciation for out-of-the-way places, and over the years we'd teamed up occasionally to track down environmental stories in countries such as Iceland and Burma.

Now a captivating drama was unfolding in our backyard, and thanks to *Foxy* we had a rare chance to examine it up close. In the opening months of 2012, as the Northern Gateway public hearings took off beneath the roar of a national argument, we hatched a fragile plan: we would sail out of Sidney in mid-June and ascend the east coast of Vancouver Island, reaching the Great Bear Rainforest/Northern Gateway in ten days if all went well. That would give us three months before winter storms became a risk; twelve weeks to explore the proposed tanker route in fair (we hoped) weather and visit a selection of communities along it. These communities, chosen partly on the basis of geography and partly on who returned our emails, included the First Nation reserves of Bella Bella (Heiltsuk), Hartley Bay (Gitga'at), and Kitamaat (Haisla). The latter, though close in name and location, was not to be confused with the decidedly non-indigenous town of Kitimat, proposed terminus of the Northern Gateway pipeline and port of call for 225 oil tankers a year. Roughly eight hundred circuitous kilometres by sea from Victoria, Kitimat would mark the northern apex of our journey, from whence we'd turn around and head back south the same way we'd come up.

The only flaw in this plan was that neither of us knew how to sail.

Humpback whales' spouts linger in the air of the Great Bear Rainforest.

2

THE
~ IRON SAIL ~

WE LEFT under a warm drizzle of rain in the late afternoon of a windless day. It was June 30 and we were two weeks behind schedule, but we were off.

Everything went fine for the first hour. Then Ilja glanced at the engine coolant's temperature gauge and saw the needle edging into red territory. A small issue in the greater scheme. We eased up on the throttle and the engine's temperature dropped from 240 degrees to 180, putting us back in the green zone.

Two hundred nautical miles of ocean lay between us and the Great Bear Rainforest, four hundred kilometres through which we were making all the progress of a hard-paddling duck. But despite the mellow pace, the sensation of movement, and therefore of progress, was constant. Every few hundred metres a new halfmoon bay arched into view, or an all-window mansion winked in and out of sight from between cedars, or a narrow channel opened up to reveal a corridor between what looked like one island but was in fact two. At five nautical miles per hour you could spot the eagles scanning the ocean's surface from the tree branches, make eye contact with the seals who thrust their snouts out of the water with the mien of curious dogs. The light current felt like a carpet being slowly pulled out from under *Foxy*'s keel.

Ever since Ilja had purchased *Foxy* six months earlier, our thoughts had been occupied almost exclusively by things we couldn't see: prime ministers and First Nations and energy policies and changing climates and oil spill probabilities—all denizens of an abstract planet, the world of the world wide web. That realm is very different from the world of five knots. In the former, Total Distraction exerts its constant pull, so that paying attention to the space around you takes a little more effort every day; now we'd cast off into the latter, and dolphins were swimming circles around us. It took tremendous willpower to think about anything else. Whatever we couldn't grasp with our five senses slipped from our attention.

Unfortunately the wind refused to blow in our new world of physical geography, so we motored myopically north: past Coal Island, up Colburne Passage, through Satellite Channel and along the western shore of Salt Spring Island, home to arguably the greatest concentration of eccentric artists in all the eccentric Gulf Islands, though none of them were visible from sea. Only trees. Over the lightest of rapids at Sansum Narrows, giving *Foxy* her first jiggle, after which the rain turned to mist and then evaporated to reveal a high summer sun setting late over the somnambulant towns of Crofton and Chemainus, until finally, as the first stars pricked the eastern horizon's velvet curtain, Thetis Island appeared below them.

Time to drop anchor. Everyone who knew anything about sailing had told us that our moments of greatest panic would involve anchoring and docking. This was our first attempt

Skipper Zach Hyde sitting in Foxy's *cockpit during the crossing of Queen Charlotte Sound.*

at either. Everything we did would be our first attempt, because this was the first time we'd taken *Foxy* outside the marina. She'd been on the hard until a few days ago, dry-docked for repairs and refurbishments that went well into overtime for—well, for instance, the leak Ilja chased for weeks, discovering in the process how water can drip subterraneously through a boat like a mole in its burrow, popping out in places far from the point of entry so that you will have to patch a dozen suspicious cracks in the deck before the drip in your galley hold stops dripping. There was also a broken bilge pump, a non-flushing toilet, a leak in the water tank, a sink faucet that wouldn't flow, and a few dozen other Achilles' heels to consider. The last and probably most vexatious of these was our discovery that the VHF cable was no longer connected to the antenna at the top of the mast. This prompted a surprisingly complex rewiring job involving twenty metres of pinky-thick cable, two soldering irons, a spool of solder, and a new appreciation for the miracle by which the human voice is transformed from sound to radio wave, dispatched into space and shunted through a wire, only to be turned back into the original voice. But none of that taught us how to anchor.

Our solution to this, our secret weapon in the potentially life-or-death battle against Sailing Ignorance, was Zach Hyde.

Zach was another friend of mine, a born adventurer like Ilja, with the kind of hands people felt comfortable putting their lives in. He grew up in Squamish, a town wedged between mountain and sea on British Columbia's southern coast. When he was still a teenager, Zach started a one-man adventure-tourism company of sorts, taking thrill seekers to the top of the Chief (the grey monolith overlooking Squamish), where he'd buckle them into a harness and belay them down the three-hundred-metre cliff face. Later, he bought a 30-foot sailboat that he fixed up in his backyard and used for a decade exploring British Columbia's coast. Three years ago, he joined the coast guard as a deckhand, work that brought him farther north and often to the Great Bear Rainforest.

Zach understood boats, in other words, and he knew the waters we were heading into. He was the person we needed. His coast guard shifts gave him a month off at a time, and he leapt aboard *Foxy* before I could even finish asking if he'd join us for the first month of our trip to teach us how to sail. Just watching him put Ilja and me at ease: thirty-eight years old, shaven-headed, lean and nimble as a lemur, Zach scampered up and down *Foxy* in long-toed bare feet that gripped the deck like suction cups, his eyes and body in constant tandem motion. Unfortunately, our delayed departure meant we only had him for two weeks instead of four, but that, he assured us, would be enough time to reach the Great Bear Rainforest and teach us what we needed to know.

As darkness settled over our first night at sea, we needed to know how to anchor. If you were a landlubber with soft pink hands like me, you might have supposed that anchoring was a straightforward matter of lowering the anchor until it hit the bottom. But that is not the case, especially when you are on a sailboat whose anchor hasn't been used in an undisclosed period of time (the previous owner having kept her tied to a dock for years, apparently) so that the entire apparatus is rusted into place. Neither Zach nor Ilja, and certainly not I, could budge the heavy metal triangle hooked like a nose guard over *Foxy*'s bow.

The three of us inspected it like an algebraic formula. The anchor's thick chain disappeared into the V-berth below our feet; beside it was a rubber ball of a button that, when you stepped on it, was supposed to release the chain but didn't.

"There must be a switch in the V-berth that activates the windlass," Zach said. He and Ilja went down to look for the switch, while I took the helm and hit reverse every so often to keep us from drifting into the smugly anchored sailboat playing Johnny Cash off our bow. Our own stereo was still on our to-fix list, and would stay there till October. I listened to Johnny for twenty minutes while Ilja and Zach went up and down from anchor to V-berth trying unsuccessfully to make something move. Finally, Zach unscrewed the metal box into which the anchor chain disappeared.

"Yyeaahp," he said, "she could use a little grease."

After a heavy dose of WD-40 and much wrench-hammering, the huge shiv that unspools the chain let out a rusty scream and started turning. Zach hauled out twenty metres of chain by hand, drowning Johnny out completely. When he yelled at me to do so, I put the engine in reverse and hit the throttle to make sure the anchor's teeth bit into the bottom rather than slide overtop. The teeth bit. All should have been complete. Then Zach stepped backwards onto the rubber button that hadn't been working before, only by now it had awoken from its slumber and revealed that its job was not to let the chain out but to pull it back in. The windlass started spinning with a vital electric whir, accompanied by the shriek of rusted metal as the anchor chain reeled itself in at a magnificent pace. Thus engaged, the windlass switch froze anew, this time in the 'on' position, so that no amount of stepping on it could turn the windlass off. Zach and Ilja swiped frantically at the chain, which now resembled a live high-voltage wire. If they didn't knock it out of the groove that fed into the spinning shiv, the anchor would come home far too quickly, bursting from the water like Jaws and biting a hole out of *Foxy*'s fibreglass nose.

Then somebody's punch connected. The chain came out of its groove and everything stopped except the now-harmlessly spinning windlass. The whole incident took maybe ten seconds. Ilja went below decks to flip a switch that doused all the electricity on board, then helped Zach to re-lower the anchor. We went down to the galley, lit several candles, opened a bottle of red and toasted our first day at sea.

"MAYDAY, MAYDAY, MAYDAY, *this is* Rainmaker. *We are going down, over.*" Our new VHF cable was working. The call came on Channel 16, which anyone from miles around can listen to or speak on. Someone, somewhere in the waters off Vancouver Island's southeast coast was having a memorable Canada Day.

It was two in the afternoon on our second day at sea and we were at the precipice of Dodd Narrows, where the ocean pinched like an hourglass between the huge bulk of Vancouver Island and a blip called Mudge Island that hardly deserved capital letters. There was only enough room for one boat to squeeze through at a time. Zach and I were standing on the bow beneath a dappled sky, keeping a lookout in case a power boat came to meet us head-on. Ilja stood ten metres behind us at the helm, his view partly blocked by *Foxy*'s midship mast, doing his best to steer with the current at our backs.

"Should we answer that?" I asked.

"No," said Zach, "the coast guard will get on it."

The water was surging faster than *Foxy*'s propeller could keep up with, forcing Ilja to steer as though he was going backwards.

"Rainmaker, Rainmaker, Rainmaker, *this is Comox Coast Guard, what is your position, over.*"

"Fourteen!" Ilja shouted.

That was for us, not the radio. Fourteen nautical miles, or twenty-eight kilometres, per hour. The future seemed to glide into reach. This was the fastest we'd go all summer.

A crowd of holiday celebrants was gathered on the low cliffs rising off the bank, watching people like us shoot the narrows. They cheered and we cheered back. The rock walls leaned in and then out, and in less than a minute we were through, spit out and back into the wide quiet blue.

The revellers' shouts had overwhelmed *Rainmaker*'s reply. The radio was now silent; Zach said the coast guard had probably moved the conversation to a private channel. A freighter came into view, piled high with gleaming blades. The apparition of a shipment of windmill vanes struck us as a triumphant omen. Visions of Copenhagen ringed by windmills came to mind. More than enough to counteract the *Rainmaker*'s bad tidings.

Ilja went below decks, reemerged with a camera the size of a grenade launcher, and snapped his first picture.

Later, when the freighter was tiny behind us, Zach said, "if you want to get rid of a body, this is the place to do it." The coast guard ship he worked on was a research vessel; scientists lowered cameras and dead pigs to the ocean floor to study the bottom feeders at work, everything from sharks to shrimp. They always got the same result. "Two hours," Zach said, "and even the bones are gone."

Time was our bottom feeder. Summers pass quickly on this coast, and farther north they sometimes don't come at all. By September, the first of winter's tempestuous grey minotaurs could start entering the labyrinth. By October, it would likely be full of them. It was July first and we were only now passing Nanaimo, still at the bottom of Vancouver Island.

Zach was explaining that the wind in this part of the world blows predominantly from the north all spring and summer, then switches to southerly in the fall, meaning it would be in our faces the entire trip. If and when it blew at all. Meaning that we would be motoring approximately 70 per cent of the time, us, whose sailboat was meant to symbolize our commitment to a fossil fuel-free future. You could hear the oil men sharpening their rhetorical swords.

"Don't worry," Zach said. "You'll still be under sail. The iron sail."

There is a term for each direction of the wind relative to your vessel's heading, he explained. If the wind is blowing perpendicular to your course, that is a beam reach. If it is coming from behind you, that is a broad reach. If the wind is blowing directly in your face, you are heading into the irons. Hence the iron sail. But no point dwelling on that now, nor the fact that in two weeks the only person on this ship who knew how to sail it would go back to his job keeping pig-plunging marine biologists afloat, leaving Ilja and me skipperless.

(Some things we had to learn in those two weeks: how to read the library of information contained in nautical charts; how to plot a course; how to read the tide and current tables in order to calculate the speed and direction of current in location X at time Y; how to dock at a busy marina; how to hoist and trim the sails; how to tack into the wind and gybe with it; how to tell which way a ship is going at night by the colour of its lights; how to operate the radar, the autopilot, the iPad's navigational software . . . and a few other details.)

A dozen small triangles appeared on the horizon, waggling at the sky like teepees on a windy plain. Zach was the first to notice. He pointed out the approaching line in the water where Gabriola Island's smooth wind shadow ended and the surface became rumpled with white flecks.

"Look at it licking up," Zach said, visibly excited. Ilja fumbled with a tangle of rope, and Zach helped him—"this is the sheet you want"—showing Ilja which rope to pull.

"Why are ropes called sheets, not sails?" I asked. "Seems sails should be sheets."

"Sails are sails and ropes are sheets," said Zach.

"And maps are charts," said Ilja.

Charts I was learning to read, but I remained illiterate in the language of the sheet. To my eyes *Foxy* was covered in a vine-like profusion of hopelessly fragmented sentences, a ropy series of non sequiturs and misplaced modifiers that looped around the decks and disappeared into the base of the mast, only to reemerge from its crown fifteen metres up without the slightest connection to their opening clauses.

Zach didn't suffer my condition. He could read the full length of every sheet on the boat, grasp all their origins and endings. When he hauled on the halyard, up went the main sail, and suddenly we were out of the wind shadow and into the wide Strait and *phwwooomp*—*Foxy* came alive. The sails snapped and tautened and we made seven knots under them for the rest of the day.

The wind blew us all the way to Hornby Island, where Zach's love was waiting for him.

Zach approached love the same way it approached him, like an unforecast tropical cyclone, and every time it did he fell—leapt—overboard and got tossed in heavy seas, having the time of his life until one day the storm dissipated as quickly as it burst and the sun came out and the ocean calmed and Zach swam back to his ship and sailed on.

Serena worked with Zach on the coast guard. Zach said she was "an old soul," which was his way of saying she was twenty-two years old and looked more like a Monaco princess than a deckhand. But she carried a relaxed self-confidence beyond her years, and her almond eyes had a serious edge. You only had to meet her to see why Zach had jumped.

Serena came around the boat a few times while we were still moored in Sidney, trapped in our last-minute errands. One evening before sunset, we were all at the boat when I thought I'd fill the water tank. My knack for causing mechanical damage with good intentions is well known to my friends, so I asked Ilja whether my idea and plan of execution was a good one. It was. I could tell the fuel valve apart from the water valve, yes? Yes.

There is a special tool whose sole purpose is to open water and fuel valves on boats. That part of my operation went smoothly. I turned the tap, water ran through a hose into the tank, I could hear it splashing into the tank, and Zach was on the foredeck with Serena, calling to me, "Check the bilge to make sure there's no water spilling out of the tank from some weird spot." I went down to have a look—the bilge was the wastewater accumulation zone below the engine... somewhere—but it was too dark below decks to see anything and the lights weren't turning on. (Ilja had an errand to run and when he left he stumbled over the jangle of cords and ropes and hoses scattered across the dock. One of those snakes was the cord connecting *Foxy* to the marina's electricity, and what none of us realized at the time was that Ilja had just yanked the plug out of the socket.)

I reemerged to ask Zach about the bilge's exact location and point of access. He was sitting in the cockpit with Serena by then and saying how great it would have been if she could have come with us, what with her having time off too.

"I know," I said, worried about where this could lead.

"It's a boy's trip," Serena said, "I get it."

"It's not that so much as...some of the places we're going, it'll be delicate. Mostly we'll be in reservations, and we have to be careful about how we present ourselves. We'd like to avoid, or at least minimize, the whole white-man-barging-into-Indian-territory-once-again thing."

"Did Serena tell you her mom is Ojibway?" Zach asked.

So, then. She probably didn't need me to tell her about the ethno-political sensitivities of reserve life.

"I didn't know that," I said, and spent the next few minutes trying to unmake an ass of myself.

"Don't worry about it," Zach said. "Check that bilge?"

"Right," I said. I'd been standing on the stepladder that led out of the galley into the cockpit, my body half in and half out of the fresh air, and now I stepped back down. "I meant to ask—"

My foot splashed audibly when it hit the galley floor. I was standing in ankle-deep water in the belly of our boat, where water should never be.

Unbidden, the memory came to me of the time I absent-mindedly tried to heat Ilja's electric kettle on a stovetop and so much black smoke poured out of his kitchen that it filled the halls and set off the fire alarm, forcing the evacuation of his entire apartment building, and I wondered if this was better or worse than that time.

We turned the water off, but a wading pool had already accumulated in the galley. Water everywhere. Zach knew where the bilge pump was but it wasn't working. Neither were any of the lights. The sun was down now and the galley was pitch dark and full of water.

Then Ilja came back. He'd been gone for perhaps twenty minutes, and the scene he returned to was incompatible with the one he'd left behind.

Ilja's anger, when it flared, was a palpable thing. You wished he would just swear more, but instead his aura sort of increased and enveloped the room in red emotion, with hardly a word being said. It felt in that moment like the whole trip might be off. We had already soaked every towel on board in a vain attempt to sponge the pond dry, and with the bilge pump still mysteriously wounded I volunteered to drive to Ilja's house in Victoria—forty minutes away—to pick up an industrial vacuum cleaner. By the time I got back they had discovered the cord Ilja accidentally kicked loose earlier and plugged *Foxy* back in; the bilge pump was working and the water had been drained, taking much of the tension with it. The scene, now lit by working lights, had improved from embarrassingly preventable catastrophe to a not-so-dry run in disaster management from which everyone (*Foxy* included) emerged unscathed.

Serena, who knew far more about boats and water tanks and bilge pumps than I, had caused none of this, but I didn't mind when Ilja, on our way home that night, blamed her instead of me.

"That was not your fault," he said. "If she hadn't been there, Zach wouldn't have let you ignore the water tank. A man can't concentrate on business when his woman's in the room." My ignorance was phenotypic, like a third nipple, something I couldn't be held accountable for. I was okay with that.

But now the sun was setting once again, and it was Canada Day, and Serena had driven up from Sidney while we were sailing and caught two ferries from Vancouver Island and was waiting with her friends on Hornby Island. They were on the beach at Tribune Bay, which was why we were putting into a south-facing bay even though a south wind was just starting to blow.

"It's not calling for more than ten knots," Zach said, "we'll be fine. We'll anchor and take the dinghy in and be back first thing in the morning! Serena's there with a couple friends."

In Zach's mind, the plan represented a zen-like harmonization of business and pleasure. We needed to anchor somewhere; he had a woman waiting for him here, and she'd you-never-knowingly brought two of her friends. We could go ashore after a full day's sail, have a memorable evening on shore, and be on our way in the morning with no time lost.

We anchored in twenty-four feet of water and sent Zach off on his own in an inflatable kayak. Ilja refused to leave the boat no matter what Zach said, and I couldn't leave Ilja alone. Zach spent twenty minutes trying to change our minds, the wind picking up all the while. Finally he blew up the kayak and paddled to shore, cheering as he went, just hollering into the wind. Three small figures standing on the brown sand enveloped him in warm feminine embraces while Ilja and I looked on like grounded teenagers. An hour later the night sky bloomed with fireworks.

If you have ever tried to sleep in a boat that is anchored in livid seas, you know: the sound of the anchor's chain scraping back and forth against the hull while the anchor itself drags along the ocean floor is second only to incoming ordnance on the scale of harrowing acoustical experiences. All through the night, Ilja and I got up every half hour to make sure the lights on shore were still a safe distance away, and that we were still in twenty-four feet of water.

We were not. That number diminished throughout the night because we had anchored at high tide, and down we dropped until, at dawn, I heard Ilja clamber past my head. I called out to him: "We good?"

"Not really."

We had two depth sounders on board; one was reading twelve feet and the other eight; *Foxy*'s keel ran six feet deep. Tide was dropping for another hour.

We called Zach's cell phone. There was no answer. His voice message sounded calm, even paternal, and we remembered the advice he'd given us a week ago, the same advice everyone gives to new sailors: never panic.

"We've got to pull anchor and move farther out," Ilja said.

This was a very straightforward operation for anyone who had done it before. We had done it exactly once—yesterday morning—in dead calm conditions, with Zach supervising. Now Zach was gone, the wind was trying to blow us into shore, and *Foxy* was lurching at the end of her chain.

"Okay," I said. "I guess I'll take the helm."

"Yeah. Just put her in gear and keep her pointed into the wind—"

"Into the irons, you mean."

"—until I get the anchor in."

We didn't trust the electronic windlass, but there was too much tension on the chain for Ilja to pull it up by hand on his own. But if I left the helm to help him, the boat would be blown ashore. We came up with a variation on the original plan. I started the engine and headed us slowly towards the spot where the anchor lay embedded in the sea floor, the chain slackening as I progressed so that Ilja could pull it in easily, foot by foot. Before we knew it we had not only retrieved the anchor but re-anchored in thirty comfortable feet of water. We felt like Ahab and Ishmael.

An hour later Zach appeared on shore, a slender bull with a prominent skull pumping his kayak up at the water's edge. He paddled towards us while Serena waved goodbye, and it was raining and windy and altogether miserable and Zach was cheering as he got closer, just like he'd been cheering when he left, and we were cheering back, pulling him aboard when he came into reach, clapping him on the back, asking what we missed.

FOXY WAS A narrow ship, which meant she cut easily through water but didn't have the galley space many other sailboats her length had. Living aboard her was like how I imagined pod-living in Japan: comfortably confined, with continual mild tremors that sometimes became turbulent quakes.

You entered her galley through a vertical stepladder in the cockpit, two thirds of the way to her stern, emerging into what would be a kitchen if it weren't in a sailboat, where certain household terms are forbidden. The non-kitchen had a gimbled stove that swiveled perpendicular to *Foxy*'s length, so no matter how the waves rocked us side to side the chili pot stayed still. There was a sink with a beautiful bronze hand-pumped faucet that occasionally worked, and if you removed the wooden panels below the sink you would behold Suzy, our obstreperous diesel Isuzu 3AB 37-horse engine, whose muffled roar you felt as much as heard if you were below decks. Suzy was like having a pet dragon on board whose dyspeptic moods could be discerned by the pitch at which she rumbled. *Foxy*'s designer had a psychopath's knack for compartmentalization; behind every flat surface, including the galley floor, was a stash-spot for spices, liquor, pots and pans, food, books, clothing, and all the minutia one could desire for a three-month voyage; three men could easily go for weeks without touching land if need be. There was also a small refrigerator with a locking door that sucked an immense amount of power and could therefore only be plugged in when the motor was running or if we were at shore. Beside the non-kitchen was the quarter berth, a body-length bench above which hung the VHF and electrical switchboard. That was where Zach slept.

The non-kitchen adjoined to a non-living and -dining room with wooden benches arranged around a non-dinner table that was rimmed with detachable rails to stop dishes from sliding off. It rested on a telescopic pole that could be lowered so the table's surface lay flush with the benches. My bed. A narrow hall led forward from there, past the head (not the bathroom), whose toilet we lived in perpetual fear of plugging, ending in the darkly cavernous V-berth, where Ilja slept amidst a chaos of backpacks, camera cases, spare sails stuffed into burlap sacks, guitars, ropes, books and, just past the clothing mound Ilja used for a pillow, a three-hundred-pound heap of anchor chain.

Altogether this made for a welcoming, womb-like aura below decks, and we spent a lot of time gestating inside *Foxy*. There I was on the fourth of July, hiding in the galley with Zach from a sun that had finally emerged after an interminable June-uary, watching Ilja struggle to replace a battery. Tests had indicated one of the three that powered *Foxy* was on the brink of death, but it wasn't clear which one. Ilja lay with his head and arms buried in the dark tight space where the batteries lay nestled, his trunk and legs jutting toes-down onto the quarter berth. A moment of silence had descended on our lazy banter when a *sizzzzle-crackle-SPARK* erupted from the region of Ilja's head; he let out a belly-yell and his legs twitched violently, like a frog in a high school biology experiment, and then everything—Ilja, *Foxy*, Zach and I, the universe—collapsed into silence.

But Ilja was fine, and even apologetic when he realized afterwards that Zach and I both thought we'd just watched our friend die by electrocution.

The flood of relief at Ilja's not being dead was soon replaced by the same brooding awareness of time's passage that had haunted us since before we even left—Independence Day already and we were stuck in Comox, a town on Vancouver Island from which we could see the same Hornby Island we'd left two days ago. Essential repairs—the windlass, the batteries, twin runners that needed to be rigged to the aft deck so as to stabilize the mast should a heavy blow come up—had bogged us down again.

Later that afternoon, Ilja and I were standing on the dock when Ed walked by. Ed was fifty-two, a retired school teacher who worked around the marina helping to repair boats and drink with their owners; he had a sun-blotched, eyebrowless face and a smile that was somehow glazed and brotherly at once. He carried loops of wires and an arsenal of tools in his belt. Every time he walked past *Foxy* he would joke, "And I'm supposed to be retired!"

This time he paused, and we got to talking about retirement finance, about the 2008 Wall Street crash, about children, about whether our generation had it better or worse than his. The crash hadn't hurt him too bad, said Ed, but he worried about his daughter. "She's about to get a science degree," he lamented, "and what's she going to do with *that*?"

"Be glad she's not taking up photography," Ilja said.

"Or writing," I added.

He asked what our trip was all about.

"We're heading to the central coast, as far up as Kitimat," said Ilja. "Checking out the Northern Gateway issue."

"Awareness and voice for BC's threatened coast," I said. "That's kind of our motto." Said so on our website, anyway. In order to raise money for our trip, I explained, we'd turned ourselves into a single-issue charity of sorts, hastily assembled and without actual charitable status (or any other kind of status outside Facebook), but with a promise to lend whatever voice we could to the cause of keeping oil tankers out of British Columbia's central coast.

"How much money did you raise?" he asked.

"About thirty thousand dollars."

"So you're going there with basically a Greenpeace outlook," he said.

"We won't be ramming any boats," I said, "at least not on purpose. Technically speaking, I'm a journalist and Ilja's a photographer."

"We just want to talk to interesting people with different points of view," said Ilja.

"Although we do kind of have a message," I said.

"It's a bit of a dance," Ilja said.

At any rate, all opinions were welcome at our table, we told Ed.

He thought about it a moment and decided to take us at our word. "Well, from the perspective of a retired schoolteacher," he said, "whose only real income is off investments, I have to consider what's going to make me money. And Enbridge has been a real good investment."

No denying it. The market had been betting on Enbridge since the moment Northern Gateway was announced; between 2010 and 2012 the company's stock price doubled from twenty to forty dollars.

"I mean I have some stocks in alternative energy, too," Ed wanted us to know. "But you can't put all your eggs in one basket. A lot of people who invested in solar over the last few years have taken a real beating." Ed was right. If the world was in a race to the bottom line, fossil fuel companies were winning.

"In a perfect world," I said, "oil companies would be investing their profits into solar and other alternatives, so they could keep their monopoly on energy markets and we could keep our climate. With their kind of money in research and development, maybe with a little government subsidy help, we could get a new energy infrastructure up and running before it's too late."

"Yeah," said Ed. "In a perfect world."

AFTER FOUR DAYS in Comox, Zach and Ilja finished the repairs and we pulled free, watched the Comox glacier first appear and then slip out of sight as we held a bearing of 310 degrees past bobbing motorboats inhabited by solitary middle-aged men waiting at the end of a pole for a lucky strike, past seals and dolphins and a pod of charging orcas, past the logging town of Campbell River with its neat stacks of white houses rising up the hill. There was a marina at Quadra Island where we docked for the night, and in the Landing Pub three young and cheerfully inebriated men were pretending to play pool while flirting with a bartendress who teased them without their quite realizing it. A sign on the wall read BEER: NOW CHEAPER THAN GAS, DRINK DON'T DRIVE.

We followed the suggestion. Thoughts of Northern Gateway slipped into the background while we watched the timeless animal pursuit of jockeying for sexual advantage unfold. Possibly weakened by a full day under direct sunlight, we fell into one of those "if only" conversations about owning a piece of land with a house on it and a family inside. We were all in our late thirties and none of us had any of these things.

"If my aunt had balls she'd be my uncle," Zach said. "Fuck if."

Next morning at dawn, we left Quadra under a breezeless blue sky and motored up Discovery Passage against a dying flood. "Navigation of Discovery Passage is very simple," Zach read aloud from a sailor's handbook, "except in Seymour Narrows. Here tidal streams, which at some stages of the tide attain sixteen knots, make it advisable for low-powered vessels and small craft to await slack water." Tidal streams—currents—were created by the tide surging up and down, which in turn was a result of the moon's gravitational force. Every six hours and twenty minutes the tide reached its highest or lowest point. The lows were lowest and the highs highest at full or new moons, when the gravitational pull was strongest. Four times a day, the current came to a brief halt as the tide maxed out and paused at high or low. We wanted to traverse Seymour Narrows during that pause.

Rather than a straight shot like Dodd Narrows, which we'd flown through with a strong current at our backs five days earlier, this bottleneck makes a sharp S-curve. There used to be a barely-submerged mountain peak in the middle of the Narrows called Ripple Rock that tore the belly out of more than a hundred vessels before the government blew it out of the water in 1958. That explosion was one of the first events to be televised live from coast to coast in Canada. But even without Ripple Rock you still had to be careful. If you timed it wrong you might show up when the Narrows was a swift-flowing river intent on flinging you into the rocky shore; and if you really timed it wrong there might be a wind blowing opposite to the current, which has the same effect on the ocean as petting a cat the wrong way. "Anyone who's sailed this coast for long enough will have a Seymour Narrows story," Zach said.

Our time had not yet come. We reached the Narrows exactly at high tide, when the current died and the pass that Captain George Vancouver described as "one of the vilest stretches of water in the world" was smooth as tarmac. *Foxy* joined a single file of a dozen sailboats, yachts, and seiners that had similarly timed their approach, and after passing through we all fanned out into the widening Johnstone Strait. The tide switched, dropping now, and the outflowing current gave us an extra knot.

The small cities and towns that had lit up the evening coast of our passage thus far now faded away. Unremitting forest took their place, all second or third growth. Rumpled green hills rolled back from the shore, checkered with the brown squares of clear-cuts. The occasional house, lonely and beautiful on a clifftop, or a clump of cabins set just behind the first line of trees, were the only signs of human habitation. We shared our marine highway with a light traffic of fishing boats and ageing yachts and tugboats hauling barges stacked impossibly high with shipping containers. But much of the time we saw no one. Only animals. A lone humpback spouting in the distance. A pod of killer whales steaming down the strait like linebackers rushing the endzone. A school of white-sided dolphins, hundreds of them, visible first as distant splashes before their bodies grew distinct, leaping after fish and one another or just for joy, a few individuals splitting off the group and bounding towards us, lapping *Foxy* on their sides to peer up at us, then charging off as quickly as they'd come.

Below us, feeding the dolphins and orcas, were the fish everyone thinks of when they think of British Columbia. There are five species of ocean-going Pacific salmon (six, if you count the fast-growing Atlantic salmon farmed here in open-ocean nets), and the only thing about them that everyone agrees on is that it would be a shame if they met the same fate as the Atlantic cod.

No one disputes that wild Pacific salmon populations, overall, are in decline, but confusion about the reason has allowed bureaucratic paralysis to proliferate. Compounding the bewilderment is the profusion of subgroupings that all fall under the general category of "salmon." It isn't just that there's five species, some of which are doing better than others. Each species of salmon is in turn most accurately considered one river at a time, because each river has its own distinct breeding population. Some are seeing record returns, while in others salmon have gone extinct; some rivers might have strong coho and chum runs but no sockeye or chinook left. But even the same species on the same river can tell conflicting stories, because each year's salmon run is a measure of the generation that was born four years ago. If one generation gets scooped up by a trawler, or stricken with disease, or buried by a mudslide before it's hatched—any of these and a host of other factors can ruin a river's salmon run for one out of every four years, while the other three years remain bountiful. Multiply that by the thousands of rivers, creeks, streams and tributaries perforating British Columbia's coastline, and you begin to appreciate the overall picture's complexity.

Even so, certain rivers are representative for their sheer size and fertility. The Fraser River, which hosts one of the province's most prolific sockeye runs, is one. Sockeye are the strongest of the salmon—they swim the farthest upriver to spawn—which is why their flesh is the firmest and, to most palates, the tastiest of all salmon species. On average, some eight million sockeye used to swim up it every fall, pulsing through Vancouver towards the Great Divide to spawn in the shallow gravelly waters of the Fraser's many tributaries (their homing instinct is so precise that each one will die in the exact stream where it was born). But in the 1990s the Fraser's numbers started plummeting, and they kept falling even after the Department of Fisheries and Oceans sharply curtailed the local commercial fishery. The situation came to a head in 2009 when only 1.4 million sockeye made it home, a record low that suggested the river's population had entered a terminal decline. The next year, however, 35 million sockeye returned, the most prolific run in a century. Then in 2011 came another, milder bust, with 4.5 million returning, to be followed by a sharper drop to 2.3 million in 2012. It was like watching a stock market on the eve of a run on the banks.

Everyone wanted a smoking gun. Seven of the twenty-first century's first ten summers were the warmest in history for the Fraser River; surely that had something to do with it? But a strange illness appeared to be attacking the fish as well. In recent years, up to 95 per cent of the sockeye ascending the Fraser were dying before releasing their egg sacks. Some sort of salmon leukemia appeared to be at work. Autopsies revealed abnormally soft heart tissue; the hard work of swimming so far against a powerful current was giving them heart attacks before they could reproduce.

It so happened that one of the Fraser's tributaries, Harrison Creek, kept hosting healthy sockeye numbers while all the rest were plummeting. Tagging revealed that the Harrison Creek sockeye followed a different migration path than the rest of their Fraser cousins: when the Harrison fry emerged from the mouth of the Fraser at the start of their life cycle, they wrapped around the southern tip of Vancouver Island and up its west coast. All the rest headed north and swam up the east coast of Vancouver Island. They took the same route we were following now, a route that took us all past several innocuous-looking open-net pens, each containing hundreds of thousands of farmed Atlantic salmon. These salmon farms had been there since the early 1990s, precisely the time that the Fraser's numbers started dropping.

The Harrison Creek sockeye run didn't pass a single fish farm.

In 2011, a scientist named Kristi Miller who worked for the Department of Fisheries and Oceans published an explosive paper in the journal *Science* identifying a potential viral cause behind the mysterious mortality rates of adult Fraser sockeye. The virus she found *might* have been the one killing wild Fraser sockeye, and it *might* have originated in fish farms; further research would be required to know for sure. Miller didn't find the molecular evidence that many were hoping to see, but even so the DFO forbade her from speaking to journalists in the uproar that followed the paper's publication. It also forbade her from pursuing her research into the matter. Finally, the department also changed certain rules; henceforth, DFO scientists needed departmental approval before submitting any research to scientific journals. In fact, from now on they would need approval just to apply for a research grant.

It may be a coincidence that the Fraser's sockeye began collapsing at precisely the moment that dozens of open-net salmon farms were placed on their migratory route. That remains an open question because it would take two years of public outcry and a $15-million federal inquiry before the DFO agreed to follow up on Miller's preliminary findings. Not until March of 2013 was Miller finally allowed to speak to journalists, and to begin the tests that would identify the sockeye's killer and trace it to its source.

But if you were wondering why the Department of Fisheries and Oceans dragged its heels for so long, that part's no mystery at all. The department is bound up in a conflict of interests, with a dual mandate to protect both the farmed-salmon fishery as well as its wild counterpart. Over the past twenty years, profits from the farmed salmon industry have risen from zero to $600 million a year in British Columbia, while profits from the wild salmon fishery have fallen in tandem, shrinking to a third of what farmed salmon brings in. From a budget-balancing perspective, those kinds of figures speak louder than body counts.

A LIGHT TAILWIND came up and we hoisted the sails; ten minutes later it died and we pulled them down; then it blew again from the west and we raised the sails once more. The blow kept picking up, ten, fifteen, twenty knots. This was nothing but it felt like something. At twenty knots, each gust shook the mast violently and we could hear all the things we'd failed to put away in the galley crash around. I took the helm while Zach showed Ilja how to reef the main, shrinking the sail so the wind had less material to grab.

But there was little Zach could do to stop the wind from wrapping steadily northward as the day wore on, until it was blowing into our faces, halting all forward passage completely. We fought for two fruitless hours, tacking from one shore to the other, but the wind only grew stronger while our landmarks stayed frozen in place. Zach was finally in his element and wanted to push on; he was sure if we trimmed the sails just right we could find a forward angle. Ilja felt otherwise. Zach's enthusiasm overwhelmed him and he shouted above the wind, "This is no problem! We can do this! It's only five o'clock, we've got five more hours of daylight. We can still make some way."

"No," Ilja said, "this is my boat. This whole trip is about not rushing things." Their captain-skipper tug of war went on while *Foxy* jounced and the galley rumbled with tossed debris, and the mystery release valve from the water tank that we never figured out burped water with every heave and soaked the galley floor. Ilja was adamant. "I know it's no problem," he said to Zach and me later that night, as we debriefed over pilsners in the calm of Neville Channel. "I know things get a thousand times heavier than what we were just in, and that *Foxy* can handle it, and we'd almost for sure be fine. I know that. But I'm totally new to this. I'm very conservative and none of us knows this boat's systems. We need to play it safe. That's the whole fucking theme of our journey."

It was Ilja, if anyone, who would make the call that saved our lives, preventing a disaster before any of us saw it coming. Zach was a cowboy; he courted disaster, ran directly into it, confident that his skill and determination could plow him safely through. While we were still in the middle of that afternoon's mild gale, we'd noticed that the wind vane at the top of the mast had come loose and was swinging wildly. The wind vane was attached to the radio's antenna, and if the antenna snapped our communication system would have been kaput. Zach had offered to climb the mast then and there, with the boat pitching heavily, and tape the antenna in place so that we could keep going. "Why would you want to do that?!" Ilja shouted, incredulous. "We have a safe anchorage right beside us! Why would you want to risk it? Just give me one good reason!" And Zach, approaching nirvana, unable to picture anything but success, clung to his vision. "It's no problem, Ilja! It's just climbing a ladder! I can do this!"

Ilja's response was his first direct order as captain. We made for a protected inlet on the east shore of Johnstone Strait; as soon as we entered, the wind died completely and we anchored 40 miles from where we had awakened. Everyone's role was now clear. Mine remained to be useless and curious as a child, Zach's was to push us both as far as we could go, and Ilja's was to know when to rein Zach in.

BY THE TIME the earth had completed one more revolution we were pulling into Alert Bay, gazing open-mouthed at the Namgis cemetery's forest of totem poles painted red by the dying sun—our first glimpse of the civilizations that populated this coast before the Parthenon existed.

Alert Bay was a two-in-one kind of town, and before we knew it three days slipped through our hands there. Half the town belonged to the Namgis, a tribe of the Kwakwaka'wakw Nation whose territory covers northern Vancouver Island. The Namgis have been burying their dead here on Cormorant Island for millennia, but it wasn't until the 1880s that the living came to join them. Back then, Vancouver was a dusty trading post and Alert Bay was on its way to becoming the unofficial provincial capital, a vibrant hub for British Columbia's fishery. Ravaged by successive smallpox epidemics and under considerable pressure from the federal government to relocate to a single population centre, the last surviving Namgis moved here and reinvented themselves as labourers for the economic motor of the province, salting and smoking and canning fish that would go on to Victoria and then across the continent. Their labour sustained Alert Bay, which entered a prolonged boom-bust cycle that settled finally on bust twenty years ago. A few mildewing trawlers are left in the marina, trying to make a living off the one or two weeks a year their permits allow them to scoop wild salmon from the sea, but visiting sailboats, whale-watching skiffs and converted tugs far outnumber the fishing vessels now.

The few remaining whites lived along the southern half of Alert Bay's waterfront crescent. That town was a kind of living museum; a recent civic facelift gave it a suitably quaint atmosphere for tourism, including several spruced-up and permanently parked double-decker buses, but when the streets lay empty, as they mostly did all day, Alert Bay had the air of an embalmed corpse.

But that was the white side of town. In 'Yalis, the reserve spreading back from the northern half of Alert Bay, the decline of white influence was experienced as a silver lining to the decline in commercial fish stocks. The Namgis, after all, had only recently stopped declining themselves—from a population of nine thousand spread across Vancouver Island there now remained but sixteen hundred—and for the first time in many generations the future was looking good.

"At last, our people are healing," said Andrea Cranmer, who, together with her mother and sister, operated an art gallery and café called Culture Shock. Culture Shock was the first place we went, like every new arrival; it stood above the marina and ferry terminal in the precise centre of Alert Bay, marking the boundary between the town's two halves, and a certain fusing of native and Western cultures was evident in the Namgis-made paintings and T-shirts and carvings and jewellery for sale in the Cranmers' gallery.

Andrea was a crackling, mischievous woman who was clearly enjoying middle age, and she made us sit on the couch after we told her what we were up to. "Last journalists came through here," she told us, "only wanted to talk. They didn't have time to listen." She told us she was dedicated to reviving the feasting, dancing and gift-giving ceremony known as the potlatch, central to all coastal First Nations' culture, back to its former glory.

The Canadian government first banned the potlatch in 1884, but didn't enforce the ruling until 1921, when forty-five Namgis were arrested and sent to jail in Vancouver for holding a large potlatch on nearby Village Island. Following the mass arrest, RCMP confiscated every Namgis mask, costume, rattle, and piece of jewellery they could find and sold them to museums and galleries across North America. Banning the potlatch didn't make it disappear, of course—it just went underground—but it didn't help matters when St. Mike's residential school was built in the middle of 'Yalis in 1929, eight years after the ban was enforced, and indigenous children from up and down the coast were sent here to what became one of the more notorious residential schools in Canada.

The potlatch ban and residential school each lasted for forty years; the damage they inflicted had no such time limit. "I see a lot of my people walking around with the weight of the world on their shoulders," Andrea said, "but I tell 'em all the same thing: Get off the cross, we need the wood!" She liked to focus on solutions, Andrea did, and potlatches were her favourite panacea. "Our kids are growing up proud again," she said. "There's a lot of healing still has to happen, but that's part of what the potlatch does. The nightmares my generation had to deal with are finally things of the past. Our kids aren't ashamed to be Namgis anymore."

St. Mike's was still the most prominent building in all of Alert Bay, a three-storey building of crumbling brick and broken windows overlooking the bay's northern shore. The question of whether to tear it down or not had divided the Namgis for several years after the government handed over the keys in 1975, but ultimately they decided to let it stand. "It wasn't the building that hurt me," one old man told Andrea, who now passed his logic on to us. "It was the people inside it."

We wanted a closer look, so after we'd been Culture Shocked we made our way down the boardwalk that led from the Cranmer family's shop to 'Yalis. The boardwalk ran parallel to the water's edge, raised a metre above the road beside it, and when I hopped off it I heard a voice behind me say, "I thought white men can't jump."

Two old Namgis fellows were walking a metre behind us, one of them rolling a rusty bicycle with a flat tire.

"We can jump down all right," I replied, "just not up."

"Me, I can jump off a roof," said the one with the bike. He grinned. "Don't dare me, now."

"Wouldn't dream of it," I said.

Ilja, Zach and I slowed our walking pace and our two new friends sped theirs up, and we all walked together in silence for a while. Both men had gaunt, leathery faces with friendly eyes, which the one without the bike directed out to sea. His more talkative friend spoke up again.

"First time here, eh."

"Yeah."

"Hopefully not the last," said Ilja.

"Welcome to Alert Bay." No one asked for names. Both men smiled a lot, revealing missing teeth. We told them we were at the beginning of a long trip. The bike-walker told us he knew about those; he'd finally graduated from high school a few years ago. Our paths diverged when we got close to the red brick building, but before we parted ways both men looked into our eyes in a way that was at once casual and intense.

"You have a safe journey, now."

A huge raven croaked at us from a broken fence post as we entered the grounds of St. Mike's. The decrepit structure was sleepily foreboding, but the surrounding scenery was bucolic. An acre of green lawn spread out before the main entrance, with a single enormous cedar planted in front of the stone stairs. Under the branches a five-year-old Namgis girl was swinging from a rope while her grandmother pushed her, both of them giggling uncontrollably. Their laughter broke St. Mike's brooding spell more effectively than any bulldozer.

The residential school was locked and barred to visitors, but not so the beautiful new building of cedar and glass that crouched beside it: this was U'mista. U'mista meant "the returning," a term formerly used to describe slaves being returned to their home villages. Now it described the centre's ongoing mission to reacquire Namgis treasures that had been confiscated during the potlatch ban. Inside was an exquisite collection of masks: ravens, eagles, wolves, giants, and many other creatures both real and mythical, hauntingly carved and painted. Their makers had captured a stark, violent beauty that came to life in a video of dancers who became possessed with the spirit of whichever mask they wore. It was easy to imagine why the church, and the state it was once closely aligned with, would have wanted to confiscate such powerful talismans. The fact that the Canadian public interpreted such a policy as an act of benevolence—saving the savages from themselves—revealed something more subtle; namely, the condescension that so often swirls beneath the surface of our good intentions.

Back on the white side of town we met Dave, an old salt who came off charming and friendly from the moment he accosted us on the street outside the liquor store.

"What's your mission?" he asked straightaway.

"We're out to stop Enbridge from ruining the Great Bear Rainforest," we told him.

"At least you have one," Dave replied. "Mine's the *Princeton I.* You'll see her docked in the marina. Come by any time. The wine's always flowing and the bullshit's free."

Dave had been sailing these waters since he was fifteen. Now he was sixty-two and ageing hard, with a bulldog's jowls and bags under his eyes that were dimpled like golf balls, and long white thinning hair. Dave had a theatrical way of speaking; "Let me tell you something," he'd say, then lean way back on the brink of his announcement, head cocked so that he was looking at his audience out of one bulging eye before following through with whatever piece of wisdom or dirty joke came next.

The *Princeton I* was an eighty-year-old wooden tug, painstakingly refurbished with live-aboard quarters where Dave hosted whatever travellers happened to be passing through Alert Bay. Dave had pulled his mission from twenty feet under in 1981, when he was our age, and spent the next nine years bringing her back to life. "I thought it would only take three years at the most," he said. "Let me tell you something: don't be afraid when something starts to take longer than you thought it would. That's a good sign."

Eventually the talk came round to oil tankers. "I'll tell you another thing," Dave said. "It isn't Douglas Channel that's going to get 'em. That's a straight shot, long and deep, plenty of room to get by each other. It's Wright Sound at the end of Douglas, *that's* where the shit'll hit the fan. And if it isn't Wright Sound, it'll be Caamaño Sound. Fuckin boulder field in there. You wanna know something? Trying to steer a 300,000-ton tanker through Wright Sound in the dead of winter is the most misguided fucking notion I've heard in my entire misfucking guided life."

Dave's pontifications took on a confrontational tack as the sun began to march down the sky. "Don't ever forget," he told Zach, in whom he saw himself as a young man, "you don't know shit." He'd invited us to the *Princeton I* that night to look at charts for our upcoming route, but he was very inebriated by the time we got there and had precious little navigational advice. Still, it was fun to hear him talk. He called Port McNeill, across the water on Vancouver Island, Port Big Deal; told us ad nauseam what a rotten idea it was to send oil tankers in and out of Kitimat; told us we were going to have a grand adventure if we didn't fuck up, which was more likely.

We spent three days in Alert Bay not because of the personalities it bred but because this was our final stop before entering the wilderness of the Great Bear Rainforest, and who knew when we'd next have a chance to use our phones or send emails? I posted a saccharine blog about how well things were going. Ilja tinkered with the engine and got as many spare parts as he could think of from the hardware store. But the main reason for delaying was that Zach had fallen in love with our journey and now wanted to spend another month with us. This struck Ilja and me as a potentially life-saving development. But seventy-two hours of begging his coast guard superiors for time off got Zach nowhere. Our gamble therefore cost us three precious days of skipperdom instead of gaining us another month. We now had Zach for just five more days. Bella Bella, the first town we'd reach inside the Great Bear Rainforest, the town where we were planning to get Zach on a plane, was at least a three-day sail from here. Optimistically. We filled our holds with canned food and fresh vegetables and renewed anxiety, then cast off the next morning at dawn.

Making north, we finally left the hulking mass of Vancouver Island behind us and entered Queen Charlotte Strait. The first pulse of swell pressed into *Foxy*'s hull, radiating from the open Pacific to the west. Hecate Strait was in sight, marking the southern edge of the Northern Gateway. Beyond that was only ocean, all the way to China. If we came back in three or four years we might see the distant silhouettes of oil tankers.

But not on a day like today, for no sooner had we left Vancouver Island behind than a dense fog descended, burying *Foxy* in a white nimbus. An hour passed before we burst onto a flock of gulls bobbing in the water dead ahead; on hearing

Suzy's rumble, they circled into the air and became a halo of white inside the whiteness of the air, until their wings flapped the fog away and we found ourselves in a spotlight of sun. The spotlight grew, pushing the fog farther back, until the mainland appeared off *Foxy*'s bow at the same time as a ten-knot blow came up from the southeast and a million white tongues started lapping at *Foxy*'s hull. We hoisted the main, unfurled the jenny and sailed for four straight hours. When the shore came close enough to make out the hidden nook our chart told us to look for, we dropped sail and fired up Suzy and motored into a network of interconnected lagoons and bays, all sheltered from the brunt of the open ocean by a slim green gate called Robson Island.

No bugles went off, but this was it. We were in. We had entered the Great Bear Rainforest.

MAYDAY MAYDAY MAYDAY. Channel 16 again. A man's voice, clear and urgent. In four seconds the next voice came, efficient, unworried, standing by.

This is Tofino Coast Guard responding to Mayday, over.

Yeah. Heavy breathing, but not from the man on the radio; from someone next to him. *We've got someone having a heart attack out here.*

What are your coordinates, over.

We're at the mouth of the lagoon in Smith Inlet.

What is the name of your vessel, over.

The Lady Evelyn. (In the background, someone muttering heavily: *"Breathe! Breathe!"*)

Which lagoon in Smith Inlet are you inside of, over.

*Hold on...I have to do CPR...*an urgent background conversation, audible but incomprehensible...*there's only three of us here.*

What is the name of the lagoon you are at, over.

A long silence.

He's got a heartbeat. Gasping heavily. *I don't know the name of this lagoon.*

Roger, we are sending someone to find you. Over.

We were drifting off the southeast edge of Calvert Island, watching a humpback meander through the vast ink vat of Fitz Hugh Sound ahead of us, the world utterly still except for the whale and the radio. There was nothing we could do but listen. It was four in the afternoon and we had been up for twelve hours, and it would have taken many more to reach Smith Inlet now. Cape Caution, a reefy stretch of headland infamous for its exposure to swell, current and wind, had let us by with no more than a blown kiss, a broad reach that pushed us at seven knots for 50 miles with two metres of swell undulating slowly and steadily beneath us all the way to Calvert. The wind died just as the headland veered north and Fitz Hugh Sound opened up, but we didn't bother to take the sails down; instead we saw the whale and dropped our hydrophone into the water, hoping for a song. We'd spent almost a thousand dollars on that hydrophone. But the whale didn't care about that; it ate in silence, and it was the *Lady Evelyn* who called out instead.

A fresh blow came up, a line of churned water barrelling towards us down Fitz Hugh, and we hardly had time to haul in the hydrophone before *Foxy*'s sails snapped taut again and we tacked northward into Fitz Hugh, zigzagging through the three-kilometre-wide pass until we reached Safety Cove, a deep narrow bay on Calvert's eastern shore surrounded by high steep mountains that returned our happy shouts with cartoonish accuracy. The *Lady Evelyn* and her heart attack belonged to another universe.

We'd covered fifty-four nautical miles, precisely one hundred kilometres, all of it under sail, and it was impossible to care about anything else. We were through the gates to another world, of fewer boats and greater trees. There were cutlines in the forests here, but not so many, nor of such size, nor as fresh, as the ones that made a chessboard of Vancouver Island. The forests here were bigger, greener, fresher. We hadn't seen another boat all day.

The northern tip of Calvert Island is perforated by a narrow, twelve-kilometre artery called Kwakshua Channel that is so straight it seems like a product of intelligent design; if you exit Fitz Hugh to follow Kwakshua westward, you will see that it stops just short of piercing Calvert Island all the way through, like an axe that cuts 95 per cent of the way through a tree trunk. A thin sliver of forested land is left to wrap around the anchorage at Kwakshua's end, protecting it from meteorological abuse, making this a safe and waveless place to park your boat even when the most furious storms are pummelling Calvert's west coast (which lies exposed to open ocean) just a few hundred metres away. You have reached an astounding piece of earth known as the Hakai Beach Institute.

Anchor, row ashore, and walk across this narrow band of earth. Behold a series of horseshoe bays with rocky promontories connected by foot trails leading through the forest to one white-sand beach after another. The trees on the outer rim of this forest are stunted and manicured like bonsais by relentless winds, while farther inland cedar, spruce, hemlock and fir grow straight into the clouds. The water on both sides of Hakai is emerald green when the sun shines on it, and studded with small teardrop islands that offer sanctuary to dozens of species of migrating birds. The subaqueous roots of those islands harbour one of the most teeming eco-systems on earth; clams, mussels, starfish, halibut, salmon, octopus, krill, herring, seal—these merely top the list, which extends to terrestrial species like Calvert's resident wolf population.

Humans, too. In the three months before our arrival, some five thousand people—mostly scientists and graduate students, and no few journalists—had passed through the beautiful wooden lodge hidden amongst the trees, according to Eric Peterson, the eccentric multi-millionaire who owns and operates Hakai together with his wife, Christina Munck.

Peterson's reputation as an unsociable but benevolent genius preceded him, which was more than I could say for mine. When Zach, Ilja, and I accosted Peterson on his way to dinner he clearly failed to correlate the solicitous journalist who had emailed him a month earlier with the three unshaven louts who all but high-fived him on his doorstep. "Welcome," he said, ruffled, "I hope you enjoy Hakai," and then he ducked his head and mumbled something about being late and disappeared into his lodge.

The next morning, I loitered alone on the grass near the docks until Peterson materialized again: white crown of hair, white goatee, a delicate pot belly. "I suppose we can have a quick coffee," he said, then turned on a heel to stride ahead of me into the lodge, letting the door shut behind him as I struggled to catch up. He was a tall man who moved like a sasquatch, fast and slouching, hands by his knees. By the time I'd followed him up the stairs to the cafeteria he was already seated by the window with a cup of coffee on the table before him. There was no one else in sight except a chef in a white hat and apron. I asked him where the coffee pot was. He had a friendly smile and a German accent and so we spoke a little German. Hearing that I could speak another language, Eric turned away from the window to look at me for the first time.

"My mother's German," I explained as I sat down.

"Do you speak any other languages?"

"Only Spanish."

"Ah!" Even better. It turned out that Peterson and his wife operated all their philanthropic activities under the aegis of an NGO called Tula, which had spent many years and several millions doing health care work in Guatemala. Eric had fallen in love with the country after travelling there as a young man in the sixties.

For the next two hours, he looked me in the eyes and spoke at great length with little prodding. Tula was still very active in Guatemala, he said; in fact he expected to find out today if the Gates Foundation would approve his application for a $20-million grant. He was casual about the amount, saying only, "It's nothing to the Gates Foundation, but it would give us some clout in the region."

He was conscious of the backlash such clout could provoke.

"It's very easy to come in as a big NGO," he said, "and completely overshadow the great people who are already on the ground. Totally counterproductive. The way to do it is, you go into these devastated communities and find a point of light to start working with. There's always a point of light. In Guatemala, that was the nursing station."

Peterson's background was in health systems; he'd made much of his fortune off some sort of medical imaging invention. His wife, who wasn't in Hakai at the moment, was a biologist, and had been president of the Nature Conservancy of Canada for some time. In addition to Tula's work in Guatemala, Peterson and his wife had done a great deal of conservation work elsewhere on British Columbia's coast before they bought Hakai and became the mayors of a transient scientist's village.

"We were never people who wanted to move into pristine areas and conserve them; we wanted to take on post-industrial places and try to restore them," Peterson said. "We worked in Campbell River, where logging has completely wiped out what used to be a thriving riparian ecosystem, and River's Inlet, where the sockeye run has totally collapsed."

River's Inlet was the nucleus of Owikeno territory, and as Peterson got to know them he realized they struggled with many of the same health care issues that Tula dealt with in Guatemala—Canada's treatment of First Nations and their resource base over the previous century was apparently comparable to one of central America's most vicious civil wars. Tula agreed to fund a nurse training program for young Owikeno, and slowly the health care programs grew alongside the conservation work, "until we had so many programs running out here that we decided we needed a home base."

The Hakai Beach Institute was part of a 1,230-square-kilometre marine conservancy, the largest of its kind on Canada's Pacific coast, a theatre of operations that Peterson described as "the perfect laboratory."

"The landscape here has been changing for fifteen thousand years, and it's never been a garden of Eden," he said. "It's extremely harsh. It's nothing close to pristine—if you think it is then you're not looking. Everywhere you look there's evidence of human behaviour. Every little bay has a shell midden, a canoe tunnel, a clam garden, a stone fish trap; the trees and forests have been modified by people for fifteen thousand years. So now we're in archaeology too. It never occurred to me that we would be. But we are on overlapping territory here between the Heiltsuk and the River's Inlet people, and when I first got here it was a very adversarial relationship; the only way we could go ahead was if we agreed to let them do whatever archaeology they wanted, wherever they wanted."

The Owikeno and Heiltsuk had come to accept his presence because he not only welcomed them to Hakai but also paid to train many of their young men and women in archaeology and ecosystem monitoring; it also helped that Hakai's programs incorporated Traditional Ecological Knowledge, a term I'd always found suspiciously New Age-ish, but Peterson pointed out that the Heiltsuk and Owikeno's deep familiarity with the habits and habitats of their region's plants and animals saved science a great deal of time, by telling the scientists where to look.

"We're studying the ocean and what's in it, we're studying the air, we're studying the forests. If I'm successful, ten years from now we'll be known as a science monitoring station," he said. "If you want to get anything done you have to stay a while; it took us ten years to start seeing results in Guatemala."

Before I left, I asked him for his thoughts about the Northern Gateway. After all, if it were to go ahead, oil tankers would be passing by his doorstep off Calvert Island's western shore almost every day.

"We tend to focus on things that we can do," he said with a shrug. "We don't get into advocacy. The Heiltsuk don't need anyone to speak for them, neither do the Owikeno. If they ask us for support, we give it as best we can." Robert Bateman and several other well-known Canadian artists had visited Hakai shortly before our arrival, fed and sheltered by Peterson while they worked on a series of paintings that were compiled into a coffee table book called *Art for an Oil-Free Coast*. "I take it for granted that Northern Gateway is a stupid idea, as much on economic grounds as environmentally. But we don't carry placards. And if Northern Gateway were to go ahead, we'd get up and go to work the next day."

Peterson frowned, then admitted he was tired of journalists who kept asking the same question. "I'd hate for people to think that Northern Gateway is the only thing going on up here," he said. "There are too many other incredible stories to be told in this region."

ZACH HAD TO fly back to work the next day. We'd planned to cast off immediately after my conversation with Peterson and make for Bella Bella, but when I got back to *Foxy* Ilja and Zach were listening to the forecast with long faces.

"Wind," said Ilja. "Lots of wind. Building to fifty knots."

Zach wanted to go for it. "It's not really picking up till tomorrow afternoon," he said. "If we leave right now we can beat it."

"I don't know. Fifty knots is fucking serious."

"They're calling forty to fifty out in Hecate Strait. In Fitz Hugh it'll be half that."

There wasn't a breath of wind where we were at the moment; I found it impossible to imagine a storm we couldn't get through. I said, "It sounds like it's now or never."

But ultimatums were not a good way to change Ilja's mind. "Well then it's never," he said. "I'm not risking this boat and our lives just to stick to an arbitrary schedule. That's how ships get sunk. We'll get Zach out of here on a float plane, but *Foxy*'s not moving till it's safe."

All of us were frustrated, with one another as much as the weather. Zach clearly felt we could make it, and in my impatience to move on I found it easy to believe him. Ilja, who had $100,000 worth of boat and camera gear to lose, preferred to err on the side of caution. He had the final word.

"Come on," he said, "we're going fishing."

Half an hour later we were bobbing in ninety feet of water, feeling better. Our tender, a ten-foot inflatable dinghy with a brand new four-stroke, fifteen-horse Tohatsu, had been under-utilized thus far in our journey, and it felt good to race around the glassy lagoon in the heart of Calvert Island. The rum didn't hurt either. Pretty soon we'd shut Tohatsu down and leaned back, content to float and let the sun shine on our faces.

The fishing pole Ilja levered casually between his legs was really an afterthought, until the tip bobbed.

"Bite," he said, startled.

Zach hooted, then I hooted, then Ilja hooted. The only thing we'd caught so far was a one-pound rockfish in Safety Cove. Judging by Ilja's strained biceps, something substantial was now on the line.

The line started angling out, as the fish moved from directly below and started swimming away.

The zodiac spun slowly and started moving nose-first in the same direction.

"He's dragging us," Ilja said. "We're getting dragged by a fish."

Anything big enough to pull a dinghy with six hundred pounds of human aboard probably wasn't going to fit inside, even if we could have pulled it up.

"Fire up Tohatsu," Ilja ordered. "I'll reel her in from shore."

I kept an eye on the rum while Zach yanked the starter cord and eased the throttle. Slowly, gently, we made for the nearest shore, a tiny outcrop of rock that could hardly be called an island. Now we were dragging the fish. Zach found a nook between two boulders where the tender's nose fit per-fectly, and I got out first to hold it still while Ilja clambered awkwardly after me, clutching the now-heaving pole with whitened hands. It was a low tide and the rocks he stepped on were covered in slime and seaweed.

"I'm good!" Ilja shouted as soon as he'd walked to a flat, dry spot. "I think." He didn't stay still but started pacing along the shoreline, hopping from rock to rock and almost falling over each time the fish made a run for freedom.

"I'm going back to get the camera!" Zach shouted, and off he zoomed, leaving me with Ilja on the island.

"Go find something to kill this thing with," Ilja ordered.

I scrambled across the rocks. Surely there was a piece of driftwood here somewhere. There was nothing. I searched and jumped and huffed and puffed, then heard Ilja cry, "Holy *shit*."

"What is it?"

"I just saw it."

He told me later that he'd thought it was a shark when it first came out of the depths. But it was a halibut, two metres long and flat-bellied like an ungainly stingray. Zach buzzed back into sight just as our catch leapt across the surface, skipping away from Ilja like a charging elephant, dragging out the line that he'd painstakingly reeled in for thirty minutes as though it was string cheese. Zach cackled and pulled his camera out, hoping to capture another such moment, but Ilja, not happy to be stuck alone with me on shore, yelled at him to hurry up and park.

Twenty more minutes passed before the halibut tired enough to stay close to the rocks, three metres off the tip of Ilja's pole. It glided sadly back and forth in the green water before our feet, as graceful as it was ugly.

"What are we going to *do* with that?" Ilja asked.

Everyone we told the story to afterwards was shocked and disappointed that we didn't kill it. What kind of men didn't kill their prey? But there was nowhere to store that much fish meat on *Foxy*. And the truth was, after staring at it so long, so close, we felt a little sorry for it.

"I can try to get the hook out," Zach said, "if you can bring it close."

Exhaustion had made it docile, this pale creature that had never seen the sun. When Zach knelt beside the water the halibut gave up and let itself be pulled into reach, one reproachful eye blinking in the air for three still seconds as it proffered a cheek to the sky; Zach stretched forward and gripped the hook with a pair of pliers and twisted it out in one fluid motion. The fight gone out of it, our fish backed slowly into the water, glided just below the surface for a moment, and then with a single twitch disappeared into the depths.

The next day, Zach copied the halibut's manoeuvre with a human inversion: instead of going down, he climbed into a float plane and disappeared into the sky.

*Bald eagles, emblematic raptors of the Great Bear Rainforest,
are particularly abundant near fishing towns like Bella Bella.*

BELLA
BELLA

THE DAY Larry Jorgenson showed up in Bella Bella, a Heiltsuk man grabbed him off the street and threw him against a wall, put a knife to his throat and growled: "No white cocksucker's gonna run *this* town."

It was 1980 and Bella Bella was at the height of a suicide wave. In a town of twelve hundred people, one teenager was committing the act every month. Desperate for solutions, the Bella Bella Community School followed a string of connections that led to the Director of Mental Health for Northern Alberta, and they hired that white cocksucker to become their high school counsellor.

Jorgenson brushed off the knife incident and set about working with community leaders to identify which teens seemed likeliest to take their lives next. Rather than talk to them in school, or even try talking much at all, he loaded them onto a fishing boat and took them for week-long expeditions into the surrounding wilderness. These forays were as much of a trial for Jorgenson, who wasn't an outdoorsman and had no experience either boating or camping, as they were for the

Heiltsuk kids he bullied aboard. But nobody drowned or died of exposure. Instead they explored forests and beaches that were littered with arrowheads and spear tips; they discovered that low tides often revealed stone fish traps painstakingly built over millennia, and ancient burial grounds lurked just beneath the ubiquitous moss. Here, far from the darkness and abuses of home, was evidence of an ancestral link to the land that stretched back ten thousand years, embedding the castaway Heiltsuk kids in a culture older than Greece.

Reestablishing this link proved to be a vital first step in getting the Heiltsuk off their knees. It helped that, soon after Jorgenson's arrival, the last residential school in Canada closed its doors, even as the potlatch ban was renounced by the federal government. As with the Namgis of Alert Bay, Heiltsuk children were allowed to be proud of their heritage once again, if only someone would show it to them.

Jorgenson was by no means the only person to do so—he had no inkling of the dances, songs, totems, recipes, and myriad other traditions that made the Heiltsuk who they were, knowledge that only the elders could pass down. But the wilderness therapy program he initiated became a rallying point for the whole community. The program grew and became an annual summer camp where those dances, songs, and recipes were taught after a day of exploring; over time, children he'd taken under his wing grew up and became camp counsellors themselves, earning enough money over the summer to pay for university degrees. Jorgenson married Marge Housty, the daughter of a highly respected hereditary chief, and they had two children, Jessie and William, who also went to those summer camps and got university degrees of their own. Jorgenson encouraged his children to keep their mother's surname, and they did. Today, William and Jessie Housty are two of the people who run Qqs Projects Society, the non-profit Jorgenson created in 1999 to house the panoply of social, environmental, economic, and scientific enterprises those early wilderness camps morphed into. Qqs, pronounced *kuks*, means "eyes" in Heiltsuk, and its mandate is "to open the eyes of our young people to their responsibility as stewards of our environment and culture."

I learned this brief history several months before arriving in Bella Bella, because Jorgenson and I had a mutual friend, a man who headed the American Museum of Natural History's department of biodiversity for the Pacific region. This department is a silent partner of sorts in Qqs, collaborating with the Heiltsuk on everything from fundraising strategies to the pursuit of environmental stewardship (it's possible the museum felt a sense of obligation because of its ample collection of Heiltsuk masks, canoes, and other regalia). Our mutual friend invited me to join Jorgenson and his wife and daughter for dinner when they were all in Vancouver one wintry night in March. We met at a Chinese restaurant near the airport. The most remarkable thing about that dinner was its silence; Jorgenson and the Houstys are impressively taciturn in the presence of strangers—taciturn but not unfriendly, nor immune to the call of Laphroaig, for Jorgenson became more voluble over the course of a post-prandial whiskey, and after telling the story of his first day in Bella Bella he promised me mine would be better. "The Qqs office is in the first building you see when you walk off the docks," he told me. "Be sure to stop in if you make it."

WE MADE IT, but it wasn't pretty. Zachless, Ilja and I navigated the 43 miles from Hakai to Bella Bella without wind or incident, motoring up Fitz Hugh, past the abandoned cannery town of Namu, where the oldest archaeological remains in North America can be found (a nine-thousand-year-old shell midden), turning west into Lama Passage and following its northward hook between Campbell and Denny Islands until, seventeen days after leaving Sidney, the clapboard houses of Bella Bella came into view.

That part all went fine. But then we had to dock.

A forty-one-foot fibreglass sailboat weighs in the neighborhood of twenty-five tons and has but a one-metre-diameter propeller to push and pull it through the water when the sails are down. It isn't Porsche-like to manoeuvre, and especially in reverse has a certain veering tendency. Aiming such a craft up the middle of a 1.5-kilometre-wide channel is one thing, but slipping it between two piers that are twenty metres apart and then parallel parking between seven-digit yachts, while an assortment of fishing boats whose pilots know what they're doing and are impatient with rookies come and go all around you, is an experience we found every bit as nerve-flaying as our pre-expedition advisors had warned it would be.

Ilja manned the helm while I stood by the rail clutching a stern line, prepared to jump off as soon as possible and tie the line around a cleat. We entered slowly and smoothly, with Ilja angling us in starboard-to—our starboard beam would rest against the dock. I tossed the line to an old salt standing on the dock who saw my uneasy face; he caught it and pulled, and as soon as we were close enough I jumped off and grabbed the line back, which was when Ilja changed his mind and executed a ponderous-yet-frantic 180-degree turn in order to park facing the exit. Not knowing what else to do, I stood still and spooled the line out, watching in anguish as the rope wrapped around *Foxy*'s rear end the way a leash gets wrapped around a spinning dog. Ilja completed the turn and eased her in, port-to now, and I pulled on the line so that *Foxy*'s ass end inched slowly towards the dock. The bow line was now just a few centimetres above the propeller. Rope-wise, we had achieved the equivalent of putting one's skis on backwards, but at least we'd made it down the hill. I held my pose with all the nonchalance I could muster, straining to keep the rear of the boat tight to the dock, until Ilja shut her down with a sigh, his heart beating as fast as mine, and there we were, safely docked and ready to fuel up.

I ignored the dozen gazes we'd attracted up and down the dock, casting my eyes upward to the heavens, and who did I see there, looking down at us from the raised road that ran out above the dock, his face a study in non-expression, but the future chief of Bella Bella, six-foot-four, three-hundred-some pound William Housty. I recognized him from the Internet, though we'd never met and there was no reason for him to know who the city idiot staring up at him was. He shook his head and walked away, and it was two weeks before I saw him again.

Humbled but relieved, we fueled up. *Foxy* had made it all this way on a single tank, 180 litres of diesel, a modest amount of hydrocarbon. Perhaps our vessel set a decent example for the future of civilization, after all: go slow, burn oil when you have to, harness the wind when you can.

Keeping *Foxy* in Bella Bella was not an option. The fuel dock did not promote lingering, as there was already a line up of boats waiting to take our place. There was a marina at the other end of town, but it was filled way beyond capacity with Heiltsuk fishing vessels of all sizes. So we carried on in search of the nearest anchorage, and found one three miles away off Denny Island, in a sheltered cove where the water was thirty feet deep at low tide. And there we stayed for the next fourteen days.

Our anchorage was five hundred metres from Shearwater, the half-town where perhaps a hundred people (most of them white) could be found on any given summer's day, either spending money or making it in a smattering of small businesses. Shearwater was a popular stopover for every class of sport fisherman, sailor, treeplanter and tour operator between Vancouver Island and Alaska, because there was nowhere else for hundreds of kilometres to do your laundry, sleep in a hotel, or get your boat fixed. Unlike Bella Bella, where there weren't many places for non-residents to hang out, in Shearwater there was nothing to do *but* hang out. In fact, Heiltsuk of all ages came to Shearwater for work and entertainment, which gravitated around the Fishermen's Bar and Grill. A seabus made the fifteen-minute crossing from Bella Bella to Shearwater every hour, but if the wind was down and Lama Pass smooth enough, Ilja and I preferred to take our tender.

To cross Lama Pass was to bridge the gulf separating Canada from its First Nations. I was thirty-five years old, born and raised in Canada, and I'd never spent more than a few hours in a reserve before. There were thousands of enclaves all over my country into which foreign countries had been stuffed, and I didn't know what any of them were like.

And then I entered Bella Bella and beheld a cascade of running children, highly revved trucks, all-aged bicyclists and young mothers walking their babies in strollers while vocally shepherding the toddlers big enough to walk: "Jimmy, get out of those bushes and come here this instant," as Jimmy wrestled his brother, who wore a Batman cape and mask, into a submission hold. Everyone but the children waved hello and smiled. The ten-thousand-gallon fuel tanks above the dock were perched upon by bald eagles and enormous ravens, as were many of the treetops; the sound of beating wings filled any silence humans left behind. Most of the houses needed a paint job and a new window or two; a third of them had "Heiltsuk Nation Opposes Enbridge" posters on display, the words stenciled around a stylized image of a Watcher totem eating an oil tanker. Many of the same windows also displayed faded Vancouver Canucks banners. Inflatable pools and portable basketball hoops were everywhere. A few of the yards were busy with families cleaning salmon, throwing the guts onto the grass for the ever-swooping birds to take away.

After our reconnaissance, we walked back towards the dock and entered Qqs headquarters. You could tell at a glance this was prime habitat for the several species of journalist, scientist and politician who migrated through these waters from May till September, all of them nurtured by the Heiltsuk who live here year round.

Tucked between the grocery and liquor stores, a wooden sign out front identified this seasonal habitat not as Qqs but as the Koeye Café. The name came from the watershed where Qqs held their summer camps and did much of their ecological research, primarily into grizzly bears and salmon. Just like the watershed, the café harboured an elaborate ecosystem whose cornerstone was a small but vibrant library that Jessie Housty, Larry Jorgenson's daughter, seeded several years ago with the help of Louise Dennys, the vice-president of Random House and a longtime admirer of Jessie, the Heiltsuk Nation, the entire Great Bear Rainforest, but in particular, of Jessie. When Dennys first visited Bella Bella several years ago, she came across a thirteen-year-old Heiltsuk girl reading the *Aeneid* on the beach. Dennys and her husband, whom Salman Rushdie described in his memoir as "the best-looking happily married couple in North America," had no children of their own, and Jessie became something of a surrogate daughter to

Jessie Housty at the entrance of the Koeye Café in Bella Bella.

the beautiful pair. Many years after that first encounter, Dennys would send boxes of books to Bella Bella that included signed copies of recent releases by Rushdie, Ondaatje, Atwood, Krakauer, and other humble friends.

Jessie Housty ran the café, but she was out of town. Her colleague, a rail-thin woman named Louise, was behind the counter, and she told us that Jessie had just been elected to band council and was in Vancouver on council business. Jessie's brother, William, and their parents, Larry Jorgenson and Marge Housty, were also out of town, forty miles south of here in the Koeye watershed, where they would be all summer (when I'd seen William yesterday, he'd only been in town to pick up supplies). But Jessie would be back tomorrow. Or maybe the day after.

We lingered before we left, browsing not just the bookshelves but also the walls above them. They were festooned with anti-Enbridge posters crayoned by children's hands, precociously accurate renderings of marine animals (mostly whales and salmon) in various states of oil-streaked duress and saying things like *Fish Oil, not Crude Oil,* or people holding hands while they stomp an oil tanker beneath their feet while a word-bubble above their smiling faces says *Thanks Enbridge, You Really Brought Us Together.* Just beside the entrance, typed and printed on computer paper in 18-point font and glued to the wall without any artistic primping, was a historical reminder:

In the days that are gone, when tribal warfare was life, and the hand of Christianity had not reached these northern tribes, the name of Bella Bella was known and feared by all the tribes from Nanaimo on the south to Alaska on the north. Not that other tribes were serfs and weaklings, but the name of Bella Bella stood for bravery, courage, fortitude, intrepidity, and fearlessness, and woe to any tribe that dared fling its fire-brand of insult to any member of this proud, arrogant, and merciless foe.

In other words, be nice.

Having organized for many months and sailed for many days to reach this, our first official stop in the Great Bear Rainforest, we abruptly felt awkward for being here. Not unwelcome, but definitely gawkerish. We didn't know anyone here. Not only were Jorgenson and his family all out of town, but so were the three other people I'd contacted in the previous months. Harvey Humchitt, a hereditary chief who headed the Heiltsuk Integrated Resource Management Department, and whose permission we technically needed to interview or photograph anyone in Heiltsuk territory, had been friendly and responsive over email but was now fishing somewhere in the outer islands, gone till next week. Elroy White, one of the few archaeologists in the world to dig through his own culture's past, was unearthing old smokehouses on Hunter Island with a graduate student and didn't know when he'd be back.

The other person was Ian McAllister, a legendary figure in these parts who didn't live in Bella Bella anyway, but rather just across the water on a beachfront property known as Whiskey Cove. A conservationist and wildlife photographer, McAllister had arguably done more than any other single person to put the Great Bear Rainforest on the map; I'd first heard of him in 1997 when he and his wife co-published *The Great Bear Rainforest* coffee table book, together with my first journalism professor—the book that helped inspire my first visit to the Great Bear Rainforest thirteen years earlier. McAllister's images of moss-draped old growth and salmon-sated grizzlies and emerald coves had transported me, then a recent coastal transplant fresh from Edmonton, to a world I didn't know existed. There was of course much more to come. Over the subsequent decade, McAllister camped, sailed, scuba dived, wrote and photographed his way through the Great Bear Rainforest, authoring several naturalist books of his own and publishing photographs in *National Geographic* and its equivalents around the world. He founded two separate environmental non-profits dedicated to studying and preserving the Great Bear Rainforest's ecosystem. He also occasionally took it upon himself to guide professional photographers through the region, and in our brief correspondence over the previous months he'd promised to help us however he could.

But now that we were here McAllister had gone incommunicado, and we didn't know why until one of the many informal proteges he has scattered around the Great Bear Rainforest showed up in his place.

Michael Reid was an enterprising thirty-year-old from the Lower Mainland with whom I'd spoken several times over the previous months, though I hadn't expected to see him until we made it farther north. For the last two years Michael had been working with the Gitga'at Nation in Hartley Bay, 160 kilometres northwest of Bella Bella; his job was to help the Gitga'at prepare for the Northern Gateway public hearings. It was a nebulous position that I gathered involved publishing many kinds of impact assessments—environmental, cultural, economic—to be used as some kind of evidence. The sound of his voice chiming unexpectedly over Channel 16 on the VHF at our first sunset anchored way out in the boondocks came as a profound delight.

Foxy, Foxy, Foxy, this is Skomalt, Skomalt, Skomalt. *You in the neighbourhood, over?*

Michael had just bought a sailboat, too. She was tied up at McAllister's dock in Whiskey Cove, where we could see each other's mast lights, and why didn't we come over for a whiskey?

Our host awaited us aboard a thirty-three-foot black sloop called *Skomalt*. He lived aboard her with his girlfriend, Sarah Stoner, a sunny extrovert who worked on communications and research for Pacific Wild, the NGO McAllister now headed. They expected to spend the next two years living and sailing between Hartley Bay, where the Gitga'at lived, and Whiskey Cove, which doubled as Pacific Wild headquarters.

It was just too bad, Michael said, that Ian was now in Victoria, picking up a new catamaran that he would sail to Whiskey Cove himself. "Actually it's his second try." The first attempt, some weeks ago, had resulted in grievous damages when a tug boat accidentally hooked McAllister's anchor chain at 4:30 in the morning, coming out of Neville Channel—the same place we'd anchored ten days ago after Ilja and Zach had their argument over whether to proceed in the gale. Like us, McAllister had anchored in a placid-seeming spot for the night, only his peaceful sleep was interrupted by a terrible, sustained lurch. The tug driver, who didn't have his radio on, dragged the catamaran into the middle of Johnstone Strait before looking back and realizing he wasn't alone. Fortunately no one was hurt except the catamaran, which was towed back to Victoria for repairs.

Some accidents, you just can't predict.

Michael was a natural storyteller who nevertheless spoke slowly, and chose his own words carefully. In this he fit easily into coastal First Nation culture, aided further by a sensitivity for the volatile waters of coastal politics. He told us he'd first fallen in love with the Great Bear Rainforest on a kayaking trip ten years earlier, and carving out a new life here represented a dream come true.

For the last two years, for better and worse, that dream had revolved around the Joint Review Panel's three stone-faced members charged with overseeing the public hearings into Northern Gateway. It was the Joint Review Panel's job to visit every town along the pipeline and tanker routes, many of them twice, and listen to thousands of hours of testimony from thousands of individuals; the process resembled a sprawling criminal court case in which the JRP was the judge, Enbridge the defendant, and the public was the prosecutor. Or perhaps those last two were the other way round. It often seemed that Enbridge was the prosecutor, and it was the public who had to defend its right to keep oil tankers out of their backyard. Certainly, the project was innocent until proven guilty, and it was up to a concerned public to convince the panel beyond a reasonable doubt that Northern Gateway's risks outweighed its benefits. The whole process would take approximately fourteen months, after which the panel would submit its report to the National Energy Board with a conclusion: either Northern Gateway was in the public interest or it wasn't.

The panel members refused to speak with the press for the duration of the review process; the only way to gauge their thoughts was to look at their faces and study their backgrounds, which were mixed. All three were jointly appointed by the minister of environment and the National Energy Board, the government agency responsible for regulating Canada's 71,000 kilometers of pipeline. Sheila Leggett, the panel's chairperson, was vice-president of the National Energy Board; the NEB wasn't known for turning down pipeline applications, but Leggett was also a founding board member of Alberta Ecotrust, an NGO that *was* known for its staunch environmental advocacy. Kenneth Bateman, the second panel member, also sat on the board of the NEB. Prior to that he'd been vice president at ENMAX, a Canadian utility that developed one of the largest wind farms in the country. The third member was Hans Matthews, a geologist and mining advocate who spent eighteen years as president of the Canadian Aboriginal Minerals Association; in the context of Northern Gateway, Matthews' job history mattered less than his ethnicity, for he was an Ojibway from Ontario's Wahnapitae First Nation, also known (to critics of the Northern Gateway, who quite universally distrusted the public review process) as The Token Indian.

Whether or not the Joint Review Panel members were predisposed to approve of Northern Gateway, the Harper Administration must have had its doubts because, shortly before we left on our journey, Cabinet gave itself the power to overrule both the panel's recommendation and the NEB's decision.

But the prime minister's life would be a lot easier if the panel sided with him. One night when we were chatting with

Michael Reid aboard the *Skomalt*, we asked him: "Do you believe in the JRP's neutrality?"

"I have to," he replied. "Otherwise everything I've been telling the Gitga'at to spend their money on is bullshit. They've spent almost a million dollars by now, on environmental impact assessments, economic impact assessments, cultural impact assessments, largely based on my advice. But in all honesty, I haven't seen anything to make me think the Joint Review Panel isn't genuinely listening. Convincing them is the best chance we've got. But a lot of people will tell you otherwise, especially the Heiltsuk. They see what happened at the last hearing in Bella Bella as proof of the panel's contempt for First Nations in general."

What happened: The most memorable of all the JRP's hearings were the ones that didn't take place in Bella Bella on April 1, 2012. That was the day the JRP members' plane touched down in Bella Bella for the first of four days of hearings. Over two hundred Heiltsuk protesters had gathered at the airport to greet the panel with anti-Enbridge, no-tanker banners, chanting the ubiquitous coastal slogan: "No Tankers, No Pipeline, No Problem!" News cameras, which followed every step of the panel's progress throughout the province, were on hand to film the occasion, and it must be admitted that the scene broadcast to the nation didn't look terribly frightening. Nevertheless, the panel members panicked at the sight of all those protesters, in particular the young man who stepped off the side of the road and rapped on their window. They declared the scene a security threat, and called the hearings off.

Said the Joint Review Panel (in an email to the Heiltsuk Tribal Council): "The Panel cannot be in a situation where it is unsure that the crowd will be peaceful...Based on our experiences this afternoon, the Panel is concerned that a meaningful hearing cannot be achieved."

Said Bella Bella's RCMP detachment to journalists at the time: "The protest was a peaceful demonstration and there were no incidents to report of."

Said Jennifer Carpenter, Bella Bella's resident anthropologist (who we'll get to in due course): "We have footage of grandmothers and children banging drums on the side of the road. *That's* what they were afraid of?"

Said Jessie Housty (once we finally met): "It actually worked out well for us, because we have irrefutable evidence that they were lying when they said they felt threatened. There was absolutely no threat in sight. It's ludicrous, and the whole country knows it."

Said Michael Reid (to us in Whiskey Cove, a whiskey in his hand): "The panel members got on the first seabus to Shearwater and that night they went to the pub. Ian and I were there. It was one of the strangest nights of my life. The pub was packed and everyone in it was drunk, including us and the panel members. They weren't shy at all. It was too good an opportunity to miss. Ian started right in on Bateman, calling him a coward for running away. I wound up talking to the First Nations guy, Matthews, but I didn't want to accuse him of anything. I just wanted to hear his side of the story."

This was Matthews' side of the story:

The chiefs of Bella Bella had agreed to roll out the red carpet for the panel members on their arrival, just as the Haida had done, as the Gitga'at had done, as the Haisla had done—as just about every coastal tribe had done when the panel came to their respective towns. Feasts were prepared, songs were sung, chiefs went to the airport to greet and escort them into town. And this was supposed to happen in Bella Bella too, but at the last minute there was a strange kerfuffle; it turned out that the grand chief of the Heiltsuk Nation, a man named Toby Moody, was on the same flight as the Joint Review Panel, and his arrival overshadowed that of the panel members. It was for him that the lesser chiefs of the Heiltsuk Nation now waited at the airport; when Moody stepped off the plane, it was to him that the entourage flocked, leaving the panel members to huddle alone in a strange airport with crowds of protesters banging drums outside and no one but a single security guard to keep them company. Their welcoming committee thus vanished, the panel waited in confusion until finally their taxi driver came in of his own volition and brought them outside to his van. No sooner had they started driving than one of the protesters knocked on the van window in an attempt to get the people inside to look at his placard; at precisely the same moment, the security guard, who had entered the van with the panel members, saw a commotion on the road ahead whereby someone happened to drive his vehicle into the ditch. The security guard panicked and made an executive decision that it wasn't safe to proceed, a decision that the jittery panel members made no effort to sway. They turned around, and later, instead of going to the community hall for the welcoming feast that awaited them, went to the dock and caught the seabus to Shearwater. Once there they went to the Fishermen's Bar and Grill, where a few drinks put everyone in a better, more talkative mood.

The panel eventually relented and agreed to resume the Bella Bella hearings, but a day and a half was lost along with a lifetime of goodwill, and several people who signed up never got the chance to speak.

"He said to me," said Michael of his conversation with The Token Indian: "'We don't *have* to come to any of these towns. The JRP has total control over which communities it visits. We made a particular point of coming here in the first place, and they treated us like enemies.'"

THE NEXT MORNING we went back to Bella Bella. Lama Pass was a sheet of glass broken only by the substantial wake of a BC Ferry; we bounced over that and tied our tender to the fuel dock, then walked past the dozen children playing around the high tide line, past the two young men smoking cigarettes and drinking canned beer beneath a tree twenty metres on, past the liquor store, and into the Koeye Café. Jessie Housty was there behind the counter.

She was just as I remembered from that silent dinner in Vancouver: friendly but guarded, a shy twenty-five-year-old with olive skin and frank brown eyes in which her Heiltsuk DNA was most evident. She greeted Ilja and me with a warm hug and told us we'd come just in time. The Joint Review Panel was coming back next week to finish up the hearings it had cut short in April.

"They're insisting on holding the hearings in Shearwater now, for security reasons," Jessie said with a wry smile. "We're thinking about paddling over in war canoes if we can't change their minds. I'm working on a letter to them right now, detailing exactly why they are legally obligated to come to us in Bella Bella. They probably won't read it until March, but as long as we have it in writing it'll stand in court later on."

That, in essence, was the reason the Heiltsuk and so many other First Nation communities were taking part in what they saw as a charade: to get it all on record. So that after the project received regulatory approval, they could tangle Northern Gateway in dozens of court cases claiming the federal government had failed in its constitutional duty to properly consult or reasonably accommodate the concerns of every tribe whose land the pipeline and tanker routes crossed.

Jessie was clearly preoccupied. Ilja and I left her to her letter-writing duties, poured ourselves a coffee and turned to join Kai Nagata and Stephanie Brown, two journalists who'd arrived in Bella Bella a week before us. They were now in the café, brainstorming with three Heiltsuk students over the video they were going to film that day.

Kai Nagata was a gifted journalist from Vancouver who had risen to become CTV's Quebec City Bureau Chief by the age of twenty-four before quitting the television news industry in a highly publicized divorce that made him a minor celebrity in Canada's journalistic community. That was just a couple of years ago. He refused, he wrote at the time, to keep churning out "easy stories that reinforce beliefs [viewers] already hold," or to work in an environment where "every question I asked, every tweet I posted, and even what I said to other journalists and friends had to go through a filter, where my own opinions and values were carefully strained out." He moved back west to become an independent videographer, writer, and satirist, and here he was now showing Heiltsuk teenagers how to do the same.

Stephanie Brown, a lean Métis in her early thirties, was a freelancer whose most recent assignment had taken her to Thailand and Burma; there, she'd covered the story of the Shwe pipeline construction, which would carry gas and oil from the Bay of Bengal to China, bisecting Burma and displacing huge swathes of Burma's ethnic minorities in the process.

The two of them were now travelling the Northern Gateway pipeline and tanker routes together, compiling a mini-documentary called *The End of the Line.*

But today they were teaching, not filming. A comically (or childishly, depending how you saw it) lowbrow Youtube video called "Shit Girls Say" had recently gone viral and become a spontaneous Internet franchise; people all over the world were making their own versions, replacing "girls" with "yogis" or "hipsters" and a hundred other tease-able demographics. Kai and Stephanie were going to help their three new students make an expletive-free version called "Stuff Bella Bella People Say" and post it online.

"What *do* people say in Bella Bella?" I asked.

"Got five bucks for the seabus?" said Chelsea, a girl with impish eyes and a sly grin.

"Also," said Jaryn, a muscular teenager with a buzz cut, "we don't have a good hospital here, so anytime anyone needs something checked out they have to leave."

"We call it a medical," Chelsea said. "We fly to Vancouver for them. We love going. There's McDonald's and Kentucky Fried Chicken."

"And Tim Hortons."

"And 7-Eleven."

They were giggling. This wasn't an indictment of Bella Bella's medical system—which was worth indicting; later, when Ilja and I were eating the worst chicken chow mein of our lives at the only restaurant in Bella Bella (the fact that it was spelled Ciao Main on the chalkboard helped), a woman with grey hair and thinning lips joined us a propos of nothing and whispered: "Someone really needs to do a documentary on the health system here. It's criminal! The doctors here have no idea what they're doing! They'll say, 'Just because your father has arthritis doesn't mean you do too,' and they'll refuse to write you a referral to see a specialist, so you have to wait forever to see one because the plane ticket to Vancouver costs money, and by the time you make it to Vancouver whatever it is that was wrong with you has become a crisis. But everyone's afraid to talk about it, people are in hiding for what they've said!" leaving us to wonder, principally, where exactly a person would go to hide in a town like Bella Bella—no, Chelsea and Jaryn weren't complaining about a health care crisis, they were celebrating the articulation of a *thing* that characterized life where they lived. A thing that set it apart from how life might be in other places.

Now Kai and Stephanie stepped in, coaching them on how to turn going-to-Vancouver-for-a-medical into a pithy shit-people-say phrase.

"Just got back from a medical!"

"Bring any nuggets?"

"Don't forget rez dogs!" exclaimed the third member of the team, Rory, who was Jessie Housty's cousin; he wore thick hipster glasses and had three days' worth of post-adolescent stubble. "We're always shouting at the rez dogs around here."

Another thing people were always doing in Bella Bella, like everywhere on earth, was gossiping about one another's romantic liaisons; in a town of fifteen hundred people descended from a small pool of great grandparents, this often took a comedic turn that was ultimately portrayed in "Stuff Bella Bella People Say" through a scene on the seabus:

Two young women are sitting at the back of the boat; the seat before them is occupied by another young woman sitting alone; at the front, oblivious to their surroundings, a young couple is cuddling, the girl resting her head on her sweetheart's shoulder.

Girl at the back, to her friend: "Look at them all serious. He's taking her to Shearwater on a *date*."

Friend, in response: "Are they even Facebook official yet?"

Solo girl in the middle, turning to face the two in the back: "Oh my god, guys, I heard they were like third *cousins*."

But that was yet to be filmed. For now, a rez dog with matted white dreadlocks sprinted past the Koeye Café, big as a wolf, kicking up dust as it raced down the inclined road and pattered to a halt on the fuel dock's wide planks. He thrust his burred chest over the water to bark imperiously at an elderly white couple pulling away in their elderly yacht, then strutted back up the pavement, pausing by the café entrance where all of us were now squinting in the sun. Ilja and I petted the rez dog's head. Rory, grinning, said, "Now smell your fingers."

Chelsea leaned over and whispered to Jaryn, "They can be the *gumshuas*," and then, realizing we'd heard her, clapped her hand to her mouth. But we agreed that this would be the perfect part for us to play. *Gumshuas*. White guys. The role came naturally to us both. We shot what would become the opening scene then and there. Stephanie crouched on the street and used her shoulder as a tripod while another girl held the camera and peered through the viewfinder. Kai, standing behind them from a director's distance, called "Action!" Ilja and I stood in the entrance to the Koeye Café and scratched our heads while staring at a map; then Chelsea and Jaryn walked past, right in front of the camera. "Who are those *gumshua?*" Chelsea muttered, her words and our confused-tourist faces soon to be added to the Internet's trillions of snowflakes.

That evening everyone was headed to Shearwater for karaoke night at the Fishermen's pub, and we invited Kai and Stephanie to stop by *Foxy* for a drink. We settled into the cockpit with a beer each, and I asked how they'd gotten interested in the Northern Gateway story.

"I was in Burma when Aung San Suu Kyi got elected," Stephanie said. "It was a very hopeful time for that country, and still is. But at the same time as all this good stuff was happening in the capital, they were building the Shwe pipeline in the countryside. Nothing good was coming out of that. The damage that construction caused was awful, both environmentally and socially." Stephanie hiked through Shan state on her own, where the final leg of the pipeline was being built, and met with villagers whose lives had been devastated by the upheaval with no promise of restitution. "Burma was being used as one big gateway for China," she said. "Then I got home and saw the same thing happening here."

Her story reminded me of my own international *déjà vu*. I'd first seen the Northern Gateway script unfold in Peru three years earlier, and it went like this:

In October of 2007, Peru's then-president Alan García wrote an open letter to his country under the title "The Syndrome of the Dog in the Manger." García's letter, published in the national newspaper, bore a striking resemblance to the one Canada's minister of natural resources, Joe Oliver, wrote five years later to lambaste the anti-Northern Gateway crowd. García had used Aesop's fable as the model for his own Amazonian predicament, a jungle full of untapped treasures guarded by "second-class" citizens who stubbornly resisted industrial development on their land. "Many resources aren't being traded, invested in, or generating employment," he wrote. "And all this because of the taboo of outdated ideologies, because of idleness and indolence, or the law of the dog in the manger who says, 'If I don't eat, no one else eats either.'"

García's letter infuriated Peru's indigenous and environmental communities, but worse was to come. It turned out the Syndrome of the Dog in the Manger was only preparing the ground for a series of 101 presidential decrees García passed without debate a year after the letter was published. These decrees had the cumulative effect of gutting Peru's environmental regulations, weakening the territorial rights of indigenous communities, and strengthening the rights of corporations that already owned industrial leases on 75 per cent of the Peruvian Amazon. García insisted the decrees were necessary for Peru to come into compliance with the free trade agreements he had just signed with Canada and the United States (in fact, as officials from both countries belatedly pointed out, Peru was already in compliance and none of the decrees had any bearing on the trade deals).

Concluding that it was going to take more than words to make Lima listen, in April of 2009 almost seventy tribes of the Peruvian Amazon rose up in collective protest and shut down highways, river ports, and oil facilities in over half the country. Commerce and industry ground to a halt across an area the size of France. The natives' demands were clear and concrete, centring on the revocation of the most troublesome of García's 101 decrees. But on June 5, 2009, after two months of half-hearted negotiations, the Peruvian army descended on the uprising's most troublesome blockade instead and opened fire on three thousand Awajun protesters. Three were killed, and another eighty-two wound up in hospital with bullet wounds.

I flew to Peru soon afterwards to follow up on the story, and I was impressed by how unapologetic García remained, in large part because the protesters had defended themselves to the tune of twenty-five dead soldiers. "A genocide against the police," was how the president saw it. He did, however, expand the category of blame, allowing that Peru's second-class citizens might not have been entirely responsible for their actions. "We watched this disaster come on little by little," he said. "It was brought on by the desperate appetites of those hungry for power, inspired by foreign interests that want to slow the velocity of our development."

Everywhere you looked, foreign interests were at work. It was hard not to be reminded of all this three years later, back in Canada. Just as the conflicts in Peru and Burma transcended any one group of people or industrial project, whatever we were witnessing at home was much bigger than Enbridge or Northern Gateway or the Heiltsuk. It was the local chapter of a story playing out in every country on earth. People were arguing, often violently, over hyperlocal issues of land, jobs, and governance, but each of these conflicts had deep taproots that drew on global issues. Can the world's biggest corporations be trusted with the power they've amassed? Is climate change an existential threat to human civilization? Up to what point is it safe to pursue economic growth on a finite planet? But it was hard for people with opposing views to discuss these kinds of questions without slipping into hyperbole. Better, maybe, to focus on concrete issues like the Northern Gateway proposal; or even, briefly, on something a little bigger, like Canada's own version of García's 101 decrees: Bill C-38.

Bill C-38 was put before parliament in March of 2012, and because of the Conservatives' majority it passed into law unaltered two months later. It was ostensibly a budget bill laying out the government's planned expenditures for the year ahead, only this particular budget had an extraordinary number of constitutional amendments tacked onto it. Almost half the

425-page document was devoted to environmental regulation, or rather deregulation, for the bill dismantled half a century's worth of laws and institutions designed to conserve Canada's ecosystems. The Bill amended sixty-nine constitutional Acts and repealed others entirely, including the Kyoto Protocol Implementation Act. To list just a few other casualties: the number of lakes and rivers protected by the Navigable Waters Protection Act was reduced from 2.5 million to 159; the Fisheries Act was changed so that fish habitat would not have to be protected from development unless a commercial fishery was at stake; the National Round Table on the Environment and the Economy, a key advisory body for the federal government, was dissolved; federal funding for the Experimental Lakes Area, a living laboratory of fifty-eight lakes in Ontario that has yielded solutions to such problems as acid rain and phosphate-induced algal blooms, was terminated; also terminated, quite audaciously given the context, was British Columbia's oil spill response centre, its duties transferred to a national headquarters in Quebec. The list goes on for a couple hundred pages. Anyone who studies it will have a personal favourite or two, and mine was this: from now on, the prime minister and his cabinet were given (by themselves) the authority to overrule the very regulatory bodies they had just eviscerated. All they had to do was declare it a matter of "national interest." This meant, for instance, that if the National Energy Board rejected Enbridge's Northern Gateway application, the prime minister could approve it himself.

Canada was still a long way from bloody military interventions—the prospect of our armed forces opening fire on a crowd of unarmed civilians remained almost unthinkable—but as I said to Kai and Stephanie, the path Northern Gateway was taking us down didn't seem to lead away from that outcome.

Kai and Stephanie had many connections in the world of news and pipeline politics. I asked what they thought the chances were of Northern Gateway being approved.

"I actually don't think we have much to worry about," Stephanie said.

"It's looking like Northern Gateway is the lame duck of the Big Three," Kai agreed. There were two other major projects-in-waiting that promised to divest the tar sands of their bitumen, and these were the ones that looked most likely to go ahead: Keystone XL, which would pipe over 800,000 daily barrels from Alberta to the Gulf Coast, and Kinder Morgan's expansion of an existing pipeline running from Alberta to the edge of Vancouver, which if approved would send an additional half a million barrels per day to BC's southern coast.

Neither of these projects had received anywhere near the negative press in Canada that Northern Gateway attracted. Keystone XL, it was true, became a rallying cry for the American climate change movement, and so got as much airtime as Northern Gateway (much more in the United States); but the fact that most of Keystone's infrastructure traversed American territory already crisscrossed by pipelines and oil tankers kept Canada's environmentalists from attacking it with any particular zeal. In any case, Canada had approved the project long ago and its fate lay entirely in American hands. And Kinder Morgan, though controversial, was simply proposing to expand an existing pipeline/tanker route whose infrastructural hurdles had already been overcome.

Northern Gateway, by contrast, was an all-Canadian project looking to go places no oil man had gone before.

The intense media scrutiny unleashed on Enbridge as a result unearthed a treasure trove of news stories. Chief among

these was the largest onland oil spill in U.S. history: in 2010—
the same year the company filed its Northern Gateway application—an Enbridge-operated pipeline spilled twenty thousand
barrels of bitumen into Michigan's Kalamazoo River, contaminating sixty-five kilometres of its length. A frustrated official
with the U.S. National Transportation Safety Board, which
investigated the spill, famously compared Enbridge's techni-
cians to the "Keystone Cops," in part because it had taken
the control room in Edmonton seventeen hours just to realize there was a leak. Three years and almost $1 billion later,
Enbridge was still embroiled in cleanup operations along the
Kalamazoo.

The Kalamazoo was not a stand-alone incident. It turned
out Enbridge-operated pipeline leaks had caused six of the ten
largest terrestrial spills in the United States over the past ten
years. This did not include the Enbridge-run gas pipeline that
ruptured in the Gulf of Mexico on the very day that the Northern Gateway public hearings opened, but that, too, made for
good reading. Unfortunately the company didn't seem to be
benefitting much from hindsight; in 2013, the National Energy
Board announced that 117 of the 125 pump stations Enbridge
operated across Canada lacked the backup power necessary to
enact an emergency shutdown as federal guidelines mandated.
Of those 117 stations, 83 were missing emergency shutdown
buttons altogether.

Enbridge's oversights weren't just infrastructural. They extended to the cultural arena, in particular its dealings with the
First Nations living along Northern Gateway's pipeline and
tanker routes. The company first put the wrong foot forward
in 2006, when a team of surveyors contracted by Enbridge cut
down fourteen sacred trees on Haisla land, near the proposed

tanker terminal outside of Kitimat. The Haisla, who hadn't even been told that surveyors were on their land in the first place, were not placated by Enbridge's belated apology. "We compared it to a thief breaking into your house and destroying one of your prized possessions, and then calling you later to apologize for it," was how one Haisla councillor put it. Native leaders throughout British Columbia were further alienated when Enbridge subsequently hired an aboriginal consulting firm to speak with First Nations on the company's behalf, instead of sending its own executives to negotiate directly. Later, when a hereditary chief from the Gitxsan Nation named Elmer Derrick announced that his nation supported Enbridge, his nation boarded up his office and threw him out of the community. These and other fumbles were all assiduously reported by every media outlet in the country, to the point that Kai and Stephanie now assumed that the two remaining years of public review were little more than an expensive and time-consuming formality that nobody had the heart to stop. Northern Gateway, they said, was finished.

And yet they didn't look all that excited.

"But isn't that fantastic?" I asked.

"Sure," said Kai, "and all it took were the tireless efforts of a thousand journalists, every environmental NGO in North America, and a few dozen politicians. Meanwhile Keystone and Kinder Morgan will go forward, and no one's done anything about climate change because we were all too busy arguing over Northern Gateway."

"Seems to me," I said, "that whatever else happens it'd be a huge victory if Northern Gateway gets denied. This movement needs a morale boost."

Kai and Stephanie smiled skeptically. So did Ilja. We finished our beers and went into Shearwater to sing some karaoke.

A SILVER MIST enveloped the seabus shortly after dawn a few days later, and we crossed Lama Pass without seeming to move at all. The fog stretched off the water into Bella Bella's streets, covering a line of maybe thirty people waiting outside the Waglisla Band Store, just above the Koeye Café. The store should have opened at nine but its doors were still locked. Across the street, a crew of six men who looked like they were still up from the night before were hanging out in the stoop of a derelict house; friendly catcalls ricocheted between the men and the grandmas in the lineup. A moment of calm, wings flapped somewhere, and one of the men hollered "ERIC WHAT THE FUCK" in a voice that could have been heard in Shearwater. Eric must have been the manager, because a few seconds later the barred doors opened and the queue shuffled tranquilly into the store.

We weren't going to the store. We veered around the lineup and kept walking several blocks down a misty road that paralleled the shore, until we reached a squat wooden building in a gravel yard opposite Bella Bella's marina. This was the Heiltsuk Integrated Resource Management Department (HIRMD), to whom we now submitted ourselves for formal vetting.

HIRMD had been created at the outset of the Great Bear Rainforest Agreement in 2006, and it was now the official body through which all Heiltsuk development decisions were made. This primarily meant things like figuring out which hillsides to log and how to log them, or where and how much to fish, or whether clam farms could be made to turn a profit, but it also included whether or not to let any particular journalists/media types poke around the territory. To that end I'd struck up a friendly correspondence with HIRMD's president, hereditary chief Harvey Humchitt, who was now back from his fishing excursion and ready to meet Ilja and me.

A heavy-set receptionist greeted us when we walked through the doors, and we told her about our appointment. She picked up her phone to tell Chief Humchitt we were here. A phone rang in the office directly across from where we stood, picked up after the first ring and followed by a soft "Ah-huh?" then, "Okay I'll be right out," and out came Harvey Humchitt, his eyes lit up way louder than his voice, a toothy grin on his face, half-conspiratorial and half-apologetic.

"Sorry it's taken me so long to see you guys," he said straight away. "We're really, incredibly busy here. You have no idea. But please, please sit down."

We felt like long lost nephews. A week later, we would be eating crab at his house with his wife and daughter and three of his friends who came every year from Hawaii and seemed (like us) to form but one thread in a constant string of guests who blurred the line between professional, political, and social contacts—Kai and Stephanie, for instance, had been informally adopted into his family already and given Heiltsuk names.

We were happy to settle for permission to take notes and pictures. But first we had to go through the formality of sitting in the board room to meet HIRMD's half-dozen permanent staff members.

Harvey led us in, and soon we were seated around an oval table with a group of six smiling Heiltsuk and one scowling woman of unambiguous European descent. She was an anthropologist named Jennifer Carpenter with Jane Goodall hair and a hearing aid that kept malfunctioning.

That was all right, because the others hadn't heard our story yet. After saying how grateful we were just to be here, we explained that we wanted to photograph Heiltsuk people and places, to write about the history and culture of their nation, and record how they felt about the Northern Gateway proposal. In particular we were hoping to visit the Koeye watershed and see what Qqs was up to there. We would eventually be publishing our stories and images in...well, we weren't yet sure about that. Somewhere. *Reader's Digest* was interested, though they were going broke and might not be around next year; I was planning to write a book, though my publisher was also going broke and might not be around next year; Ilja had an Art Project in mind.

"Why don't I show you some examples to give you an idea," he said. He produced an iPad on which he'd saved several portraits: each was a double-exposed photograph in which a human subject was superimposed over a landscape to which that person had a particular connection. There was one of a logger, his chainsaw-holding silhouette visible overtop a pile of milled trees; in another, a woman's face looked out of the garbage dump where she worked; a third revealed a waterfall in the shape of a woman's body. Ilja hoped to gather a few dozen of these over the summer; when we got home, he would frame them in light boxes and find a suitable exhibition space.

"If these were digital I could do this kind of thing in two seconds," he explained, while Humchitt and the rest took turns looking at the pictures. "But I do it with film, which is a lot more time consuming." A more accurate term would have been pain in the ass. I myself didn't yet fully appreciate the procedural implications of Ilja's Art Project, but it wasn't long before they were driven home. To get the "subject" half of each double exposure, Ilja needed to hang a white screen on-location and surround it with a number of remote-operated flashes whose positioning gear was almost entirely homemade (duct tape, rolled-up beer boxes, etc). These items, plus the unwieldy Linhoff camera that looked more like an accordion and required an even more unwieldy tripod, all had to be hauled out of *Foxy*, loaded onto the inflatable, and lugged to wherever the person to be photographed was waiting; then, during the half hour minimum it took Ilja to set up his portable studio, it was my job to keep the subject entertained and generally distracted from the fact that what they'd thought they were signing up for—a snapshot—was obviously a much more involved, nineteenth-century-esque operation, for which they would next discover, once Ilja called them over, one of the conditions was maintaining absolute rigidity of pose for up to thirty seconds at a time while he made sure subject/lens/screen/flashes were all precisely lined up. That part included firing the flash several times, which if it was dark (it always was), was a blinding experience. Given that more than one of the people we would eventually subject to this operation was well into their ninth decade of life, and that the environment in which we had them impersonate strobe-lighted statues was often filled with mosquitos or rain, or both, one could argue that the brief description Ilja gave HIRMD's staff of his project was among the more disingenuous moments of our trip. But there was no arguing with the motivation.

"I do it this way," he said, "because the same piece of film has been touched by sunlight that struck both the person and their landscape. There's a physical connection between the film and both of its subjects that you lose when you replace film with digital technology. And physical connections are exactly what we're trying to tell Canadians about."

Everyone at the table admired the photographs except the anthropologist, who had been frowning since the moment we sat down. Her expression didn't change when Humchitt handed her the iPad.

"I think they look weird," she said. She swiped at the screen, her eyes flicking from side to side, and handed the iPad back to Ilja. "I can't imagine why you'd want to do something like that." Everyone else looked momentarily at their hands. "Have you got release forms?" We did not. Jennifer Carpenter frowned. "You can't go interviewing and photographing people here without release forms."

We promised to write and print release forms, as we should have done in the first place. In the chaos of preparing for the trip we'd forgotten some important things. "Our mistake, definitely," we said.

She turned to me.

"What exactly are you planning to say about the Heiltsuk?"

"I don't know yet."

"A lot of journalists come through here, you realize, and not all of them can be trusted to report with honesty or accuracy."

By way of example, she told us that the students of Bella Bella, whom Global News had called "environmentalists" in a recent documentary, were not, in fact, environmentalists. This was a group of teenagers that had gone on a forty-eight-hour "hunger strike" two months ago to symbolize the hunger that would ensue if an oil spill wiped out fish stocks. "They studied *case law*," she said proudly. "They're not some fringe group of environmental radicals."

The subject of hunger strikes was in fact one that I found interesting in an unmentionable sort of way. I wondered: If you were never in danger of actually starving, wasn't it more accurately a cleansing strike? Or possibly a fasting strike? There was always "hunger action," a compromise I'd heard elsewhere. But I couldn't deny those kids had skipped more meals for this cause than I ever had, and so, when she summed up the situation with "the myth of the noble Indian has got to be done away with," I joined Ilja in a round of conciliatory nodding.

Once she got going, our anthropologist friend harnessed the power of inertia. We learned that she first came here as a graduate student several decades ago and soon fell in love with a Heiltsuk man. This was back when marrying a Heiltsuk made you one—in the eyes of the government at least—and now, though her husband had died, she had a daughter born and raised in Bella Bella who, according to her mother, considered herself to be 100 per cent indigenous. She, the mother, was wary of the outsiders she'd once belonged to, though she still quoted them like theatre buffs do Shakespeare. "Franz Boas," she said, "recorded an oral tradition that says 'In the beginning, there was nothing but water and ice and a narrow strip of coastline.' So Heiltsuk stories capture the fact that they've been here since the last ice age." She told us how exciting the news was coming out of the recent digs. "The so-called pioneers who pushed up here in the 1800s thought they were entering virgin territory. They were amazed at the emptiness of it. They had no idea that there used to be people living everywhere they looked. There was a smallpox epidemic that pre-dated the 1860's epidemic, so by then the First Nations were already down to a small portion of the civilization we now know flourished here for thousands of years. We've been mapping it!" And she showed us a laminated map with hundreds of blue and red dots illustrating where towns and villages and small cities once thrived. They were everywhere, blanketing the forked ocean shores like alveoli on bronchial tubes, shores that the past two centuries had returned to the spruce and hemlock and cedar trees from which those ancient villages had been painstakingly built.

With that, the monologue wound down, as did the meeting. We were granted permission to interview and photograph people on Heiltsuk territory. None of the other First Nations we visited required any such vetting, but in retrospect we were glad for the experience. It was instructive that the only person on our entire journey who gave us the slightest bit of pushback was a white anthropologist who, after thirty-eight years in Bella Bella, considered this place to be home. Who could blame her for being suspicious? She knew her former people well.

ONE MORNING, instead of sinking and dying someplace like we would have if I had been captain, Ilja started the engine to see how it sounded. Sure enough, there was a strange wheeze and rattle.

He shut the engine off and pulled aside the wood panel beneath the sink and shone a spotlight inside, and after fifteen minutes saw that a bolt had rattled off.

"Is it an important bolt?" I asked.

"It holds the engine to the boat."

The bolt had fallen into the hand-torture chamber of metal that was Suzy. Ilja spent the next hour fishing it out and screwing it back into place, while I sipped coffee and hoped for the best. He finished and looked at his grease-stained hands and let out a heavy sigh. "It's been three weeks and I haven't taken a single good picture yet," he said. A sailboat, so perfect for sightseeing, was not a place from which to take professional photographs. It was constantly moving, and you were never at the right angle to/distance from your subject, besides which you were too busy sailing to even try. When we weren't sailing, Ilja was constantly checking the engine, for this wasn't the first morning Suzy had made a strange sound; that happened almost every time we travelled under engine power. Some wire or screw or hose was always coming loose and requiring a two-step diagnosis and intervention that could easily chew up an hour of the day or more—much more. Now that Zach was gone, Ilja had no one to help him with the ongoing task of engine maintenance. My helplessness in that regard became a thing that pained us both, like hemorrhoids, flaring up each time Suzy developed indigestion.

Jessie Housty had invited us to her house for a drink that evening. She felt bad for not making time yet to have a proper conversation. I suggested to Ilja that she would probably submit to a portrait if he asked her, and his mood improved ever so slightly.

The wind had been building all day, and Lama Pass was livid. Trying to pilot our small inflatable across to Bella Bella would have been like driving a golf cart through a boulder patch. Instead we caught a seabus whose clientele demonstrated the population boom in effect, a four-to-one ratio of children to adults, half of them absorbed in iPhones and handheld video games and the other half in some combination of gossip and hand-to-hand combat.

Jessie lived in a small square home with an aluminum-hulled skiff parked in front and a beautiful deck on high slender stilts out back. We knocked on the front door and after a moment she opened it, a sheaf of papers in her hand from which she didn't look up. We followed her into a living room packed floor to ceiling with books; on the floor beside the bookshelves, dozens of folders were stacked in neat columns: the entire written testimony provided to the Joint Review Panel thus far by every tribe and environmental organization in British Columbia. Her dinner table had four bowls on it, one filled with an assortment of worn beach glass, another with feathers, a third with driftwood, and the last with small bones.

"Good thing I put away the book on cannibalism that I was reading earlier," she said, seeing me eye the bones.

A tangle of roots lay drying next to the bones, and Ilja asked her what it was.

"Hellebore," she said, putting down her papers. "Very strong medicine. It'll kill you if you have more than a pinch."

"Where do you collect it?"

"In Koeye." She pronounced it *kway*.

"The café?"

"Don't be dense."

The Koeye river valley was the primary theatre of operations for Qqs, the organization that Larry Jorgenson had founded, and for whom Jessie was now director of Traditional Ecological Knowledge. Koeye was sixty-five kilometres south of Bella Bella on the mainland; we had unknowingly sailed past it on our way out of Hakai. This was the site where Jorgenson made permanent his formerly peripatetic youth camps, and after spending her childhood summers there Jessie had put in several seasons teaching children how to forage for food and medicine amongst the old growth's understory.

"I practically grew up there," she said. "But I don't go to Koeye nearly as much as I'd like to now that I have council duties and Enbridge to fight," she said. "If there's anywhere you should see before you leave, it's Koeye."

Ilja and I looked at each other and nodded. "Agreed," Ilja said, and we all clinked bottles.

"My family's there right now," Jessie said. "They're building a new lodge. The old one burnt down last winter."

Like Hakai, Koeye had been taken over by a private fishing lodge in the 1990s that barred access to all non-paying visitors. It hadn't been much of a commercial success, in part because of regular protest flotillas that the Heiltsuk sent down from

Bella Bella. When the owners finally put the land up for sale, Qqs secured a major donation from the Buffett Foundation and bought the land for $1.2 million. They used the old lodge, just as Eric Peterson had at Hakai, to house scientists and staff for the summer camps.

But last winter, a young Heiltsuk man burned the place down to the ground.

"He was a really sweet person," Jessie said. "My parents used to take him in when he was between foster homes as a kid, so I grew up with him. He had severe fetal alcohol syndrome. We brought him into the Qqs programs, and he improved a lot. Eventually, we got him to be caretaker there during the winter, a time when no one's around much. He's in his early twenties now and he was doing better than ever, or so we thought. Seemed happy to be there, grateful to be given a position of authority. We'd send someone to see him every few days and there were no warning signs whatsoever. Then we got an emergency signal one day. We went to check what was wrong, and the lodge was gone—reduced to ash. Larry spent that whole night at the police station swearing up and down that there was no way this kid could have burnt the lodge down on purpose, that it could not have been arson. Meanwhile, the kid's in custody with William keeping watch over him. He's raving mad, totally hysterical, and he attacks William, which doesn't get him very far." I pictured William from the one time I'd seen him standing on the dock: half man, half bear. "Eventually the police took him in," Jessie continued, "and we haven't seen him since. He told the police when he calmed down that he'd done it, that he was glad he'd done it, but nobody knows why. It seems he had a psychotic attack, but at the same time he was extraordinarily methodical about it; he poured gas onto the floor of every room in the lodge and opened up all the propane tanks, then walked outside and lit a match. Then he waited until the next day before sending out a distress call, to make sure no one would get there in time to put the fire out. Apparently he's living in Prince Rupert now, but no one here really knows."

Jessie shook her head. There was no trace of anger in her voice.

"More than the lodge, I'm sorry for losing him. For him having lost himself, and us. The lodge we can rebuild, but I don't think we'll ever get him back."

Jessie slid open a glass door and stepped out onto the patio. Ilja and I followed her into the cool air and beheld a stunning view.

"Just don't lean on the rail," she said, grabbing a rotten beam and wobbling it to and fro like a loose tooth. "I don't have time to hide your bodies."

A family of eagles was flapping its wings at a family of ravens in a tall spruce near the beach, vying for branch supremacy. The ocean beyond them was a hammered sheet of metal, and on the far side of the pass, two kilometres from us, patches of forest on Denny Island were spotlighted by a July sun setting through the slowly marching clouds.

"Do you own this place?" Ilja asked.

"Even if I could afford it, there's an eight to ten year wait for housing here," she said. "I'm renting."

Jessie had a wistful air about her. Competent people in communities like this one quickly found themselves weighed down with more responsibilities than they wanted, and Jessie was more competent than most. On top of being a librarian and a director/fundraiser for Qqs and an elected band councilor and Bella Bella's foremost anti-Enbridge activist and a medicine woman whose grandparents had taught her to see the forest as a pharmacy, she was also a self-proclaimed "medievalist" who was finishing her Masters in Literature from the University of Victoria. All she needed, she said, was three uninterrupted weeks to write up her thesis. "It's on Medieval ethno-ecology and cryptobotany," she said.

"Specifically?" I asked.

"Specifically, the literature of John Mandeville." Mandeville was a fourteenth-century travelling knight whose fantastical literature made him more famous than Marco Polo for centuries, until academics realized that he'd invented almost every story he wrote, and that in fact there may never have been any such person as John Mandeville in the first place. Whoever wrote *The Travels of Sir John Mandeville,* however, had done it well enough to dupe several generations of European scholars, and that was what fascinated Jessie. "I thought I'd focus on the most timely and relevant subject I could find," she said.

Jessie told us she could spend a happy lifetime gathering medicine in the forest and reading books under a tree. But the more we talked, the more it seemed that a part of her thrived on adversity. On being the underdog. She told us the story of how the oldest member on the Heiltsuk Tribal Council, sixty years her senior, came up to her the day she was elected and said condescendingly, "I'm not sure about electing kids to council. This is grown-up work." It was clearly a fond memory.

"The funny thing is I never even wanted to be a councillor," she said. "I only joined the race so that I could push for there to be a proper campaign. In all the previous elections, no one ever laid out their platforms or policy ideas, there were no debates—everyone voted for their family, or if they didn't have family running, for their friends. All I wanted was for candidates to talk about policy, and then I wound up winning."

In fact, there was a fair amount of antipathy to the very idea of elected band councils, a sentiment that runs through virtually every First Nation in Canada. The institution of democracy was an imposition of the Indian Act; as a result, every band in the country has two sets of leaders, an elected tribal council and a cast of hereditary chiefs. The former gets its authority from the Canadian constitution, the latter from tradition, and the relationship between the two groups isn't always harmonious.

Jessie's father had talked about this divide when we met in Vancouver months earlier. "The elected council was generally very pro-industry, pro-jobs, while the hereditary chiefs were more focused on environment and cultural conservation," Jorgenson told me then. "There was a lot of tension. But over the past few years the two groups have found a middle ground."

During the last election, however, a number of old-school candidates had been in the running whose attitudes worried Jessie enough to run against them.

"You mean they're for Enbridge and Northern Gateway?" Ilja asked.

"No, no one's that extreme. Everyone in Bella Bella is against Northern Gateway. I've never seen anything like it in my life. A year and a half ago, hardly anyone in Bella Bella had even heard of Northern Gateway. Now every single person in town knows about it and is outraged. I went into a kindergarten class to talk about it the other day. They're kids, so I'm thinking I don't want to go in and be all depressing, so I said to the class, 'What are some things that you love in the ocean?' And a six-year-old answered me by saying 'Fish! But did you know there's a company called Enbridge that wants to kill them?'

"Before, you couldn't get more than five or ten people to show up at a community meeting. Now, we're filling rooms.

We've organized rallies where two or three hundred people came out. We had six hundred people show up at the JRP hearing—that's more than come to potlatches! And it hasn't just been within the Heiltsuk that Enbridge has united people. All the coastal nations have come together on this. The Haisla, Gitga'at, Kitasoo; they all sent chiefs to stand with us when the JRP came to Bella Bella, just like we went to their communities when it was their turn. Nothing like that has ever happened before."

We pondered that for a moment, then Ilja said: "Jessie, at some point between now and October, would you let me take your picture?"

Jessie gave him a withering look before answering: "If you absolutely must."

Then we all fell quiet. Heavy wings flapped and filled the silence; the eagles had won the contest and kicked the ravens out of the tree. It was almost dark now, and calm, and time to go. We thanked Jessie for her hospitality and walked back to the fuel dock to catch the last seabus back to Denny Island.

The next day, British Columbia's premier, Christy Clark, who had thus far refused to take a stance on Northern Gateway, announced that her Liberal Party would support the project on five conditions: 1) That the Joint Review Panel recommend its approval; 2) That "world-leading marine oil spill response, prevention and recovery systems" be put in place to protect British Columbia's coastal waters; 3) That "world-leading practices for land oil-spill prevention, response and recovery systems" be put in place to protect British Columbia's land; 4) That "Legal Requirements regarding aboriginal and treaty rights are addressed;" and 5) That British Columbia "receives a fair share of the fiscal and economic benefits" of the project.

The vaguely worded statement (what constituted "world-leading practices"? Who would decide if aboriginal and treaty rights had been satisfactorily addressed? What proportion of royalty payments amounted to a "fair share"?) served as a balancing pole for Christy Clark's tightrope performance in this, an election year. The coming winter campaign would hinge largely on British Columbia's potential to become an energy-export hub for Asia. In addition to Northern Gateway and Kinder Morgan, there were almost a dozen major proposals to pipe shale gas from northeastern British Columbia to various coastal terminals. These raised the prospect of tens of billions more in foreign investment. And yet Northern Gateway loomed over this field, taking the brunt of the media's glare in a slow-burning spectacle that laid to rest the tired adage that any publicity is good publicity. Up to 65 per cent of BC residents were opposed to Northern Gateway, according to polls. The New Democrat Party, who the same pollsters gave a comfortable and growing lead over Christy Clark's Liberals, practically revelled in its opposition to Northern Gateway. Now the Liberals, anxious to catch, were also...sort of opposed. Or sort of for it. It all depended.

Clark insisted that the first four conditions would have to be met before she would even discuss the money, but the media refused to discuss anything but the money; pretty soon, Clark played along. Speaking to the University of Calgary's School of Public Policy three months later, she would note that British Columbia was currently slated to receive only 8 per cent of the profits, while assuming almost 100 per cent of the risk of an oil spill. "If you were in business," Clark asked her audience, "would you take that deal?" By then, relations between Clark and Alberta's premier, Alison Redford, who refused to negotiate any royalty sharing scheme whatsoever, had already degenerated into icy silence.

Clark's announcement of the five conditions made the Liberals no new friends in Bella Bella. Kai Nagata and Stephanie Brown sprang into action that morning, interviewing Jessie Housty for a story that ran in an online magazine before the day was out.

"She has conditions in there around making this safer," Jessie told Kai for the record. "That's not the same as making it safe. We've been very clear as coastal peoples that no amount of risk is acceptable to us with this project."

Ilja and I found Jessie at the Koeye Café that afternoon and joined her for a coffee. She was in a good, if combative, mood, and laughed at how Bella Bella's chief councillor, Marilyn Slett, had dodged the press and sent every journalist inquiry to her instead. Publicity annoyed Jessie, but she knew how to keep her composure and find the right words. "Clark's position is no position at all," she said to us. "It lets her stay on the fence until the price is right. If a First Nations leader does that, everyone calls it selling out, but when she does it, they call it sticking to principle."

Whatever you wanted to call it, it was enough, ten months later, to win Ms. Clark the election.

The phone at Qqs started ringing again—more journalists— and we left Jessie to give the world its quotes.

Ilja and I wandered around this town where everyone is constantly playing and saying hello and striking up conversations with you. We ran into Jaryn, from the "Stuff Bella Bella People Say" video, who grinned at us and said the video had been posted. A block farther on, we heard someone call out, "Hey, it's the *gumshua*!" and thought someone must have watched the video already. A weathered fellow who looked fifty but was probably thirty was walking our way on unsteady feet, arm in arm with a beautiful woman whose black hair fanned over her shoulders like a shawl. We high-fived the guy and said hello to the girl. "I guess we're local celebrities now," we said, only half joking, but it turned out neither he nor his girlfriend had seen the video; he was just calling out the *gumshuas* on the street. "You're not as white as me though," he said. "I'm the biggest white man in town!" The girl laughed at our expressions and explained. "His name's Daniel White." Then they carried on towards the liquor store.

THE STORY OF disappearing species is already so familiar (even now, at its beginning) as to belong somewhere in the realm between proverb and cliché. But the fact that its *human* population has declined over the past two centuries does make the central coast of British Columbia somewhat anomalous. The region's hyperabundance once supported one of the greatest population densities ever seen in non-agricultural societies, with conservative estimates putting just the Heiltsuk's pre-contact population at thirty thousand. That was (and is) just one of seven other nations sharing what is now the Great Bear Rainforest, a region whose present-day population barely matches that of the original Heiltsuk clans alone. Today there are some twenty-six hundred living Heiltsuk, about half of whom live in Bella Bella. That's no small miracle considering that in the early twentieth century the Heiltsuk population dropped to below two hundred.

One of them was a woman named Magaga, the great great great grandmother of Jessie Housty and, give or take a great, about six hundred other living Heiltsuk. The woman had twenty-two children—"she pretty much single-handedly kept our culture going," Jessie told me—and their descendants were celebrating a family reunion at the community hall. Everyone we'd met so far insisted we pop by for a free meal.

The reunion had the air of an indoor fairground. A microphone, into which someone was constantly speaking or singing, was set up under the basketball hoop. Bands played, a wedding ceremony was conducted, extended families took turns telling their matriarchs and patriarchs how much they loved and owed them, all while dozens of people looked on from the bleachers. Kids dashed in and out of the building, shooed out by their parents or older siblings whenever they made too much noise, then shooed back in when something important was about to happen. A line of booths at the foot of the bleachers were manned by plump women selling jam and preserved vegetables, bead necklaces, homemade perfumes, knitted sweaters, No-Tanker hoodies, drums. The food tables were bowed with dishes of tradition and convenience: salmon and bannock, spaghetti and potato salad, a steaming pot of chicken gumbo. The family tree was printed out on a wall, twenty pages long, beside a sign that read: *"Her children arise and call her blessed; her husband also, and he praises her: Many women do noble things, but you surpass them all." Proverbs 31: 28-29*

Sitting under that sign, his long black hair tucked under a trucker's cap, was Elroy White, the pre-eminent Heiltsuk archaeologist who specialized in uncovering the stone fish traps by which his people harvested salmon until the 1930s.

"Nice to finally meet you," he said when I introduced myself. We'd exchanged emails, but he was constantly in the field and this was our first encounter. He gestured for me to sit beside him.

Elroy White was an early protege of Larry Jorgenson, and explained with pride that he'd been the first camp counsellor at the Koeye Rediscovery Camp, from 1998 to 2001. "My whole staff was Heiltsuk university students," he recalled. "The younger generations are really going for it now, and Larry Jorgenson was right behind all that. He wanted Heiltsuk people running their own affairs, which was of course what we wanted too. But he really knows how to make things happen."

Once he completed his archeology degree, Elroy White left the Koeye camp and set about tracking down long-abandoned fish-smoking camps, as well as the stone fish traps the Heiltsuk used until the 1930s to harvest salmon. "We've found about 300 fish trap sites," he said, "and in each of those bays there are usually two or three actual traps set up. And we've only just started looking." A Heiltsuk fish trap is visible only at extremely low tides, when the ocean pulls back to reveal the circle of small boulders in which Magaga's forebears not only trapped the salmon as they pooled in front of river mouths, but selectively bred them as well. "The strongest and healthiest fish would be pulled out and sent upriver to spawn," he explained. "The rest were killed and smoked, so they could be stored for winter."

Far from depleting the numbers of the coast's most emblematic fish, oral history gathered by Elroy White and others suggests that the Heiltsuk and their neighbours actually boosted salmon populations; not only did they select the best individuals to reproduce while keeping the weakest for dinner, they also transplanted salmon into streams that didn't originally support a run. When the Heiltsuk first arrived here, after all, there were no rivers for salmon to spawn in, only ice fields. The rivers formed later, as the ice melted and trees began to grow. The Heiltsuk were here already when salmon first entered the newly formed watersheds, and as the streams filled with fish, either naturally or with a helping human hand, each family was given a creek to call its own. Their winter supply of smoked salmon depended on how well they maintained that creek. If it was choked with debris, they would clear it so the spawning salmon could make it through; if it was too exposed to hot sun or too fast-running, a strategically placed log or a boulder might provide cooling shade and calm eddies in which the exhausted fish could rest. We may never know exactly how much this contributed to the legendary runs that the first Europeans to arrive witnessed; but the idea that First Nations were somehow separate from the evolution of their ecosystem has been thoroughly debunked.

More than fifty abandoned Heiltsuk villages have been unearthed by archaeologists like White, along with hundreds of seasonal campsites where the Heiltsuk not only smoked salmon, but tended clam gardens or harvested herring roe. Like all coastal First Nations they were constantly moving to capitalize on the seasonal opportunities that nature proferred. Spring herring, fall salmon, seaweed, abalone, clams, mussels—every plant and creature had a season and a place, and the Heiltsuk knew them all.

And this was their state of affairs when Europe arrived and time accelerated. The experience of being plucked out of one century and thrust into another is something that unites every indigenous society on earth; it is a temporal equivalent to the physical uprooting that tears them off the land and into a market economy. It's probably impossible for anyone who hasn't experienced this dislocation to grasp fully how disorienting it is, how difficult to stop hunting animals and start hunting money. The game is a good one if you know how to play; if you don't, you are as fucked as any bush dweller who doesn't know how to kill.

MARILYN SLETT, chief councillor of Bella Bella, was a soft-spoken woman in her mid-forties with sleek black hair and worried eyes. She met me at quarter before eight in the morning in the low wooden building that served as headquarters for the Heiltsuk Tribal Council. I was curious to know if any Enbridge executives had been here before me.

"Yes," she said, "they sent a delegation in August of 2010. It was a beautiful day like today, so we asked if they'd ever been here in the winter, because, of course, conditions are not like this for most of the year. We get ice storms with hurricane winds quite frequently. In the fall, the fog is often so thick you can barely see your own hands. We told them we were extremely worried about oil tankers attempting to pass through our territory in those kinds of conditions."

"What did they say?"

"They said don't worry, there will be two tugs on each tanker to make sure there's no accidents, and even if there is, all tankers will have double hulls. They said they would insist on all the latest technology. And we said if you look at the history of marine accidents around here, it always comes down to human error. It's rarely a problem of technology."

I asked what she thought would happen if there was to be an oil spill in Heiltsuk territory; the oil tankers would be passing directly by the outer islands where they do most of their fishing.

"That's our nightmare," she said. "If we lose our access to the sea, we cease to be Heiltsuk."

"Do you think the Joint Review Panel will listen to your concerns?"

"We're very aware that the whole JRP process is..." she paused, searching for the diplomatic words. "Not adequate. The process is inadequate. But we go through with it because we need to be on the record."

When I asked her about Jessie Housty's role in mobilizing Heiltsuk opposition to Northern Gateway, Slett lost her worried look and, if only for a moment, became happy.

"Jessie's been integral to this process from the beginning," she said. "She's the one who organizes the community rallies, she was the one who made sure that the Heiltsuk were registered for the public hearings in the first place. She's so knowledgeable in all these matters—probably more so than anyone else in the community."

"What happened when the panel came in April?"

"We had prepared a feast and invited them, but after what happened at the airport they said no. At first we didn't realize anything was wrong. We were all waiting for them to join us when I received an email saying 'we really don't think your community understands what this process is all about, and we don't feel safe in your community.' That came as a total surprise. I called them and asked if I could come to them in Shearwater to talk about it and clear the air. It was 8:30 in the evening and they said no, it's too late. Now the panel is coming back next week to finish what they started, but they're making us go to Denny Island. That's an insult to our community. Many of our elders can barely walk; they won't be able to join us. We have guaranteed the panel no harm will come to them in Bella Bella, but apparently they are still afraid."

26 June 2012
To Chief Councillor Marilyn Slett and Ms Carrie Humchitt,
Legal Counsel,

Dear Ms Slett and Ms Humchitt,
On 12 April 2012 and 18 May 2012, the Panel wrote to your community with respect to scheduling the remaining oral evidence of the Heiltsuk. In its 18 May 2012 letter, the Panel asked that you write to the Panel, to confirm that your community would be available to present the remaining oral evidence at the outset or conclusion of the session scheduled for oral statements. No written response to these letters has been received by the Panel.

The Panel understands that staff has been in contact with you on a number of occasions since March 2012, to discuss scheduling the remaining oral evidence at the outset or conclusion of the oral statement sessions originally scheduled to begin on 25 July 2012. However staff has been unable to confirm when and where the Heiltsuk would be able to present its oral evidence from the six remaining witnesses (Jennifer Carpenter, Rory Housty, Murray Reid, Mavis Windsor, Mary Brown and Dr. Vigers.)

The Panel also understands that our staff has recently taken steps to book a venue in Bella Bella, but has been unable to do so. Specifically, the Community Hall is not available on 26 and 27 July and there may be construction at the school during the summer months. Staff also contacted the Elders Centre and was advised that the venue could not be booked.

Panel staff have looked into other venue options in the area and determined that Denny Island Community Hall on Shearwater Road is available on 26 and 27 July. In light of the ongoing scheduling issues, Panel staff has confirmed a booking at that venue. This venue is in close proximity to your community and easily accessible by water taxi.

The Panel confirms that it is available to attend on Denny Island on 26 and 27 July to collect the remaining oral evidence from the Heiltsuk. At that time, the Panel also plans to hear oral statements from those individuals who registered to provide an oral statement before the 6 October 2011 deadline and have scheduled a time for their presentation through the online scheduling tool.

I was at Jessie's house, getting lost amid binders of correspondence between the Heiltsuk Tribal Council, Enbridge, and the Joint Review Panel, when I came across that letter. I looked up and asked her about the missed deadline, the unavailable bookings. "Oh, that," she sighed, with an apologetic wince. "Our lawyer has a hard time making deadlines."

But as far as available bookings were concerned the JRP was simply lying, Jessie said. "We called the Elders Centre after we got the letter and asked them about this, and they said no one from the JRP had ever called. So when we wrote them back to tell them that we had a place to hold the hearings in Bella Bella if they wanted, they changed their reason for not coming here."

16 July, 2012
Dear Ms. Slett and Ms. Humchitt:
The Panel received your letter dated 6 July 2012...

In selecting locations for hearings, the Panel considers which locations would be conducive to a respectful, accessible, efficient and effective process in which to receive evidence. In

the case of the hearings for 26 and 27 July the Panel has con-
cluded, using the above criteria, that Bella Bella is not the
optimal location for collecting the remaining oral evidence
and oral statements from the Heiltsuk.
The Panel has decided to continue, as announced, with
the Denny Island hearing location.

JULY 27, 2012, was an overcast, windless morning in Heiltsuk
territory, and Lama Pass was syrup-smooth when two canoes
set forth from Bella Bella with ten young Heiltsuk in each of
them. Jessie Housty sat at the front of the lead canoe; a drum-
mer in the following canoe kept a beat for the paddlers to row
by. Ilja and I slow-jogged beside them in our tender, me holding the throttle at a low hum while Ilja juggled several cameras. Eric Peterson from the Hakai Beach Institute was right
behind us in his beautiful speed boat, which had made the
journey from Hakai in less than an hour; Kai and Stephanie
were aboard with him, Kai sprawled belly-down on the foredeck, filming. Peterson and I waved to each other and tried to
keep out of our respective camera men's frames.

When the canoes reached Shearwater half an hour later,
William Housty was there to greet them with a voice that came
from the belly of the earth. "We come not in peace, we come
in war!" he roared, and the paddlers knocked their wooden
oars against the hulls of their canoes. "Now hurry up," William added, "it's twenty after nine!"

The Denny Island Community Hall was a tenth the size of
Bella Bella's, and the sixty-some people who showed up that
day filled it to capacity. The panel members were seated at the
front, wearing the poker faces for which they'd become legendary. Their masks didn't crack until I approached Sheila Leggett
during the coffee break to ask if she'd be willing to tell me her

Twenty young Heiltsuk travelled in two canoes from Bella Bella to Shearwater in order to attend the final round of Northern Gateway public hearings.

side of the April Fool's Day story. An emotion that looked like happiness flashed across her face, accompanied by a smile, and she sang out "abso*lute*ly not!" before turning away.

And then who should take the stage but Rory Housty, the hipster-glasses-wearing co-star of "Stuff Bella Bella People Say," quivering like a drumskin as he swore an oath of honesty on a feather and drum. I'd never seen a man so visibly nervous; we all fell in love with him at once, and even the panel members twitched. The notion that this whole process was a meaningless sham evaporated the moment it actually began. Each person who testified, when their turn came, believed they had the power to stop the dreaded monster from attacking, if only they found the right words to touch its heart.

Rory had prepared his in advance, and after raising a trembling glass of water to his lips, he opened a laptop and proceeded to read:

"We as Heiltsuk are still fortunate enough to be able to have salmon, herring roe, halibut, cod, seaweed and shellfish. A chief shows his wealth by being able to serve his people traditional foods. Our hereditary chiefs cannot practise our cultural ways that our ancestors have passed on to us from generation to generation when an oil spill occurs."

And who else: Jennifer Carpenter, the anthropologist from Heiltsuk Integrated Resource Management Department, displaying a map of the hundreds of stone fish traps that archaeologists have discovered in Heiltsuk territory:

"You know, there's a perception that folks living in this area were just lucky they were born into this teeming wilderness of abundance. It's quite the opposite, we're learning.

"My late husband told me he was told by his grandmother and great-grandmother that the fish trap was used to enhance the salmon. The good breeding stock would be allowed to go up to spawn. The amount harvested in any given year would be carefully monitored so not too much was taken. And the medium species would be harvested for smoking and drying for the winter and distributing to family and relatives and trading up and down the coast. We have also learned that salmon and herring were transplanted to extend their breeding grounds."

And one Dr. Gary Vigers, an environmental consultant with a PhD in biochemistry who has been working on British Columbia's coast for forty years:

"Imagine, if you will, a sheen of oil as a sheet of Saran Wrap. Take a piece large enough to cover your face, chop it up into a hundred small pieces, approximately the number of toxicants in oil, and eat it, and you might have some indigestion or not even notice the difference. However, place the uncut sheet of Saran Wrap firmly over your nose and mouth for about ten or fifteen minutes, and you'll probably die of suffocation.

"This is exactly what happens when herring eggs are exposed to oil slicks and entrained oil. Oxygen transferred from water to spawn is cut off and the eggs quickly suffocate."

Those three and seven more spoke that day, each given ten minutes, each applauded like Leonard Cohen. After it was over, the panel members slipped out a back door and disappeared from our lives forever. But the day's testimonies were duly transcribed by the Government of Canada and can be read online for as long as the Internet lives. Their voices joined a chorus that included over a thousand men and women, children and elders, cowboys and Indians, scientists and teachers and fishermen and mechanics. Some of the speakers were poignant, some were banal, some were witty, some were insipid, some cried and some shouted and some stuttered. But when the hearings finally closed in February of 2013, the final tally showed almost all of them had one thing in common. All but two of the 1,161 British Columbians who spoke out were opposed to Northern Gateway.

It's worth adding that many British Columbians who weren't able to deliver oral testimony before the Joint Review Panel submitted their opinion in writing instead; for that cohort, the final tally was 239 in favor, 9,159 against.

And a few weeks after Christy Clark won the provincial election, her government registered its formal opposition, too.

One more thing. It turned out that while we were cooped inside the Denny Island Community Hall, an Enbridge pipeline was rupturing in Wisconsin. It was a relatively new line, built in 1998, and it had passed two safety inspections in the past five years. The twelve hundred barrels it leaked went into uncelebrated earth, contaminating no oceans or parkland. It was a minor mishap that flashed briefly across the next day's news cycle and sank into the fallow ground of unremarkable events. These kinds of things happen all the time.

The presence of grizzly bears is a key indicator of healthy ecosystems.

4

WHISPERING BEAR

O F THE SIXTY or so grizzlies who dine on the Koeye River's salmon each fall, Ilja shot six. He shot them all in the space of three hours, two days after the Joint Review Panel left Denny Island.

We left the morning after they did, motoring south down Lama Passage, thrilled to be on the move until, an hour in, Ilja noticed the batteries were overcharging once again. We anchored in a bewitching harbour called Canal Bight where fish jumped all around us, and Ilja found an alternator wire that had sheared off, and he replaced it, and we were good again.

On we pushed, Lama Pass opening into the lake of Fitz Hugh Sound, south through the current-laden junction with Burke Channel, on past the ghost town of Namu and its ancient middens. Calvert Island came into sight off our starboard bow, the Hakai Beach Institute hidden on its far shore. Between Calvert's northern tip and the island chain above it there was a narrow gap through which you could see Hecate Strait. That was Hakai Pass, and it was the chink in the armour of outer islands through which an oil tanker's spill could easily flow if the tide was rising and the current flooding in. Directly in the current's path, open as a warm embrace, was the Koeye rivermouth.

The Koeye River empties into a round bay and we anchored there in twenty feet of water that breathed beneath *Foxy* with the mild swell pulsing through Hakai Pass, across Fitz Hugh Sound and into the bay, a swell that crested and broke into white foam when it finally struck the shore's coarse yellow sand.

An overgrowth of cedars and spruce that predated the Renaissance obscured the river's passage into the northeast corner of the bay. On the opposite shore a rough worker's camp was visible above the gravel pullout where barges delivered the materials that would become the new Koeye Camp Lodge. Ilja and I inflated our kayaks and paddled ashore, offering brief hellos to the dozen tired-looking men who were finishing dinner around a bonfire. They pointed us towards Marge Housty, Jessie's mother, who was washing dishes on the patio of a small cabin that the arsonist had spared.

Marge had a luminous smile that she bestowed on us at once, dissolving our vague anxiety at being outsiders in a sacred place. She remembered our months-ago meeting in Vancouver. "I'm surprised to see you here," she said, "and delighted. You haven't really seen Heiltsuk territory until you've seen Koeye." Marge was a different person here, surrounded by forest and ocean and stars and firelight, than she'd been in the city. Brighter, less muffled. "I'm afraid you've just missed dinner, but please join us tomorrow if you can," she said. We thanked her and told her we were hoping to take our tender up the river tomorrow to take some pictures. "We don't normally allow any motorized craft up there," she said.

But Ilja had over a hundred pounds of camera gear to bring; an exception would be made.

We saw Larry Jorgenson, too, and he was exactly the same as he'd been in the city—gruff and distracted. He was staring at an immense pile of boardwood, his eyes flicking from the lumber to the acre of empty land beside it. Those boards would form the lodge and several cabins that would occupy this peninsula. The land was flat as a parking lot, rimmed by cliffs whose edges were lined by tall firs that shielded the lodge from storm winds without obstructing the $1.2-million view. We left Larry alone to his mental blueprints, said good-night to Marge and the workers, and paddled back out to *Foxy*.

And then it was morning again, the earth spinning relentlessly, and we were loading Ilja's Linhof Master Technika into the tender (Jessie had suggested devil's club, her favourite plant, as the appropriate backdrop for her upcoming double-exposure), along with his Nikon D3, his Nikon D7000, his 500mm "mega-zoom" (Ilja's term) lens, and nine more lenses with varying parameters of focus and range, until our beloved inflatable was piled so high with grey camera cases that I had to climb over them and perch my ass on the dinghy's rubber nose while Ilja folded his long legs into the back and nestled in beside the 15-horse Tohatsu. And off we sped.

A group of camp kids was swimming and snorkelling in a deep eddy around the river's first bend, splashing and laughing in their bathing suits as though this were the Mexican Riviera and not a ten-degree river in bear country. They waved, we waved back. We slowed as we approached two submerged boulders that Marge had warned us about, underwater shadows that you couldn't see until you were right on top of them; next came the old quarry pilings that emerged from the water

Ilja Herb kneels to photograph a black bear on Princess Royal Island.

like giant, shredded toothpicks. After that the river deepened, the obstacles disappeared, Ilja opened up the throttle, and we flew through the middle of an ancient forest.

The flight of the Nikons lasted two kilometres, after which the river became too shallow to motor up safely; Tohatsu's propellor was tinging off the gravel bottom. The forest fell back here and gave way to an estuary of chest-high grass through which narrow moats of riverwater carved brown channels. We were still in the intertidal zone, for orange seaweed covered the pebble islands that rose into the middle of the river. We stepped out of the dinghy and pulled it farther upstream, wading against a sluggish thigh-high current, until it became knee-high, then ankle high and the dinghy's bottom scraped the rocks and ground to a halt.

We were floating back downstream with the motor off when we saw the first grizzly swim across the river.

It paddled a hundred metres downstream from us, brown head bobbing above the surface. I'd never seen a grizzly bear before. I whispered, "Bear," and pointed. Ilja scrambled amongst his gear, opening one case after another, struggling to get his 500mm lens mounted onto the right camera body without making a sound, all whilst trading places with me so that I was at the tiller and Ilja sat at the front, our absurdly small and overloaded rubber raft tottering beneath us. By the time we'd readjusted, the bear had made it across. It emerged from the water and paused to shake itself dry just as the current brought us alongside, and before it disappeared into the grass Ilja opened fire. They were his first wildlife shots of the trip. His relief was orgasmic.

"Thank Jesus," he sighed when the bear was out of sight.

We drifted a few hundred metres more and pulled out onto a gravel section of riverbank. Yesterday, when we stopped to replace the alternator wire, we'd also caught our first coho, and now we ate the leftovers—in hindsight, perhaps not the wisest menu selection in bear territory. But Ilja washed the tinfoil in riverwater before putting it back in his pack, and then he grabbed his camera and we went for a walk. We followed the river bank where it curved into the grass field, hugging a thin strip of rock against the forest's edge. The sea of green spread out across from the moat of water beside us, the grasses flattened by crisscrossing bear trails that ran between the canals. We reached a promontory two and a half metres above the channel just as a mother grizzly burst from the grass a hundred metres away with two cubs at her feet; they plunged into the channel and sauntered slowly out the other side, and Ilja shot them too.

They shook dry together, the cubs looking like raccoons with their sharply thin pale faces and dark eyes. Their mother was lean, her flesh hanging off her frame in long folds, for the fall's salmon feast hadn't yet begun and all they'd been eating was berries and grass. Too shortsighted to see us, she nevertheless caught a whiff of something strange in the wind and let out a few precautionary *whuffs*. Then she started walking. Her path brought her and her cubs closer to us. The only thing I knew about bears was never to get between a mother and her cubs. They kept coming closer. We backed away, and the mother reared onto her hind legs, sniffing hard. We kept backing off, Ilja shooting all the while, and they stayed put. Then we turned a sharp corner along the bank and ran back to the boat and that was that.

Ilja was elated now, and so was I. I took my clothes off to jump in the river while Ilja rolled a celebratory joint. I dunked my head underwater, and when I looked up, there was another bear swimming across the river towards us. More shooting. Ilja said, quietly, "If anything happens, don't run. We'll calmly get into the boat, and if he gets closer we'll pick up our paddles and wave them above our heads so that we look bigger than he is." The thing not to do was panic. Our paddles were pathetic little plastic things that came with the inflatable kayaks, because we'd misplaced our wooden paddles in Bella Bella. Maybe the Heiltsuk used them to paddle their canoes to Denny Island. I hadn't minded until now. I felt naked, because I *was* naked, but also because we didn't have bear mace or guns or any reliable means of self-defense other than not panicking, and the bear kept swimming closer.

But he came ashore fifty metres from us, slow and lumbering and almost-blind, non-aggressive and in no hurry, and

Some sixty grizzlies visit the Koeye watershed each fall to feast on salmon. This sow and her two cubs arrived early, in July, and are still lean from a winter of berries.

disappeared into the grass. There was no reason to be afraid, after all.

Still, it seemed wise to get back in the boat and finish rolling our joint there. I put on my clothes and we packed the boat up and eased it back into the river. The current was so slow we hardly moved. A few moments later, another lean grizzly emerged from the trees directly behind where we'd been standing. It ambled snout down to our picnic site and licked the rocks where Ilja had washed the tinfoil after our picnic.

We spent the next half hour floating beside him, twenty metres away as he strolled down the shore, pausing to chew the grass or glare dimly at us, then walk on. Eventually he reached a side channel that stretched back towards a mountain, and we let him disappear into the distant forest. By then, the mama had returned to the main branch of the Koeye and paddled halfway out with her two cubs, then turned back and sauntered upstream and out of sight.

And that was our first day in Koeye. We would spend two more there (sans grizzlies, but full of devil's club, Marge Housty's cooking and fire-side chats), then return in October to witness the salmon spawn on our way home. But all we really needed was that day.

Until then, the phrase "bearing witness" had been little more to me than an overused pun for all sorts of activist-journalism-type stories intended to inspire reader/viewer empathy with the Great Bear Rainforest. The experience of fulfilling the pun's dual mandate made it a great deal less annoying.

It was after all the grizzly bear, not the spirit bear, for which the Great Bear Rainforest was originally named. Spirit bears may be more unusual, phenotypically speaking, and on the whole more teddy-bear-esque, but really they are just black bears with the same gene that causes red hair and pale skin in humans (a term referred to, in their species, as kermodism); as such, they are less of a keystone species than grizzlies, which despite being the deadlier predator are far more sensitive to human development and habitat disruption. Where once grizzlies roamed as far south as Mexico and as far east as Manitoba, today they have been all but extirpated from the lower forty-eight—less than two thousand can still be found south of the Canadian border. They are gone from the prairies entirely. In the Yukon and Alaska they are doing relatively well, but in British Columbia, grizzlies have already disappeared from twelve large provincial parks and are declining rapidly in seven more.

The province's ministry of environment estimates that some sixteen thousand grizzlies are left in British Columbia, a number falling steadily as habitat fragmentation takes an ever greater toll. Their gradual decline marks more than the disappearance of the North American food chain's second-highest predator; it serves as an early warning of imbalance in the whole convoluted web of life required to sustain them, and ultimately all of us, too.

That web is still intact in the Great Bear Rainforest, which supports the largest and most densely concentrated population of grizzlies in Canada, estimated at up to three thousand in total. The Koeye watershed, spectacular as it is, is but one of dozens in the region to which these oddly skittish predators migrate every fall (and as we learned that afternoon, many linger there year round). It is a rare sign of ecological vibrancy that so many grizzlies would be willing to share such close quarters. The reason they do so wasn't obvious in July, but in two more months, when the Koeye and all its tributaries became choked with a smorgasbord of egg-laying sockeye, pink, and chum, and the normally territorial grizzlies waded shoulder-to-humpbacked-shoulder in knee deep water, and the whole forest reeked of fish and the bears grew so complacently stuffed that humans could practically tap them on the shoulder—when that happened, you no longer wondered why there were so many grizzlies here. You wondered instead what might happen if an oil spill were to occur in the wrong time and place. If, say, instead of spreading contaminants during the spring herring run as did the *Exxon Valdez*, a tanker were to founder in September or October. The never ending cycle of currents and tides would flush said tanker's payload into the Koeye or any of a thousand rivers like it at precisely the moment that all those waterways were acting as delicate riparian wombs, incubating millions of salmon eggs destined to become the winter-sustaining fish on which thousands of the world's last grizzlies might one day feed.

In case any doubt remains about an oil spill's deleterious effect on ecosystems in general, or British Columbia's coast in particular, I did consult a few specialists once our journey was over. They had several ways of saying the same thing, all of it easily confirmed with a little laptop research. To avoid redundancy, I nominate Otto Langer as their spokesperson. Langer spent thirty-two years working for the Department of Fisheries and Oceans and the Department of Environment (before it became a ministry); he worked on habitat protection and water quality as both a biologist and program manager, before leaving government in 2001 to help the David Suzuki Foundation create its Marine Conservation Program. Among other accolades, he was voted Conservationist of the Year in 2009 by the BC Wildlife Federation, and in 2010 by the Canadian Wildlife Federation.

The most immediate effect of spilling oil in the ocean, Langer told me, is "acute toxicity"—poisoning. "Fish death can occur at a few parts per million" of oil in the water, he said. Any fish in the immediate neighbourhood of an oil spill will be exposed to much more than a few parts per million, and "once that happens they do not have any hope of survival. That also applies to otters, seals, and birds. The oil will harm the waterproof coating on the feathers and fur of those organisms. The animals can die from hypothermia—especially birds—and can lose their ability to float in water. Also, the animals try to get the oil off of them and will lick it off and end up swallowing it; once this mess is in their body it can exert a very toxic effect indeed.

"But the greatest concern of oil on our coastal waters is what we see in the press—the massive coating of the intertidal environment, the beaches and the life in those key, essential and highly productive habitat areas." Koeye was a prime example of those areas, a zone where river, ocean, and land, and all the organisms they support, intermingle, gorging and breeding in an orgy of life that sustains land and sea alike. "Some of our most productive ocean areas are the eel grass and marsh beds," Langer said. "Once oil gets into these areas it also coats these plants and can kill them. These marsh and eel grass areas are essential for wildlife habitat, and even young salmon will feed on the shrimp, amphipods, and other small organisms that live in these shallow marine habitats. Even bears and deer depend upon the marine plants that thrive in these areas. Accordingly, a significant oil spill can harm the food of land animals that would not normally swim in or be associated with the ocean. However, bear, beaver and deer and even wolves do swim from island to island and their fur will rapidly uptake any oil from the surface of the water, like an oil skimmer. They will lose their insulation and lick the oil off, and that can kill them."

The proof is in the body count after the *Exxon Valdez* disaster: excluding fish, invertebrates, and all the animals that simply disappeared, the dead included 250,000 seabirds, almost 2,500 sea otters, 300 seals and 14 orcas.

Of course, that kind of thing could happen in British Columbia only if there were an oil spill to begin with. And that is a very big if. What we're after here is an accurate sense of the Northern Gateway's long-term compatibility with the Great Bear Rainforest. Something quantifiable. And for that it isn't ifs or puns we need, but numbers.

Before they die, salmon are morphed by freshwater, the effects varying according to species. Some develop hooked snouts, while others grow humped backs.

5

EVERY
PRECIOUS
DROP

OVER TWELVE hundred marine traffic "incidents" were reported off British Columbia's coast in the decade leading up to our trip, but *Foxy* did not feature among them. The closest we came to an incident was on August 2, as we motored up the middle of mile-wide Seaforth Channel. We'd left Koeye and were heading north again; up Fitz Hugh, through Lama Pass, past Bella Bella and Shearwater—just two hours past, in fact, when Suzy made a sound like her 37 horses were beset by wolves. Ilja slammed a greasy fist into the kill switch and dove below decks, leaving me at the aluminum wheel. The sun was shining. To starboard, a tug was overtaking us with a football-field-sized barge in tow, laden with machinery and oblivious to our predicament, as were the three sportfishing boats bearing down off our port beam. Ilja, absorbing different information in the engine room below me, shouted up in expletive-laden terms that the impeller hose had burst.

"What's an impeller hose?" I called back.

"The Pacific fucking ocean is pouring into our engine room!"

That I could picture. But Ilja swiftly resolved the crisis by turning a valve that stopped the water coming in. Never panic. No longer sinking, we unfurled the jenny and gybed downwind, sailing away from the rocks towards a narrow bay sheltered from the wind by a steep mountain. As we entered the mountain's lee, our sail deflated and *Foxy* drifted to a halt in time for us to drop anchor in forty feet of hazel water, and we were safe.

We weren't alone. Michael Reid and Sarah Stoner were right behind us in the *Skomalt*. They were headed to Hartley Bay, home of the Gitga'at Nation and our next stop, as well. There were a dozen routes we could have taken through the labyrinth to get there, but Michael said he knew of a good one, so we'd arranged to meet up in Whiskey Cove and sail north together.

The *Skomalt* followed *Foxy* to safe harbour and rafted up as soon as we'd anchored. "Thanks guys," Sarah said as they tied on, "Bowie was ready to go for a walk anyway."

Bowie was Sarah's enormous live-aboard mutt, who didn't have the best sea legs; she took him ashore for a beach walk while Michael and Ilja went below to look at Suzy.

"Pretty grim," Michael said.

"I think I can patch her up at least enough to get back to the mechanic at Shearwater," said Ilja. I was relieved to hear it. A tow would have cost over a thousand dollars.

"I think you guys should have a beer with me," I said.

They did, and Sarah paddled back to join us too, which was a good thing because the smell of her dog had attracted company. A guttural howl arose from the woods and a pack of pale wolves trotted out onto the rocks where she'd been five minutes earlier, sniffing intently. Ilja hustled down the hatch to retrieve his camera from the V-berth, but by the time he came back up the wolves had already flitted back into the trees.

"Fuck," he muttered. "Today's not our day, is it."

"I don't know," said Michael. "Doesn't seem so bad."

But Ilja was staring back into the bowels of the engine room now, and for the next two hours he abused Suzy with a stream of vitriol that had its intended effect, for at last he reemerged with a triumphant look on his face. He'd taken the impellor off and patched it up with a collection of parts cannibalized from non-essential items.

"Fire her up," he said, "I think we're good."

Suzy started without a problem, her timbre was healthy, the engine coolant stayed cool, nothing leaked. No water flooded the engine room.

Unfortunately, she'd lost her capacity to stay neutral.

"Are you in drive?" Michael asked. He'd looked up while we were all still looking down and noticed that *Foxy* and *Skomalt*, lashed tightly together, were spinning around inside the tight quarters of our rock-walled little cove.

"What the fuck," said Ilja. He checked the gear shift. "We should be in neutral."

"Pretty sure you're in drive," Michael said. "I think that's our cue." And he and Sarah and Bowie hopped back into the *Skomalt*, started her engine, and cast off at a strategic moment when the *Skomalt*'s trajectory shot her out of *Foxy*'s orbit into the safe, open waters of Seaforth Channel, making westerly into the setting sun, shouting back to us "Good luck! See you in Hartley Bay!"

We let *Foxy* keep turning while Ilja went back down to the dungeon and pulled experimentally on cables whose existence I could only imagine, calling up to me to put her in neutral, in drive, in reverse, until he'd sleuthed out the cause of our problems and *Foxy* stopped spinning circles. Finally he told me to kill it. He came back up grimy and exhausted, and I did the only thing I knew how to do in these situations: I rolled a joint and poured two drinks.

"What are the chances of our gears going bonkers at a time like that?" he said as we leaned back into our seats.

"Probably pretty good," I said. "When sorrows come, they come not single spies but in battalions." He gave me a look. "That," I said, "is Shakespeare."

"You mean when it rains it pours."

"Uh huh."

"I think it has more to do with the butterfly effect," he said. In just about any system, from old sailboats to planetary climates alike, pressure applied to one point often manifests as trouble in another, seemingly unconnected, point. He was pensive now. "Remember that engine-mount bolt that fell out? Who knows how long we ran Suzy before I noticed it. I think that might have been enough to shake Suzy just a pubic hair out of alignment, and now everything's a little out of whack."

"I'm sorry I'm so useless to you when it comes to this stuff," I said. "I know how stressful it is, you having to take every mechanical issue on by yourself."

"It's all right," he said. "You saying that helps."

"Communication," I said. "That's one thing I can do."

It wasn't all bad. We had performed a flawless sail-to-anchor under some duress, a manoeuvre Zach surely would have been proud of. We'd seen our first wolf pack. That night after dinner, we watched a full moon rise over our port bow, close enough to touch. Ilja went to bed but I wasn't yet sleepy, so I stayed up watching the moon. I heard the *psshh* of a spouting whale, distant at first and then louder as it swam invisibly closer, the intermittent gasps amplified by the island amphitheatre flanking *Foxy*. And then it emerged from the glistening metallic water less than a kilometre away. Not one but two: two orcas. They breached beneath the moon, lunging towards it, their white bellies reflecting its light in tandem as they shot fin to fin into the sky and arched onto their backs, slapping the water over and over, just far enough away for there to be a lag between the sight striking my eyes and the sound reaching my ears. The disturbance travelled more slowly through the water, but no less surely; a few moments later, the miniature waves from their splash rippled under *Foxy* and ricocheted around in our cove, rocking us long after they'd dived deep and swum away.

In the morning, the world was a grey-white shroud. We couldn't see five metres or hear a thing. We made our coffee and let the fog burn off, luxuriating in the silent anonymity of our grey cloak.

Eventually the fog receded to the centre of Seaforth Channel and we fired Suzy up, limping back towards Shearwater at three knots, keeping close to the shoreline where tongues of mist licked the trees, peeling away one layer at a time, revealing patches of unadulterated sky that grew and coalesced until there was nothing left but clear bright blue, *Foxy* running hot but not exploding, all the way to Shearwater, where we docked without incident, half defeated, half triumphant.

HOW MANY POETS and storytellers and musicians and hecklers and lovers of double entendre does it take to keep a language alive? Nobody knows. Probably more than a dozen, which is about all the Heiltsuk have left.

"How do you even say Heiltsuk?" I asked Jessie Housty, on the day we spent waiting for a new impeller to be flown in from Vancouver.

"Don't trouble yourself," she said. "White people don't have enough saliva in the right places to pronounce it properly."

Something else I wondered: "What does it mean to be an Indian in the twenty-first century?"

"That is the most asinine question a journalist has ever asked me," she replied.

And yet, I wondered. Were the Heiltsuk different from the rest of Canadians in a way that Cambodians, say, or Kenyans or Peruvians were not? The answer had always seemed to me to be an unequivocal yes. The experience of watching an orca breach under the full moon, or of having a wolf pack howl at you, or of watching a grizzly mother and her two cubs splash about within rock-throwing distance—these were experiences from which most cultures in the world have long since dissociated themselves. We no longer adjust our diets to the seasons; we do not know when salmon or herring are spawning. This contact with the rhythms of the natural world, so lost to city dwellers (less so to farmers, but they make up an ever-diminishing minority of our society), was something I'd long presumed to be a fundamental quality of being for indigenous societies. When I asked what it meant to be an "Indian" in the twenty-first century, I was partly teasing but partly, earnestly, wondering how she reconciled her people's ancient traditions with Google and motorboats and penicillin and online banking and all the other techno-markers of our age.

"My culture isn't defined by technology," Jessie told me, "it's defined by values." First Nations have the same relationship to modernity as all of us; the spectacle of modern innovation is no more or less incompatible with their worldviews than it is with the world of Judaism, or Christianity, or Islam. By the same token, the experience of nature is available to everyone, even city-dwellers—here I was, experiencing it, however fleetingly. I was in thrall, but not fundamentally changed, so far as I could tell. If anything, these experiences only served to confirm beliefs I already held about nature. I got those beliefs from the same urbanized culture that was causing climate change, a culture that had shown itself capable, from time to time, of inventing solutions to the problems it created.

The principal thing setting "them" apart from "us," I was coming to feel, was the experience of having been invaded, conquered, and shunted into ghettoes. Of living in a democracy that doesn't work for you. That experience is primarily a result of politics, not culture, though it has indeed been passed down from generation to generation like a family heirloom. Poverty, the ongoing injustice of broken treaties, an anachronistic Indian Act that forbids on-reserve "Indians" from owning the houses they live in, to name but one of a thousand degrading institutional slights—that is the history that divides us. The democracy that has functioned so well for most Canadians has, for this collection of minorities, been experienced as mob rule.

It will take enormous goodwill on behalf of both parties to sort this intractable mess out. If you only watch the news, it often seems like that goodwill was used up a century or two ago. But Bella Bella demonstrated that empathy is available, abundant as the ocean. Friendships are there for the asking. When we're face to face, stripped of our governments and reduced to being fellow humans in tumultuous times, camaraderie trumps antagonism. If—a romantic but surely not impossible if—we can push that simple spirit of shared humanity all the way into our politics, viable compromises might start to appear on the horizon. And surely that is one good reason for non-indigenous Canadians, myself included, to stop wondering what sets our cultures apart and start appreciating how much we have in common.

AT 6 PM on August 4, another beautiful day Ilja spent in the belly of his boat (he installed the new impeller himself), *Foxy* was ready to go. "First you think there's no way you can possibly find what's wrong," Ilja said. "Then you do find it and you take it apart, terrified the whole time because you're pretty sure you'll never be able to get it back together again. Then you put it back together again and you sail off, bracing yourself to be terrified all over again next time."

Off we sailed, leaving Shearwater for the second time in as many days, making it that night back to the cove we'd left yesterday. No wolves or killer whales this time (Passenger's Log: captain unamused at not being woken up to see the breaching orcas; had to downplay the magic). We awoke early the next morning and set forth under blue skies into Seaforth Channel, overheating slightly, but not disastrously, at 1100 RPMs all the way to the shelter of Ivory Island, where we tucked in just before Seaforth opened into Hecate Strait.

A pod of orcas was lounging at the narrow entrance to Reid Passage. No theatrics this time. They resembled bullish Holsteins of the sea, their metre-long dorsal fins wagging in the air as they rummaged lazily in the shallow water. It looked like Hakai, this collection of miniature white-sanded islands with bonsai trees blasted by their exposure to the open Pacific. The water grew calm and clear enough to see through to the bouldered bottom.

The mountains grew taller the farther north we went; steeper, closer, eating up more and more of the horizon. They were like an army that has walked across the bottom of the ocean, and as they emerged you could see first their heads, then their shoulders, and now they stood with the water around their waists, their torsos fully exposed.

We were in Kitasoo territory, approaching Klemtu, that town I'd visited thirteen years ago. (Forgive me, Klemtu—or perhaps you're already grateful—for not stopping in this time. Weeks behind schedule. Geese flying south. No contacts on the ground.) The tide was dropping as we passed the small island that shielded Klemtu from sight, and the draining ocean clawed at *Foxy*'s hull, slowing us to three knots, two knots, one...maybe we should have stopped in Klemtu after all. But a ten-knot broad reach picked up just as we were about to turn around. It blew us against the current all the way to the southeast edge of Princess Royal Island, where I'd huddled in my tent for a rain-soaked week in 1999.

Thirteen years later, I still didn't see any spirit bears, but just as before that didn't mean they weren't there. Kermodes comprise 30 per cent of the thriving black bear population of Princess Royal and her molar-shaped neighbour to the north, Gribbell Island. Their population is greatest on these two mountainous giants, but because they occasionally swim from island to island you can see them throughout the Great Bear Rainforest, making this the only place in the world where kermodes are more than a demographic aberration.

This is the land of the Only. The only place on earth where wolves rely on salmon; the only place on earth where five species of salmon fertilize the forest with their bodies, hauled in by wolves and bears and birds and weasels who all have a gluttonous tendency to leave half-eaten carcasses rotting into the moss, in turn to feed the trees—scientists have found salmon-specific nitrogen isotopes in the uppermost needles of these conifers, the only place on earth you'll see that. If you can't find an only, other superlatives will do. This is the biggest contiguous stretch of temperate rain forest on earth. The trees that grow here are some of the oldest on earth. Despite the industrial onslaughts of the twentieth century, this ocean-forest hybrid still harbours the greatest biomass density of any ecosystem in the world.

It's a marketing ploy, this trumpeting of mosts, biggests, oldests, bests; environmentalists have caught on but corporations remain the masters. When the average Canadian living east of the Rocky Mountains hears the words *Northern Gateway*, chances are they think not of tall trees or three colours of bear gorging on five varieties of salmon, but of the $6.5 billion the pipeline would cost to build—the most expensive industrial project in modern Canadian history, accompanied by a $5-million marketing slogan: "It's more than a pipeline. It's a path to our future."

At any rate, the spirit bears stayed hidden in the trees. Spawning season was just around the corner, and the whole world was waiting in the shadows. Over the next two days we wrapped around the southern tip of Princess Royal and crawled up her western shore. There was a lonely white beach there that Michael had told us about; in the forest behind it lay a place called the Colliseum. This was where chiefs from several tribes throughout the region once held congress: Haida, Heiltsuk, Gitga'at, Kitasoo... It was dug into the ground, huge timbers piled around it, benches terraced into the earth like a Roman senate. We found the beach and anchored nervously in ten feet of water, winched out the tender, and zoomed to shore over magnifying-glass-clear green water. Just inside the trees we saw NO TRESPASSING, Signed By The Kitasoo Nation. We felt their spirits looking down at us. So we drank a beer on the beach and looked out to windy Laredo Channel and Caamaño Sound beyond, where the oil tankers would maybe one day go. "We're supposed to be here to raise awareness of the threatened coast," Ilja said, "but it seems like so far all we've been doing is becoming aware of the coast's threats."

The beach was too exposed to keep *Foxy* anchored there for the night. Two miles farther north we found Kent Inlet, a narrow cleft between the cliffs that opened into a chain of blue lagoons that allowed us passage into Princess Royal's nether regions. Fish jumped everywhere we looked. But the water was nerve-wrackingly shallow, ranging from forty feet to ten as we passed through one tight hourglass after another; underwater islands loomed from the depths, poking their heads out in small rock outcrops here and there with a single tree on top.

Our paper charts did not go into enough detail to guide us through Kent Inlet. Instead, I was navigating by iPad. We'd downloaded GPS software that turned navigation into a simple video game, showing our position and progress on a digital map that zoomed with a pinch of the fingers from big picture to minute detail, laying out every corner of Kent Inlet's lagoons and showing where the shallow spots were. How satellites have softened us. Imagine the terrors Captain Vancouver and all the other Europeans endured as they explored these waters with no motor, no depth sounder, no GPS, only a pole to tell them how far the bottom was from their keel.

But our digital map had small glitches of its own, and so, as Zach had warned us repeatedly, one should never rely on it exclusively. As we inched along I saw that the images on the screen didn't quite correspond to reality; mansion-sized islands that were clearly marked on the glowing map appeared not to exist before our bow, and vice versa. I veered sharply once, then twice, causing Ilja, who was standing at the bow to keep an eye out for rocks, to snap: "Quit staring at the screen and use your eyes. This is exactly what Zach was talking about."

There were no disasters. We made our way towards a small waterfall and anchored in sight of it. The sun was setting and we'd barely relaxed before a chubby fellow paddling a long inflatable kayak that looked dangerously overloaded came into view; he unloaded his gear on the shore beside the waterfall, then paddled back and requested permission to come aboard.

"I have six weeks," he said in a Russian accent. "I'm hope to photograph wildlife, especially the spirit bear, yes. But without rain, none of them are come out. We need rain to fill the creeks. Then the salmon come. Then the bears come."

Mikhail was his name. He had bulbous glowing cheeks and a week's worth of greying stubble and he smelled like we must have, too. He'd paddled out of Klemtu a week ago and was circumnavigating Princess Royal Island with five more weeks to go. He was a strange blend of ignorant and hard core. He didn't know anything about tides or currents, and he had a hell of a time getting in and out of *Foxy* from his kayak; when he paddled, he wobbled uncertainly. Yet he'd made it this far and seemed unfazed at the prospect of paddling alone for five more weeks of waves, wind, and weather, with no help in sight should anything go wrong. He refused our offer of a drink because he had to get back to camp, less than a hundred metres away.

Precautionary measures can be taken too far, we told him, but Mikhail was resolute. He gave us his email address—"I'll hear from you in two months, yes, when you are home"—and we lowered him into his kayak, awkward as a child, and pretty soon everyone went to sleep.

Big orbs of white foam entered our lagoon overnight, ghostly beach balls that *Foxy* parted as we pulled away under a thin morning sun.

The current was mildly against us in Laredo and we made three knots as we entered the giant fishbowl of Caamaño Sound. This was a titanic aquatic traffic circle whose watery exits fanned out into Laredo Channel, Campania Channel, Principe Channel and others, all their currents and wind flows meeting and roiling about in Caamaño's giant ink vat. Hecate Strait came in sight off our port beam. We slowed down and caught our biggest salmon yet, another coho. They were gathering in the inlets now after four years of marauding god-knew-where throughout the Pacific, up into the Arctic, and would soon be entering the rivers of their birth to lay their eggs and die and feed the forest. But they needed a rain to fill the dry creeks and allow them passage.

A light tail wind came up. We raised the sails and killed Suzy. Instantly, the *brrrroop RRRRUUUUUP, bbrrrrrooooowwww* roar of a sea lion colony reached our ears. A rocky island sixteen kilometres off our port bow was covered in their fat brown bodies. They looked like slugs through the binoculars.

Just behind them, Gil Island.

This was the heart of the tanker route. One day, if we came back here, we might see the iron leviathans coming around Gil Island on their way in and out of Kitimat, not dwarfing *Foxy* so much as eclipsing her. The Northern Gateway proposal called for three classes of oil tanker: Aframax, the smallest, averages 220 metres long with a carrying capacity of 700,000 barrels; Suezmax (some classes of tanker are named after the canals they're designed to fit through), 274 metres long, would carry up to 1 million barrels; and the Very Large Crude Carrier, 344 metres long and weighing 320,000 metric tons, with a capacity of 2 million barrels. It is more than six times bigger than the largest ship yet to call on Kitimat. A VLCC has a two-kilometre turning radius and, when fully loaded without assisting tugs, takes up to three kilometres and fifteen minutes travelling at speed to come to a full stop.

Even so, the thought had crossed our minds that if the weather was always this good, this wouldn't be such a bad tanker route. If we could sail these waters without incident, surely teams of experienced professionals with vast arrays of modern technology at their disposal could as well. But the sight of green Gil Island dead ahead undermined our confidence.

Shortly after midnight on March 22, 2006, Gil Island sank the *Queen of the North*. She was the fifth largest vessel in the BC ferry fleet, 125 metres long and 8,800 tons with room for 700 passengers, though only 101 were aboard that night. They were a third of the way through their trip from Prince Rupert to Port Hardy when their ship struck what happens to be the first obstacle in the Northern Gateway's tanker route.

Prevailing winds were 20 knots that night, and a northern squall was blowing through with rain and recorded gusts of 40 knots (just shy of 80 kilometres an hour; "hurricane-force" winds, by comparison, start at 118 kilometres an hour), which was still well within the ferry's operational limits. There was no fog, no strong current, no waves. The *Queen of the North* did not go down because of weather.

Nor was technology entirely to blame. The engine and steering system were both running perfectly. The ship's navigational aids were designed to be redundant, including a global positioning system, automatic pilot, three radars, and electronic charts that displayed her course and position in real time. As the president of BC Ferries said in the immediate aftermath, "There was enough electronic information there that one would think this shouldn't happen." And yet it did.

What happened, as pieced together by the Transport Safety Board of Canada and the Crown prosecution for the criminal trial that eventually ensued, was this: the autopilot failed and no one noticed. It happened despite, or more likely because of, the fact that the autopilot system was a new one, recently installed and certified by Transport Canada on March 2, less than three weeks before it failed to execute a slight but mandatory two-degree turn where the long straight shot of Grenville Channel opened into the wheel of Wright Sound, with Gil Island directly in its path. The radars, electronic charts, and autopilot each had their own alarm that should have sounded independently of the rest; the sound on every single one of these alarms was deactivated, either during the ship's recent retrofit or at some point thereafter. Several visual alarms did start blinking, but someone would have had to look at a screen to notice them.

That someone was Karl Lilgert, Fourth Officer in charge of bridge that night, assisted by quartermaster Karen Briker. Being midnight, the captain and the rest of the officers had all gone to bed. Neither Lilgert nor Briker realized they'd gone off course until treetops appeared inside the orb of the ferry's lights, by which time it would have been too late to avoid the jagged shore even if Briker had known how to turn off the autopilot so that Lilgert could take manual control of the ship, as he ordered her to do. But she didn't know how (she would later testify that she had never been trained to do so), and by the time Lilgert had crossed the bridge to flip the switch himself and then return to the controls, well…he didn't even hear the sound that came next and woke up everyone on board, so total was his shock. With her belly ripped open, the *Queen of the North* took one hour and twenty minutes to sink. During that time, incredibly, all but two of the passengers were hustled out of bed and onto lifeboats. Gerald Foisy and Shirley Rosette, a couple from 100 Mile House in British Columbia's interior, were never seen again and are presumed drowned.

It came out almost immediately that Karl Lilgert and Karen Briker were former lovers, and that the night of March 22, 2006, was the first time they'd been alone together since Briker ended their affair a few weeks earlier (both were married at the time). These details were sensationalized by the press and incorporated into the prosecution's case when Karl Lilgert was charged with two counts of criminal negligence causing death. The trial, obstructed for years by the BC Ferry and Marine Workers' Union, finally began in January 2013, seven years after the sinking. If found guilty, Lilgert faced up to life in prison.

The Crown charged that Lilgert and Briker were either fighting or fornicating when the autopilot malfunctioned, and in their state of reckless abandon they hadn't bothered to check any of the screens that would have indicated the ship was making for a piece of land twenty-seven kilometres long and twelve kilometres wide. Lilgert, who broke down repeatedly under questioning during the trial, pled not guilty. As the officer in charge of the ship when it went down, he accepted responsibility for the disaster, just as he acknowledged having had an affair with Briker; but he insisted—as she did—that nothing untoward happened between them on the night in question. The case hinged on this salacious question, because only if the jury believed that Lilgert's mistakes were a result of recklessness (fighting or fornicating while people's lives depended on his vigil) instead of ignorance (insufficient training in the face of extraordinary conditions, as the defense maintained), could they characterize his negligence as criminal and judge him guilty.

According to Lilgert, it wasn't the autopilot that failed but the radar, its screen going white after he'd deliberately headed off course to dodge first a tug and then a fishing boat that appeared in the ferry's path. He also claimed that the squall coming in that night was climaxing in Wright Sound at precisely that moment, hurling heavy rains against the windows and pushing the *Queen of the North* around with greater-than-reported gusts of fifty knots, almost a hundred kilometres an hour—not far off hurricane strength. In addition to pushing the vessel off course, Lilgert said, this sudden storm blotted out the radar. Unfortunately for Lilgert, there were no local weather-observation stations to confirm his estimates of the storm's strength in that particular location. And no record exists—at least none that the defense could find—of the fishing boat he claimed to have been dodging. No one other than he and Briker saw it, and no one ever came forward as the operator of what the Crown prosecutor called "the fake boat." The tug Lilgert mentioned did exist, but was much too far away to have forced the ferry to dodge it. Most damning of all, the ship's version of a "black box," extracted by submersible (the *Queen* slid to a resting point some 440 metres below the surface, where she remains today), revealed that in the final twenty minutes of her life, the *Queen of the North* followed a ruler-straight course out of Grenville Channel and into Gil Island without a single course alteration.

The jury found Lilgert guilty, and sentenced him to four years in jail. But regardless of whether you believed the prosecution or the defense, the *Queen of the North*'s fate is instructive of the way things tend to go wrong at sea. Quickly, for one.

And collectively; every explanation of the tragedy involved a perfect-storm combination of failures in modern technology and human judgment, compounded by at least some measure of meteorological duress. It was also worth noting (as the prosecution did) that Lilgert had sailed this exact route 795 times before in his career with BC Ferries; it wasn't until the 796th time that everything, or maybe just a couple of things, went synchronously wrong. No one but a novelist could have imagined that night's particular assemblage of mistakes and malfunctions, and yet the story's arc is eerily familiar. Nothing makes for a better parable of human hubris than the ship that shouldn't have sunk.

BUT HUBRIS IS not against the law, and anyway Enbridge wasn't planning to sail any ships, because Enbridge is not in the oil tanker business. Enbridge is in the pipeline business. Their responsibility for the oil would end the moment each tanker left the terminal.

Who, then, would be left holding the bag in the event of an accident at sea involving a Northern Gateway tanker? To understand just how problematic this question might be to resolve, consider the provenance of the last oil tanker spill to make headlines around the world: the *Prestige*, which dumped nearly half a million barrels onto the shores of southern Europe in 2002, was controlled by a Greek company, flying a Bahamas flag, under Liberian ownership, insured in Great Britain and certified in the United States. Such a scenario is typical for the industry.

The Marine Liability Act, which governs all vessels in Canadian waters, stipulates that ship owners are responsible for any costs associated with an oil spill. Assuming we can find the owners, the maximum amount we can get out of them is $1.3 billion. That sounds like a lot until you consider that the *Exxon Valdez* cost the state of Alaska upwards of $5 billion. More recently, the cost to BP for their 2010 Deepwater Horizon spill in the Gulf of Mexico amounted to $42 billion. Even that record-setting amount could not prevent the annihilation of the Gulf Coast's shrimp and shellfish fisheries; cleaning up a marine oil spill, it turns out, is still a contradiction in terms, even in the twenty-first century. By industry standards, recovering 10 per cent of the oil is considered a success. And that's before delving into the differences between light oil and Northern Gateway's product: bitumen.

Bitumen is essentially old, old oil that has rotted in the ground and is no longer as light and liquid as the stuff we think of as oil. It has the appearance, consistency and odor of tar, which is why many people call Canada's most famous petroleum deposits the "tar sands." Raw bitumen is too thick to flow through a pipe—think refrigerated molasses—so in order to deliver it to an upgrading facility, or to an oil tanker that can then sail to an upgrader, shippers must first mix in gas condensates or synthetic oils known as "diluents." These decrease bitumen's viscosity and enable it to flow. The whole Northern Gateway pipeline/tanker complex was therefore scheduled to be a two-way stream, sending "dilbit" (as the combination of bitumen and diluent is known) west to Asia, and diluent east to Alberta. Since it is only recently that the world has run low enough on light oil for bitumen to be a profitable substitute, we don't yet have much evidence as to what happens when dilbit is spilled. The best example we do have was serendipitously provided by Enbridge itself in 2010, when the Kalamazoo absorbed twenty thousand barrels of the stuff. The diluents separated from the bitumen and mostly evaporated, while the bitumen sank and stuck like glue to

everything it touched. Sixty-five kilometres of the Kalamazoo's bottom needed to be dredged as a result.

But that experience raised as many questions as it answered:
in salt water, which is more dense, and therefore more buoyant than fresh water, mightn't the separated bitumen float? Or
would it still sink to the bottom? What about the fact that the
waters of the Great Bear Rainforest are over ten degrees (Cel-
sius) colder than the Kalamazoo? Could that, combined with
salt content, make the bitumen neutrally buoyant so that it hov-
ered somewhere below the surface? Or worse, would it frac-
tionate into myriad different toxic organic compounds, each
contaminating its own depth and some of it lingering on the
surface to leave those familiar rainbow streaks swirling and
shearing in the wind?

Good questions. It turns out no one, least of all Enbridge,
knows the answers. I didn't learn this until after our trip, when
I looked for a scientist who might help shed some light on
them; in doing so I learned as much about my government's
approach to science as I did about bitumen.

A journalist friend of mine, Anne Casselman, had told me
about a scientist employed by the Department of Fisheries and
Oceans named Kenneth Lee who had been doing the kind of
research I was interested in. Lee was the executive director of
the Centre for Offshore Oil, Gas and Energy Research, a DFO-
sponsored outfit based in Dartmouth, Nova Scotia. According
to DFO's website, the centre was established in 2002 "to coor-
dinate the department's nation-wide research into the environmental and oceanographic impacts of offshore petroleum
exploration, production and transportation." As its director,
Lee was arguably the foremost expert in the country on the
subject of how bitumen behaves in saltwater, and my friend

Anne had been happily surprised by his candour during an interview he granted her for a *Scientific American* article on the subject.

By the time I emailed Lee, however, DFO had evidently gotten wind that he was saying more than he should. The email I sent him got the following response: "Thank you for the interest, our communications contact Mr. —— will contact you regarding an interview. Regards, Ken." I never heard from Lee, or any other government-employed scientist, again. Instead, the communications department commandeered the conversation and supplied me with a series of bureaucratic talking points in place of answers to the questions I submitted.

Fortunately Anne Casselman was already able to report some of the things Dr. Lee might have liked to say, in *Scientific American* online. "It's not cast in stone exactly what dilbit is," Lee said in Anne's article, which explained that the exact combination of condensates and synthetic oils added to the bitumen vary from company to company. "The fate and behavior of the product—the character of the product when it's spilled in the water—will depend on what the final formulation is," Lee said. "We have to understand the physical behavior of the oil before we can design the optimal cleanup technologies."

"One of the big questions when we're talking about dilbit," he added, "is does it float or does it sink?...If you talk to Enbridge or some of the people in industry, they say, 'well, it floats.' You look at what happened in the Kalamazoo River, and it sank."

Lee had much more to say that never made it into the story. Fortunately, Anne was generous enough to share the rest of the interview with me, and because of who Lee is and what he said, I take here the unusual step of sharing parts of it with you:

"Everybody thinks that oils float. But if you have a heavy crude oil, as it evaporates the lower molecular weight compounds disappear and the oil can become more viscous and sink. Even heavy crude oils can sink. But dilbit is a very heavy crude oil that's diluted with condensate or a light oil. And when that light oil evaporates, chances are it will sink."

Not always, though. "In Canada we did have a spill of dilbit," Lee told Anne. "It was a small spill and in this case the product floated and they could put a boom around it. And they found they could recover the floating oil using existing equipment, called skimmers." Which sounds like good news, except: "You cannot boom oil in areas where you have high current flow, because there's so much stress against the boom...after two to three knots you can't put a boom in the water." Currents throughout the Northern Gateway reach three knots up to four times a day, as the tide sloughs in and out. "What would happen," Lee wondered, "if you had a spill in a more remote area, a much larger spill and the weather conditions weren't ideal and you couldn't boom because of sea state conditions?"

He didn't know, because nobody knows, but he did offer a relevant analogue. He'd spent four months in the Gulf of Mexico to assist with the cleanup of BP's 2010 spill (of light oil), and drew on that experience to illuminate the problems cleanup crews would face in British Columbia:

"In the Gulf of Mexico, you saw on television all those boats with booms recovering oil. It was almost ideal weather conditions, warm water, no big storm event at all, and the overall conclusion from the National Oceanic and Atmospheric Administration was that they only recovered about three to four per cent of the oil by booming and skimming." Which raised the $1.3-billion question: "If they could recover only 3 to 4 per cent of the oil in the Gulf of Mexico in almost ideal conditions, what can we do with this product?"

It was some consolation to know that at least Canada had such a thing as the Centre for Offshore Oil, Gas and Energy Research, where people like Dr. Lee were studying these problems. But don't get too excited. The Department of Fisheries and Oceans, reeling from Bill c-38's massive budget cuts, was in the midst of downsizing the centre just as I was trying to get Lee on the phone. Soon afterwards, he resigned and moved to Australia.

RATHER THAN SPEND too much time dwelling on the mysteries of bitumen, diluted or otherwise, Enbridge and the federal government did their best to shift the public's focus from spill response to spill prevention. Here, they could rightfully say that the oil tanker industry has learned from its mistakes.

In both relative and absolute terms, there are fewer oil tanker accidents today than ever before. That's an important point, considering how heavily Northern Gateway opponents relied on the prospect of an oil spill to make their case—*not if but when* would become the movement's unofficial slogan, often accompanied by references to a handful of spectacular spills seen as proof of history's repetitive tendency when, in fact, those very spills spurred the kinds of regulations that have prevented hundreds more like them from occurring.

According to statistics kept by the International Tanker Owners Pollution Federation (ITOPF), there have been approximately ten thousand oil tanker spills great and small since 1970, the year they started counting. These have dumped some 42 million barrels of crude into the ocean. But over half that amount was lost in the 1970s alone. Throughout that decade, the world averaged 24.6 "large" oil tanker spills (five thousand barrels or greater) per year; by the 2000s that average had shrunk to 3.3 large spills per year, with medium and small spills following a similar trajectory. This is despite the fact that almost twice as much oil is transported by sea today as in the 1970s. We're currently shipping about 15 billion barrels of it around the world each year, aboard a fleet of roughly 4,400 oil tankers. Oil, the world's primary transportation-energy source, itself accounts for 40 per cent of the world's marine trade, and every drop is precious.

Oil tanker spills aren't just decreasing in number but also in severity. Today's average tanker spill, again according to the ITOPF, is one twelfth the 1970s' average volume. The worst oil spills in history are ones we've never heard of; they all happened decades ago, for the most part in faraway seas. The title goes to the *Atlantic Empress*, which let 2 million barrels into the waters off Tobago in 1979. In fact, all but one of the twenty worst tanker spills on record occurred more than two decades ago. The exception was the aforementioned *Prestige*, coming in at #20 after she ran into heavy weather off the coast of Galicia in 2002.

I happened to be living in Spain at the time, teaching English in Sevilla—far from the northwest coast, but close enough to be transfixed by news images of Galician fishermen struggling to scoop tar balls from the surface with homemade skimmers, soon followed by images of haz-mat-suited volunteers shuffling along the shore. The drama caught the whole country in its grip, provoking an impotent outrage because of the way it unfolded.

The *Prestige* first sent out a distress call on November 13 when one of her tanks burst amid a growing storm. Her Greek captain, Apostolos Mangouras, requested permission to bring the ship to port so that her cargo could be offloaded and any spill contained, as per emergency contingency plans. But the Spanish authorities refused the request and ordered him to take the *Prestige* out of Spanish waters. "The ship was cracked and they sent it out to the ocean," Captain Mangouras later told reporters. "It was the worst alternative." Mangouras refused to move the *Prestige* farther offshore and was promptly airlifted from the ship and arrested. Tugboats arrived on the scene and threw ropes around the *Prestige*, while Spanish authorities begged their French and Portuguese counterparts to let them drag the dying vessel into one of *their* harbours; these requests were predictably refused. For six days, a horrified southern Europe could do nothing but watch as their leaders hot-potatoed a ruptured oil tanker through ten-metre waves. The *Prestige*'s trajectory resembled a toddler's Etch A Sketch, heading north and then south and then west out to sea, until finally, on the morning of November 19, when the *Prestige* was a hundred kilometres from the Galician coast, she split in half and sank. Just under half a million barrels of oil were distributed by current across nearly three thousand kilometres of Spanish, French, and Portuguese shoreline, exactly as captain Mangouras had predicted. None of the Spanish authorities involved in the debacle were ever charged, but Captain Mangouras did spend two and a half months in a Galician prison for refusing to follow their orders, then another nineteen months under house arrest in Barcelona, before he was allowed to go home to Greece on bail. Nine years later, he would return to Galicia to stand trial on charges of disobeying authorities and causing environmental damage. The court case began in October of 2012, exactly one decade after the *Prestige* sank, and the trial unfolds as I write. Mangouras, now seventy-nine, faces twelve years in jail if found guilty.

The *Prestige* was a single-hulled tanker, just like the *Exxon Valdez* had been thirteen years before it. The twin nightmares spurred international lawmakers to ban single-hulled tankers from entering North American or European waters, and as of 2010 the rest of the world has followed suit. Henceforth, every oil tanker on the planet must have a double hull; that is, not one but two skins of metal standing protecting the ocean from the cargo's deadly hold.

Double-hulled tankers are certainly sturdier and have a better safety record, but that isn't to say they're unbreakable. In 2010 alone there were two major spills from double-hulled tankers: the *Eagle Otome* in Port Arthur, Texas, and the *Bunga Kelana 3* in the Strait of Singapore. Both ships were torn open following collisions with another large vessel; combined, the two accidents loosed thirty thousand barrels into the ocean— nowhere near the volume unleashed by the *Prestige* and *Exxon Valdez*, though it's worth keeping in mind that colliding with another ship is far less traumatic than striking a reef. After the *Exxon Valdez* catastrophe, the U.S. Coast Guard testified that a double hull would not have saved the ship or prevented an oil spill. At best, it would have mitigated the amount lost by somewhere between 25 and 60 per cent, meaning a minimum of 120,000 barrels would still have been spread across the Alaskan panhandle.

This is important because double-hulled tankers have been one of Enbridge's principal aces right from the outset, cited by everyone from Enbridge Northern Gateway President John Carruthers to whoever pens the company's website as an example of Enbridge's commitment to the "latest technology" and "world class standards."

The company spelled out its commitment in a Marine Safety Plan whose details would govern all the oil tankers coming in and out of Kitimat, no matter who owned or operated them. Part spill-prevention strategy, part public relations strategy, the plan's principal measures were for each tanker to be accompanied by two "supertugs"—immensely powerful tugboats that would haul a tanker to safety or push it like a bumper car in the event of a power failure—throughout the confined channels; each tanker's load would be held in segregated tanks, meaning that if one were to rupture, only a portion of the total shipment would be compromised; operational weather limits would bar tankers from travelling in excessive sea conditions; each tanker would have two BC pilots aboard, who would undergo simulator training before the project's launch date, as would the tug crews; a radar system would be installed (at Enbridge's expense) throughout the tanker route that would link up with the Coast Guard's central command; and every tanker would be double-hulled (never mind that it would have been illegal for them not to be).

Based on these measures, computer simulations calculated that a major tanker spill (defined as 250,000 barrels or more, the same as the *Exxon Valdez*) could be expected but once in fifteen thousand years. This, then, was the answer to the question that the Joint Review Panel heard 1,159 times: *Not if, but when?*

That figure, one in fifteen thousand, was the crowning achievement of the Qualitative Risk Analysis carried out by the consulting branch of Det Norske Veritas, a Norwegian firm that described itself as a provider of "services for managing risk." Founded in 1864 to verify the seaworthiness of Norwegian merchant ships, DNV enjoys a stellar reputation. It was hired by the U.S. government to study the Deepwater Horizon disaster and, it was chosen to analyze Enbridge's Marine Safety Plan for Northern Gateway by a group of stakeholders that included Enbridge, several First Nations, and other industry groups. In 2012, Transport Canada gave its imprimatur to the findings in a report approved by the Department of Fisheries and Oceans, Environment Canada, and the Pacific Pilotage Authority.

"We look at it from a strictly navigational perspective," Kevin Obermeyer, president of the Pacific Pilotage Authority (PPA), which supplies the pilots who guide all vessels on Canada's Pacific Coast, told me when I called him after our trip ended. "The bottom line is you can get these vessels from deep sea to Kitimat and back very safely."

Obermeyer stressed that the PPA's support for Northern Gateway was contingent on Enbridge's following through with all the promises made in its marine-safety strategy. "People are going to jail for causing oil spills these days," he said. "You've got to look at this and make damn sure you're not going to be one of them."

Obermeyer's confidence surprised me. The week before we spoke, a 278-metre-long container ship called the *Hanjin Geneva* ran aground just outside of Prince Rupert, a hundred kilometres north of Kitimat, when it swerved to avoid a fishing boat. A BC pilot had been aboard the *Hanjin Geneva* at the time of the accident. Wasn't this, I asked, precisely the type of unpredictable event that Northern Gateway critics were afraid of?

"The *Hanjin* didn't have two tugs," Obermeyer answered. "If we used the same mitigation factors we have in place for tankers with every ship on the coast, incident rates would drop to zero."

Or at least, to once in fifteen thousand years.

Not everyone agreed with Obermeyer. Another person I called was Mal Walsh, a retired master mariner with forty years of experience in the international oil shipping industry who now lives on Vancouver Island. "Could you take a tanker out of Kitimat with two tugs and not have an accident?" Walsh asked. "Yes, of course. Could you do it nearly every day of the year? That's another question." Walsh made it very clear that he had nothing against the principle of transporting oil by tanker; that was how he'd made his living. It was sending 220 oil tankers a year into Kitimat that he considered foolhardy. Nowhere on earth were oil tankers forced to navigate through a hundred kilometres of confined water, executing four right-angle turns in close quarters along the way, in a region renowned for spontaneous bad weather. There were too many obstacles and not enough room to avoid them in the event of a heavy-weather emergency, for as Walsh pointed out, a Very Large Crude Carrier weighing in at 350,000 tons doesn't stop or turn on a dime. "In the event of power loss or steering malfunction, trying to stop a laden VLCC doing 10 knots—that would take everything in the world going right for you," he said.

Those tugs would accompany oil tankers only as far as the edge of Hecate Strait, the Northern Gateway's final and most harrowing gauntlet, where an entirely different set of meteorological dangers awaited. Today, Hecate Strait is a wide, shallow sea separating Haida Gwaii from the mainland, but when humans first laid eyes on it some ten thousand years ago it was a dry flood plain. Long since submerged by rising seas, it remains much, much shallower than the deep canyons over which *Foxy* was sailing. As a result, when hurricanes collide in the Hecate (as they are literally known to do, blowing in two at a time from north and south at up to two hundred kilometres per hour) the troughs between the resulting waves can expose the ocean floor. For this and a few other alarming reasons (colliding currents, whirlpools, blink-of-an-eye storm formations) Environment Canada rates Hecate Strait the fourth most dangerous body of water on earth. In his west coast classic, *The Golden Spruce*, John Vaillant calls it "one of the most diabolically hostile environments that wind, sea, and land are capable of conjuring up."

It's hard to say exactly how many ships the strait has claimed over the years, but a study conducted in 2009 for a proposed windfarm development examined a narrow band of the seafloor running across the top of Hecate Strait, where the wind mills and transmission cables would have been installed (the project never went through). The study area covered about one twentieth of Hecate Strait, and within that sliver almost three hundred shipwrecks were identified, all dated within the past century.

In 2012, a group of three British Columbian engineers who spent their careers assessing risk probabilities for industrial projects ranging from iceberg impacts on Arctic oil platforms to ship collisions on Vancouver's Fraser River became concerned that no independent assessment had been conducted of Det Norske Veritas' analysis. So they decided to do it themselves. Among the quirks they discovered in DNV's methodology was the use of oil-tanker incident statistics taken from routes elsewhere; in fact, DNV's figures excluded all shipping incidents along the Northern Gateway route itself.

When Enbridge Northern Gateway Pipelines allowed me one ten-minute phone interview with their president, John Carruthers, I asked him why people should trust statistics based on different tanker routes from the one his company had in mind.

"The reason they didn't use local data," he told me, "is that there hasn't been an incident on the coast of British Columbia."

As far as oil tankers were concerned, this was true. More than thirty years ago, U.S. and Canadian authorities established a voluntary Tanker Exclusion Zone to steer oil carriers around the west side of Haida Gwaii, the archipelago lying roughly 150 kilometres off the BC coast. This zone was designed to ensure sufficient leeway for a drifting, damaged tanker to be rescued by tugs before running aground. There hadn't been any incidents, because there hadn't been any oil tankers.

Carruthers was quick to point out that the TEZ was aimed solely at tankers on their way to and from the oil terminal in Valdez—which, at the time the zone was erected, was responsible for all the tanker traffic in the region. Since there had never been an oil terminal at Kitimat, no rules were ever put in place to bar tankers from going there. Carruthers claimed that using numbers from "comparable locations" like Norway's North Sea or Canada's east coast "actually gave us better data" than statistics that included smaller ships such as the *Queen of the North* would have.

I asked Mal Walsh, the retired master mariner, how he thought Norway's fjords compared to the ones leading into Kitimat. Walsh, who had commanded vessels in Norway for six years, told me that the Northern Gateway tankers would be battling far more brutal conditions. "The seas generated in the Pacific in winter cannot by any stretch of the imagination be compared to those in the North Sea," he said. "Nor does Norway have anything like the Arctic outflows that sweep out of Kitimat."

The engineers who assessed the Qualitative Risk Analysis found other flaws, too. Brian Gunn, one of those engineers,

told me over the phone, "We know there are three liquid natural gas projects being considered for Kitimat, which would
add three times as many tankers to the route. Enbridge does
not consider that in its analysis." Another critical concern
was the arbitrary manner by which mitigation values were
assigned; the use of tugs, for instance, was assumed to lower
the risk of an accident by 80 per cent, without any explanation
of how that number was derived. Gunn also pointed out that
Enbridge's method of expressing risk in "return periods" was
misleading. The company's own report put the likelihood of a
spill 5000 cubic metres (31,000 barrels) or greater at once in
200 years; that sounds better than admitting there's a 22 per
cent chance of a spill that size occurring in the project's lifetime. And that's using the company's own numbers. After factoring in variables like the coming liquid natural gas tankers
whose traffic Enbridge ignored, Gunn and his colleagues calculated there was a 78 per cent chance of a Northern Gateway
oil tanker accident occurring at some point in the project's
fifty-year lifespan, and a 30 per cent chance that the accident
would lead to an oil spill of undetermined size.

The closer you looked at Enbridge's Marine Safety Plan and
the Qualitative Risk Assessment that validated it in the public's eye, the less there was to see. Nowhere in the entire document had Enbridge estimated the financial cost of an oil spill
of any size, despite the fact that quantifying the consequences
of an accident is a basic first step in Canada's industrial risk
assessment protocol. But perhaps most damning of all were
the weather conditions that both Enbridge and DNV assumed
for their risk models. The maximum wind speeds were forty-
eight knots (almost a hundred kilometres an hour), and the
highest waves were ten metres; yet long-term buoy reports had

recorded winds in excess of a hundred knots throughout the Northern Gateway and, in Hecate Strait, waves up to twenty-six metres high.

When I challenged Carruthers about these numbers, he insisted his were accurate. "We have a very informed basis to make some of our determinations," he told me. Although tankers "are capable of operating in extreme weather conditions," they would "manage their time in order to avoid those conditions. We've imposed operational limits to cover those wind and sea conditions." When the forecast calls for truly fierce weather, Carruthers said, outgoing tankers would stay in Douglas Channel, tethered to tugs near the Kitimat terminal, while incoming tankers would wait out the storm at sea, on the far side of Haida Gwaii. "Certainly," he added, "marine weather forecasting has improved over the years."

This struck me as the same kind of magical thinking that Enbridge employed in an infamous animated video that it posted on its website, in which the tanker route was depicted as a straight, wide-open shot between Kitimat and the open Pacific; every single island was erased from Enbridge's map. It was clearly a public-relations ploy—no one doubted that whoever drew the animation knew exactly where each of those islands were—but despite eliciting a substantial public uproar, Enbridge left the video on its website. The company evidently calculated that more people would watch the video and conclude the route was harmless than would hear about the video's gross inaccuracy. The more I studied their Marine Safety Plan, the more it seemed its authors had a similar calculation in mind.

I wanted to put these same questions to the government regulators responsible for protecting nine hundred kilometres of British Columbian coastline. Had none of the details that struck me as worrisome given pause to the people who okayed Enbridge's Marine Safety Plan? But that proved to be impossible. The Kenneth Lee phenomenon kicked in once again: Transport Canada, the Department of Fisheries and Oceans, and Environment Canada all refused to grant me an interview.

AUTUMN
OF THE
MATRIARCH

Hartley Bay, world capital of the Gitga'at Nation, is a roadless town of 150 people tucked beneath a green arrowhead of a mountain at the mouth of Douglas Channel. Getting here, our emotional barometers told us, was a benchmark. Michael and Sarah were at the dock, calling "Sailors, you made it!" and for that moment, for the first time, we actually did feel like sailors. Ilja, confident now, motored without hesitation in between the yachts and live-aboards and the extremely fast-looking aluminum-hulled RCMP boat, and Michael caught the bow line that I threw him, and then we had overcome a burst impeller and oncoming winds and various narrows with currents and tides and a constantly overheating Suzy and *caught up* to two people who, five days ago, there was no telling if we'd ever see again.

Hartley Bay looked and felt like a movie set. Its wooden houses were connected by a raised boardwalk, and the only people in sight on the evening we showed up were a gargantuan young woman in a Guantanamo-orange hoodie riding a three-wheel bicycle along the wooden planks followed by a preteen girl and boy doubling on a dirt bike, *revving* and laughing laughing laughing. The boardwalk became a bridge that traversed Hartley Creek and wound up a hill to every doorstep in town, tall bushes sprouting up on all sides, before continuing out the back of town into the forest, all the way to a swampy lake. Some of the nails in the boardwalk were missing, so that if you stepped anywhere but the middle of certain planks the other side would swing up like a teeter totter and create all kinds of potential mishaps.

Most Gitga'at don't live in Hartley Bay, including their chief councillor. There are maybe six hundred Gitga'at in all, a nation of six hundred, more than two thirds of them expatriates living in Prince Rupert or Vancouver or Edmonton. Few countries have such a diaspora—I thought of Burma, of Zimbabwe, of all those countries run by despots whose fatherly faces look out at you from billboards. There was no despot here and no billboards, just a grandmotherly matriarch named Helen Clifton who, by all accounts, was universally loved.

Gitga'at territory extends north up Douglas Channel almost all the way to Kitimat (according to the Gitga'at, that is—the Haisla who live near Kitimat have their own maps) and south past Gil Island, just around the corner from Hartley Bay, encompassing much of Princess Royal Island and Laredo Channel, and all the outer islands west of us. Seventy-five hundred square kilometres, one and a half Prince Edward Islands, six hundred people. Any success a people like the Gitga'at had in their land claim struggles with Canada's government would, were it achieved, represent a triumph of justice over power. So far power was winning. Gitga'at territory, with its forest and its fish, was worth billions, and there were 33 million non-Gitga'at Canadians who wanted a piece. But the David and Goliath script had a way of playing out in places like this.

Unfortunately we'd come at a bad time, Michael told us. There was an impending death.

There were two people we'd heard of in Hartley Bay. One was Marven Robinson, the Spirit Bear-whisperer, who could personally recognize every white bear in Gitga'at territory.

The other was Helen Clifton, the eighty-six-year-old matriarch presiding over Hartley Bay and its surroundings like the pope in his Vatican. Clifton was just about the last person alive who spoke her language fluently. She'd compiled family trees. She organized the fall and spring fishing camps, decided which families got how much halibut and ling and seaweed and sockeye. She knew the Gitga'at name for every bay, channel, island, mountain and lake in the territory. But Clifton had fallen off the boardwalk while she was laying seaweed out to dry not long ago, and hurt her hip badly. Also, Marven Robinson's mother, who was Clifton's good friend, was dying at a hospital in Prince Rupert and expected to go any day now. So Marven Robinson was at his mother's side, Helen Clifton was in pain and pre-mourning, and neither one was accepting visitors. No one was accepting visitors. The whole town was in pre-mourning. When a town of 120 people in a nation of 600 loses one of its elders, all the doors stay closed.

Even the wireless Internet was down. But there was cell service. Ilja had dropped his iPhone in the ocean three weeks earlier and I never had one to begin with, but Michael did, so we tethered our laptops to his connection and spidered into the sticky strands of the world wide web. I avoided my email account and checked the news. Fresh battles in Syria. Obama neck and neck with the Mittster. America's corn harvest was withering in a drought. This year's July was the hottest in

U.S. history, surpassing the previous record set in 1936 at the height of the dustbowl era. Globally, the world's land masses had just experienced the hottest May and June in recorded history.

AFTER WALKING THROUGH an open door at the cultural centre, we met Duane Jackson, who invited us inside.

Jackson wasn't from Hartley Bay, was not a Gitga'at, not in mourning; he was Kitselas, from the mainland. He was a stoutly athletic basketball coach, life coach, mentor, baker, cultural ambassador, First Nation representative to the world, and a helluva talker.

"Everyone's got tribe," he said to us. "People ask me if I'm aboriginal, I say no, I'm Kitselas. But I never get offended. Just try to offend me! That's one of the big problems we've got to sort through in Canada, this getting offended business. Call me an Indian—I like it! If you ask my daughter—she's ten years old—if you ask her if she's an aboriginal she'll say no. What if we erased all European countries and just referred to everyone living there as Europeans? No Germans, no French, all just Europeans? Well that's what it's like for us—we're all aboriginals now? There's sixty language groups in BC alone, and we're all just one nation?

"We've got to find the commonalities. Sometimes kids in my community make fun of my wife because she's Norwegian. She's white, they say. I say, you know who the Norwegians were until recently? Longhouse people. Canoe people. Ocean people. Sound familiar?"

Jackson was an educator, to his people and ours. "We've had two complete generations that never had parents, never learned how to parent. Canadians don't realize this, they don't realize how recent it is—the last residential school wasn't shut down until the late 1980s. There was the sixties scoop, when the government sent authorities into the homes of First Nations all over Canada and took thousands of kids out of their houses and put them up for adoption. Anyone could adopt an Indian, it was like going to the SPCA and getting a puppy."

When he wasn't entertaining strangers, Jackson spent most of his time offering creative counsel to First Nations youth. The motto printed on his card was *A Journey to Be Whole*. "I don't tell boys how to become a man, I talk about becoming whole," he said. He told us about the coastal First Nations basketball tournament in Prince Rupert each February. "It's the biggest basketball tournament in Canada. It's an opportunity for everyone to meet each other, to bond, to make connections. People ask me, why can only First Nations teams compete? It's because we weren't allowed in your tournaments for the longest time. We had to create our own. That's what Canadians often forget—we weren't allowed to do anything, until so recently. We weren't allowed in restaurants—my mother, my father, everything was closed to them. They weren't allowed to vote. They weren't allowed to leave the reserve without a pass. They weren't allowed to throw a potlatch. We were banned from everything. So we had to create our own tournaments, our own feasts, our own parties. Many of these we had to hide from the public. This isn't ancient history.

"How many Indians do you think were in the room when the Indian Act was being written? Not a single one. And now, today, we have Enbridge come along, and it happens all over again. The prime minister directing our lives from Parliament Hill, which is its own country, and the people who work there, their job is to stay there. That's their primary task. And they are going to push Northern Gateway through as hard as they can, and they aren't going to relent any more than we are, and it's going to lead to seventy-five-year-old grandmas laying down in front of bulldozers. That's where this whole thing is directly leading to."

WE DID MEET one resident of Hartley Bay during that first visit. Danny Danes owned the *Bojangle Too*, a beat-up old gill-netter parked beside *Foxy*, and there he was one morning, fir-ing up the engine to charge *Bojangles'* battery, a wiry codger in fresh blue jeans and a black biker's jacket. We stepped out onto the dock and said hello, and Danny Danes said hello back.

Danny Danes, like Duane Jackson, had plenty to say to any-one who cared to listen, though his philosophy was more com-bative. He spoke without moving his upper lip and squeezed "fuck" or some conjugation thereof into all kinds of sentences. As in, Mr. Danes was an ornery old fuck who launched into story mode from the moment we said hello.

"You seen the hatchery up the creek?" he asked. We had. If you followed the boardwalk behind town it took you past a falling-down wood shack with two large green silos beside it; those silos were filled with swirling water, and you could slide a hatch open to see the thousands of salmon minnows swim-ming in their treadmill.

"Ran that place for thirty-two years," Danes said, showing us the silver-rimmed watch he'd been given on his retirement last year. "Look," he said, taking it off so we could read the inscription on the back, "they fucked it up. Says I only ran it thirty years, but it was thirty-two. Fuck 'em anyway."

He explained what he did for three point two decades: Divert a channel of water from the creek that runs through Hartley Bay; when spawning season begins, trap a few female and male cohos; bleed the female after you kill her (because exposure to blood kills the eggs), then take the eggs out of her belly and put them in the cool diverted riverwater; now milk the male for his sperm (get three or four males, because some males are infertile), collect the sperm in a zip-lock bag half full of water—"looks just like milk"—then pour the spermwater over the eggs; raise the resulting minnows in green silos, and after a year bag them up and set them loose in whichever river you want them to colonize. "In nature maybe four, five per cent of the eggs get fertilized; in my hatchery I was getting ninety fuckin per cent! I was hatching half a million eggs a year and feeding five rivers around here with coho. We counted about six thousand coho made it back up the river when spawning time came. Fuckin right."

Where did he learn how to do that, we asked.

"I took nine courses at Malaspina college," Danes said. In Nanaimo. "You shoulda seen my professor, straight outta fuckin *Playboy* magazine." He told the story of her conquest: a chance encounter at the bar, pot cookies, a trip out on his boat. "She said to me afterwards, I knew you were a good fucker from the second I laid eyes on ya." He laughed. "That was over thirty years ago. I was in good shape then, boy."

I said he looked like he was still in pretty good shape if he asked me.

"How old you think I am?"

I said, honestly, he looked sixty. He gave a satisfied grunt. "I'm sixty-nine. Got some friends over on the Queen Charlottes," as he still called Haida Gwaii, "they ask me how I keep so fit, I tell em every year I go over there and kill me a black bear, I stick my hands in its fat and I rub the grease all over me. That's why they're running out of bears." He coughed out a *ha!* then got serious. "Used to be all kinds of animals here, everywhere. When I first started fishin, I was fourteen years old; we'd just count the mountain goats on the hills beside Grenville Channel. You wanted to shoot a deer from the boat, no problem. Now, nothin. Them hunters got everything. Killin animals just to kill em. Fishin like crazy. It's this greed that's gonna kill *us* in the end, too. DFO, them fuckers, they had a meetin up in Kitimat some years back and tried to tell us how many fish we're allowed to catch. Well I gave it to em. I said, you handed out commercial licenses to everyone who could toss a net, watched em fish the salmon right down to nothin, and now you're gonna tell us how to save fish? You can all go fuck yourselves," he said, capturing perfectly the collective coastal First Nations' attitude towards the DFO.

"You know the story of the kermode?" he asked. We shook our heads. "Long time ago, everything was ice, whole world. Man was havin a hell of a time stayin alive, so the Lord took pity and He said 'all right! I'm gonna make things start to grow.' Sure enough, green plants started shootin up, then trees, then animals started comin in and pretty soon there was food everywhere and life got a lot easier. But the Lord he said 'I'm gonna leave this one bear white to remind you how things used to be; and if you don't keep him alive, things gonna go back to the way they used to be.' Well, look at things now, we got the whole world fallin apart on us, climate's starting to change up, and the ocean's runnin outta fish. We got us here one of the last places left on earth still producin fish, and now they want to go fuck it up by runnin oil tankers through it. They can go fuck emselves is what."

But inside his own home, where he invited me to visit later on, the ageing stud turned into a quiet (though still foulmouthed) grandpa. His twin grandchildren raged about the living room, the girl stabbing everything in sight with a pink umbrella and squealing 'It's raining!' while her brother drove a toy dump truck over the couch where Danny Danes slouched, watching TV. His wife, Mona, was in the kitchen baking blackberry pie. The ghost town that Hartley Bay appeared to be from outside was a false front; it came alive the moment you pulled back the curtain.

"I'd just gone to bed when the call come over the radio," Danny Danes was saying, about the night the *Queen of the North* sank, ten kilometres from here. "We keep our VHFs on pretty much all the time; if anything happens, everyone hears." He pointed to the radio in the kitchen, just like the one in *Foxy*'s galley, through which the town communicated on Channel 9. "Call came out, 'Mayday mayday! We've hit a rock in Wright Sound!' And I thought, the only fuckin rock in Wright Sound is Gil Island!" He sniggered. "I know damn well what happened that night. First mate was gettin hisself a piece of tail."

Danny Danes' boat was the first one out of the marina that night. He didn't know where exactly he was going but as soon as he rounded the corner into Wright Sound, there she was, all lit up: the *Queen of the North*, water up to her passenger deck, twenty minutes from sinking to the bottom. "Everyone's already in lifeboats when I get there," he said. "I call out, who's in charge? And the captain shines a flashlight, shouts 'I am!' I said we should probably get the kids and elders in first, it's pretty cold out here." It was after midnight and many of the people in lifeboats, especially the kids, were in pajamas. Danny put eight of them in his boat, and by then every other functioning boat in Hartley Bay was starting to arrive on the scene. As Danny made his way back, one of his passengers shouted, and he looked back just in time to see the *Queen*'s bow rise, salute the sky, and slip under the surface forever.

"There was just over a hundred people on that ship," he said, "but the next sailing was scheduled to have over four hundred. Can you imagine? Woulda been a fuckin disaster."

His wife put the pie in the oven and sat down to join us. Mona Danes was plump and full of exhausted energy—she'd been entertaining her twin grandchildren all morning. "Oh lordy yes," she exclaimed when I asked if many journalists had been through Hartley Bay this summer. She seemed to regard us in the same light as her grandchildren: exasperating but not unwelcome. "If you had come tomorrow, the kids would be gone and we could have had a better interview," she said, as her grandson drove his truck up my leg.

While her husband was ferrying shipwrecked passengers back and forth from the *Queen of the North* that night, Mona set up a makeshift camp at the cultural centre, brewing coffee and organizing the blankets and jackets and food that poured in from Hartley Bay's residents. The whole town woke up and pitched in. "By the time those poor folks started arriving, we had baked goodies and sleeping bags and extra clothes for everyone," Mona said. "It was emotional. People were crying, and we cried with them. But it felt good to help. That's what we do! We're always helping people. Now we need people to help us. Christy Clark said this morning, Northern Gateway is inevitable, it's just a matter of how much money can we get for it. Them politicians are determined to get that thing going. Well, if that's the case, what's there gonna be left here for *them*?" She pointed her chin at the two four-year-olds swinging a pink umbrella and a truck at each other, oblivious to the geopolitics at play outside their window.

Just then a woman's voice came over the VHF in the kitchen—in every kitchen in Hartley Bay. "Ethan," the woman called, "Ethan, where are you? Dinner's ready. Get on home, now."

WE DID EVENTUALLY get to meet Hartley Bay's matriarch, though we had to go to Kitimat first, and then to a place called the Kitlope, and only after almost a month had passed between our first and second visits to Hartley Bay were we granted an audience.

It was September by then, and a four-day rain had set the rainforest's autumn feast into motion. From the Alaskan Panhandle to Oregon, a hundred thousand rivers, streams, creeks, and flooded ditches filled with salmon. Some filled so completely the water boiled with thrashing tails; others hosted schools of a hundred at a time that rushed from one deep pool to the next; in some creeks, only a few dozen furtive shadows could be spotted; each year, a few more waterways stayed empty altogether.

In Hartley Creek, schools of pink, coho, and chum all mingled at the rivermouth, acclimatizing to the fresh water and the changes it wrought on their bodies—hooking their mouths into beak-like snouts, humping their backs, causing their flesh to rot and fill the air with putrefaction—before pushing upstream. The town's kids usurped the bears and wolves and eagles that gathered on other banks, and fished nonstop, hanging their poles over the wooden bridge or casting off the boulders piled along the shore, catcalling one another as they hooked one glittering prize fighter after another. The bridge's planks were covered in scales and pink egg sacks; the fish themselves were picked up by the youngest children and delivered to the mothers and grandmothers who filleted them and hung the long strips of red flesh in their backyard smokeshacks.

Marven Robinson's mother had passed away while we were gone, and the town was finished grieving. Marven himself was away on the far side of Gribbell Island with a *National*

Gitga'at kids fish from the bridge in Hartley Bay at dusk; the salmon they catch go straight to their grandmothers' smoke shacks.

Geographic film crew, shooting spirit bears. But Helen Clifton was feeling better and she would see us now.

Clifton lived in a well-kept bungalow that she'd turned into a museum of medicine baskets and carved masks and totemic paintings; a ten-point buck gazed out in perpetual surprise above the fireplace, and an old ship's steering wheel hung on the wall by the door. An enormous photo Marven Robinson (her nephew) had taken of a white bear sleeping in the forest, its chin in its paws, covered one wall.

When she opened the door we beheld a small woman with a wavy shock of white hair and intense black eyes. She wore golden feather earrings and a gold necklace that glittered beneath a buttoned-down mauve blouse, and after flashing a smile, she made us sit down so she wouldn't have to look up when she spoke.

Helen Clifton wasn't someone you interviewed. A hundred journalists, anthropologists, and well-wishers from near and far passed through her door each summer, and their—our—job was to listen. The ambassador of one of the world's smallest nations already knew what to say.

"History has a way of repeating itself when it comes to First Nations," she began. "My father, who was a leader respected up and down this coast, sent two of his boys to residential school; one of them came down with tuberculosis and never came back. So he said no more of my kids are going to go there, and he instructed us to build our own schools—but then the missionaries came in as teachers, so the suppression of our language and our culture continued."

I noted that Hartley Bay, like Bella Bella, had a church of its own. It was right next door to her house.

"Yes," she sighed. "People are slow to change, but I believe we're catching on. Less people show up on Sundays every year. The boardwalk in front of the church entrance is perfect for drying seaweed in the spring, it gets sun all day. Of course, that was the boardwalk I fell off of last month." She smiled a smile that could have cut diamonds. "Maybe God's trying to tell me something."

Clifton told us about the abalone, the shellfish that the Gitga'at and other coastal nations prized above all others, which once proliferated on the shores of the outer islands.

"Have you ever eaten abalone?" she asked. "I'm not surprised. It's because there aren't any to be had any more. Abalone grow in deeper water than clams or mussels. We used to harvest them every spring, but you had to wait for a new moon or a full moon when the tide dropped low enough to expose them. But then came the commercial divers with their scuba gear and the government started handing out licences to everyone except First Nations, and pretty soon there were no abalone left. Our people checked every year and there was nothing—until this spring! My grandsons found some off —— Island. Wonderful, you know, but now we're not sure if we should tell the Department of Fisheries and Oceans, because look what happened last time. Will they tell us not to harvest and then hand licences out to the divers again? We want to cooperate, but the trust has been broken."

Clifton talked about the spirit bear's reminder of how the world here used to look. But the kermode was no different, really, from its black and brown and grizzled cousins in the forest. "They haven't got much time. They get a couple of months each year to eat as much salmon as they can and then it's time to start moving into their winter caves. When you're watching this, when you watch bears and eagles time their cycles with the salmon, when you see whales breaching and sea lions shouting from the rocks, it has a deep effect on your psyche. It makes you a different person. It makes you healthy, and only a healthy person can gather medicine." Clifton was a medicine woman; her favourite, most powerful medicine was hellebore. Dried tangles of the roots were placed strategically throughout her house, near the entrance, beside the window. They kept bad dreams and other unpleasant things away.

"And now Enbridge and the government want us to prove that we know something about our land and our ocean," she said, sadly. "They want statistics. If there's one thing the white man understands, it's statistics. So our people are out there collecting them; they are counting the salmon and the whales and the bears. They are sampling the toxins that the *Queen of the North* has put in our shellfish. But in the end I worry that all it will serve is to tell us what we've lost after it's gone."

She brightened quickly. Helen Clifton was not a woman given to depression or defeat. The Gitga'at were fighters, she said, always had been.

"You know the Haida raided our Old Town once, about a hundred years ago. They came when the men were out fishing, and they took all the women. They loaded the women into their canoes and set the town on fire and left. Well, the fishermen saw the smoke and they raced back, and they caught up to the Haida before they could get past the outer islands, because nobody knows these waters like the Gitga'at. And they slaughtered every last one of 'em and hung 'em upside down so that when the Haida came back they'd see what happened to their raiders." Helen smiled as though remembering a childhood sweetheart. "I have a Haida daughter-in-law now, so when I tell her that story I just call 'em raiders and don't mention where they came from."

She spoke to us for an hour that day, and then one of her thirty-six great-grandchildren came through the door and hugged her, and one of her nieces came through another door and started cooking, and then more and more children came through the door and it was time for us to go. We thanked her for her time and her words.

"Hey," she winked, "as long as Granny's got a voice."

IT'S CONCEIVABLE THAT some people might find Granny's voice a little on the cutesy side; more pathos than logos, appealing to our emotions by conjuring images of delightfully edible animals, rather than to our minds with facts and figures. She wouldn't be surprised to hear it. The white man, as she said, does love his statistics.

But it bears mentioning that some of the protagonists in the pro-Northern Gateway camp—white men, for the most part—who are renowned for their grasp of numbers, whose offices and reputations rest largely on their ability to interpret and deploy all manner of numbers, have betrayed a certain selectivity in this respect. Some numbers matter more to them than others.

Let's say, for instance, that the federal minister of natural resources, right-hand man to the prime minister and an outspoken advocate for mining Alberta's tar sands as fast as we possibly can, tells the editorial board of a Montreal newspaper in April of 2013, "I think that people aren't as worried as they were before about global warming of two degrees," adding that "scientists have told us that our fears are exaggerated," but subsequently can't recall which scientists have said so or who it is that's not as worried as before. When something like that happens, those of us with younger voices than Granny's should really be saying, ahem. We have some numbers, too: The Intergovernmental Panel on Climate Change (IPCC) is composed of a thousand of the world's leading climate scientists, and it has not withdrawn or in any way scaled back its warning that a two-degree rise in the average global temperature relative to conditions preceding the industrial revolution is about the most that civilization as we know it is likely to withstand. These people are not telling us our fears are exaggerated. To the contrary, the IPCC's warnings grow more urgent every day. Must we really go over this again?

Apparently. To be clear, then, two-degree warming means, among many other things, a catastrophic disruption of global food production and potable water supply and planetary ecosystems like boreal forests (as the pine beetle has demonstrated for Canadians) and coral reefs (because of the way carbon dioxide is acidifying the ocean); it means pandemics, a multiplication in the number and intensity of extreme weather events, and a rise in sea level of *at least* four metres, which, when you picture New York and Hurricane Sandy or New Orleans and Hurricane Katrina, has some interesting implications for a world in which 40 per cent of humanity lives within a hundred kilometres of the sea. This isn't some abstract future scenario. We are already at 0.8 degrees above pre-industrial revolution temperatures, and rising at a rate of 0.1 degrees per decade. Hence twelve of the last fifteen years being the hottest in recorded history. Hence the amount of Arctic ice coverage now being half what it was in the 1980s. Hence weather- and climate-related insurance losses more than doubling each decade since the 1980s, reaching today's average of $50 billion a year, according to the journal *Science*, a figure that comes nowhere near covering the $1 trillion or so that climate change is now sapping from the global economy each year.

The IPCC was initially very cautious about attributing all this to human behaviour, avoiding categorical conclusions about a causal link in its first 1990 assessment; the climate has been warming and cooling for as long as the earth's had one, after all. But by the time a thousand of the smartest scientists in the world released their fourth assessment in 2007, they had accumulated enough evidence to state that there is a 90 to 99 per cent likelihood that industrial emissions are indeed causing climate change (one key determinant is the rate of change—whereas the last two-degree warming took twenty thousand years or so, this one will take barely a century). Even if we stopped burning all fossil fuels this second, the greenhouse effect is such that the industrial emissions already in the atmosphere would continue to warm our climate for the rest of this century. If we wish to keep long-term climate change to within the still-disastrous scenario of two degrees maximum, we as a species will have to figure out a way to cap the amount of carbon we're burning within this very decade.

But, the numbers-people protest, Northern Gateway has very little to do with climate change. Adding half a million barrels a day or so of bitumen into global circulation represents somewhere in the neighbourhood of just 0.002 per cent of the world's fossil fuel consumption, whereas its impact on our economy, on jobs and GDP, would be immense and beneficial and enable us to craft solutions to the aforementioned looming problems.

It is true that Northern Gateway's contribution to climate change would, in and of itself, be statistically negligible. But the same cannot be said of Northern Gateway's source, which is 170 billion barrels or so of recoverable oil lying inside the tar sands, which our government has shown every indication of wanting to liquidate as fast as possible—Prime Minister Harper, for one, has stated his desire to up tar sands production from almost 2 million barrels a day to 4 million barrels a day. Once that goal has been achieved, it seems pretty obvious what will happen next. The only way to keep doubling production in the world's largest deposit of bituminous sands is to keep building more pipelines out of it, and in every case we will be able to say that pipeline X's contribution to climate change is statistically negligible. It's a hideous example of the problem of cumulative impacts, which plagues all manner of human meddling with the biosphere. We just keep piling on the straw. In the case of the tar sands, the problem is this: if we keep building statistically negligible pipelines until we've liquidated the entire resource, those 170 billion barrels of oil will raise the earth's temperature by some 0.4 degrees—that is, half the total amount that the world's climate has already heated up since the industrial revolution.

In the process, we're going to use relatively clean-burning natural gas, whose extraction method may or may not be contaminating our aquifers, to power the extraction of the dirtiest-burning oil on earth, whose extraction is poisoning much of the water flowing into the Northwest Territories. We are going to do this—are doing it—in a century during which fossil fuels (and water) are primed to become ever more strategically valuable, a century during which we could be putting fossil fuel's profitable energy towards building the next generation's energy infrastructure. But no. Instead of piping Alberta's energy to eastern Canada and thereby achieving energy self-sufficiency, we continue importing oil from Saudi Arabia and Venezuela and Nigeria for everyone east of Toronto, whilst further importing a huge volume of toxic diluent from Asia, in order to be able to sell them the raw bitumen we're mining too fast to upgrade ourselves. Selling oil to Asia instead of America is now what we mean by economic diversification.

This is the logic that old Granny and all her emotional acolytes are too fuzzy-minded to grasp.

They just don't get that to live well, humans must have energy. No country on earth has achieved first world status without burning a great deal of fossil fuel to get and stay there. That's why a graph plotting the world's energy consumption over time resembles a portrait of the approach to Mount Olympus, with the summit lost in the clouds—who knows how high it will go, or whether it leads to a sustained plateau or a peak that plummets just as steeply down the other side? No one, yet. What we do know is that the world is currently burning through 15 terawatts of energy a day, equivalent to 85 billion barrels of oil. We know that 85 per cent of that energy is derived from fossil fuels. We know that renewables account for just 15 per cent, most of which is hydropower, nuclear, and wood; wind, solar and biofuels together provide less than 1 per cent of the world's energy mix. Stopping a pipeline won't change any of those numbers.

What *would* change those numbers is if countries like Canada—that is, the richest countries in the world—started investing in research and development on energy alternatives. One good way to do this is through subsidies, which after all have helped fossil fuels gain their current dominance; according to the International Energy Agency's 2012 *World Energy Outlook* report, fossil fuels are subsidized to the tune of $500 billion a year worldwide, six times what renewables get. In Canada, we spend $26 billion on these subsidies, or nearly $800 a year for every man, woman, and child. No, that money doesn't all go into the pockets of greedy oil barons, but rather towards making central heating and gasoline and electricity affordable for Canadians of all income levels. That made sense before we realized that there are some serious hidden costs to these benefits, and by ignoring them we're simply passing the bill on to our grandkids. Or more likely, by this stage, our kids.

Now we know better, and yet we're still, as it were, stepping on the gas when it comes to fossil fuels in Canada. Virtually every penny our government spends on R&D for energy alternatives goes not towards developing renewables, but to sequestering carbon dioxide. Whole books have been written about the long-term unviability of stuffing carbon dioxide into underground caverns. Whether or not we can figure out a way to make it work, the larger point is that every dollar spent on that is a dollar taken away from things like wind and solar farms, or better transit, or more efficient homes. This larger point has been spelled out by people like the International Monetary Fund, hardly a bastion of radical environmentalism, which recently calculated that shifting subsidies away from fossil fuels and towards renewables would both stimulate economic growth *and* reduce global carbon dioxide emissions by 13 per cent. That could, and should, be just the beginning. The International Panel on Climate Change, for its part, has calculated that renewables could supply almost 80 per cent of the world's energy by 2050, if the international will and $12 trillion in research and development were only there.

Big picture stuff, no question, and pretty damn speculative to boot. But if all these alternative numbers add up to a single truth, that truth is the dark poetry of Enbridge's "more than a pipeline" slogan. Even critics must agree: Northern Gateway is, absolutely, a path to our future.

The waterfront is industrialized at the head of Douglas Channel.

GARDEN CITY
AND THE
PEOPLE OF TOMORROW

IF YOU VISIT the Kitimat museum, you will learn that this town of nine thousand (or so, depending where the boom/bust cycle is at) was born in 1953, a planned birth resulting from the BC government's invitation to the Aluminum Company of Canada—"Uncle Al" in happier times—to build one of the largest aluminum smelters in the world here. You will learn about Kenney Dam, then the third largest rock-filled dam on earth, which the company built on the Nechako River, several mountain ranges away, in order to power this most energy-intensive of industries; the Nechako Reservoir sluiced its waters down a 16-kilometre tunnel bored by Alcan's engineers through DuBose Mountain, dropping 800 metres along the way and yielding a kinetic energy harvest of 500,000 horses who galloped through an 82-kilometre transmission line to power Uncle Al's factory, where barge-fulls of bauxite were converted into 100 million pounds of aluminum shipped each year down the blue carpet of Douglas Channel.

The fifties were a good decade for Kitimat, publicity-wise. *Harper's* magazine called it the "Colossus of the Northwest." *National Geographic* celebrated "Canada's Aluminum Titan." *Canadian Geographic* declared it "Tomorrow's City Today" in an article that gushed over the "Garden City" design of visionary urban planner Clarence Stein, who made sure Uncle Al's workers lived far from the smoke-belching smelter in a town graced by kilometres of walking trails, plenty of parkland, a yard for every home, and not one centimetre of shorefront. The entire town is parked on a hilltop a kilometre or so from the water's edge.

What you won't learn anything about at the Kitimat museum is the Haisla Nation.

For that, you must drive a little ways out of town. Kitimat sits on the mainland, plugged into the continent's network of highways by a long and lonely asphalt artery, but before you get past the "Hitchhiking Is Dangerous" sign you'll see a turnoff; take it. The narrow country road winds south for eleven kilometres, down the eastern shore of Douglas Channel, and ends at Kitamaat, "People of the Snow," the town where half the Haisla's population of fifteen hundred lives today. Ilja and I saw it from the water first, at the end of another stressful day of sailing up the wide tunnel of Douglas Channel, too worried about catastrophe to enjoy the sight of all those glaciers creeping in off the horizon. Ilja had discovered a dire crack in the engine mount just before we left Hartley Bay. Suzy was rattling in her cage and had nearly broken it; if she shook hard enough, she could turn into a torpedo that would crunch through *Foxy's* hull and kill us all. Anyway that's how Ilja described it. The forecast had been for following winds and we'd hoped to sail all the way to Kitimat, where welders could rein Suzy back in, but of course what blew instead was a head wind that forced us to motor for eight nerve-fraying hours.

But, we made it. Welders ahoy. Our day-long panic gave way to a two-week contemplation of the much more than eleven kilometres that separated Kitimat from Kitamaat.

The reserve, at least, was on the water. Its collection of white box houses stretched along the Douglas Channel's eastern shore before pushing back into the trees, all overgrown lawns with rusting boats and half-carved totem poles lying in the grass. Kids jumping on trampolines. Friendly nods galore. It hardly looked desperate, but you wouldn't have guessed this was one of the wealthiest First Nations in Canada, or soon to be, because the land they occupied and the shores they laid claim to were coveted by people with products to ship, billions to spend, and a healthy respect for the damage that Indians with unresolved land claims can inflict on a corporation's bottom line. The Haisla had learned the lesson Uncle Al taught them sixty years ago.

"My dad used to talk about the day they saw a barge parked at the rivermouth," said Gerald Amos, the sixty-three-year-old environmentalist, adventurer, fish enthusiast and former chief councillor of the Haisla Nation. We met at the Kitamaat village marina, where the Haisla had let us tie *Foxy* up for free when we arrived in the middle of August. This marina was more wind-protected, more chilled out, and a more enjoyable place to be in pretty much every respect than the all-white, wave-knocked, teeming-with-raucous-sport-fishermen MK Bay Marina two kilometres to the north. The Haisla kids played in the water here, running out on the breakwater and asking us for food when they smelled something cooking on our barbeque, laughing at us for living on a sailboat. "Sailboats

Backyard bliss in Kitamaat.

are creepy," we were told. At night the older kids came down to the docks to drink and smoke and high-dive off the pier. In the morning, a dozen old Haisla men with coffee mugs in their hands would take their place. They'd ask us what kind of engine we had for our tender, offer us a jar of salmon, stare into the channel in silence.

Gerald Amos kept a renovated halibut boat called the *Suncrest* in Kitamaat's marina. Almost every day, he would wander down from his house and tinker with her engine for a couple of hours. He used the *Suncrest* to give ecotours of the Great Bear Rainforest, and in a couple of weeks he was taking a group of clients to a valley called the Kitlope. In the meantime he let Ilja and me come aboard the *Suncrest* and hound him with questions while he worked.

Gerald had a perfectly round face, brown and smooth except for the creases dug into the corners of his mouth by a lifetime of smiling. When I'd called him three months earlier and told him I was hoping we could meet, he said: "We're building a magic canoe up here! Everyone's welcome aboard." He smiled even when he was telling unhappy stories, like the Genesis of Kitimat.

"My dad told me how they held a village meeting to decide who would go meet the barge, and he was chosen along with a couple other guys. So they got in a canoe and paddled over." He nodded across the channel, to where Uncle Al's smoke stacks stood against the western shore. "When they got to the barge they welcomed them to Haisla country and asked them what they were doing here. The guys on the barge told them they were here to build an aluminum smelter, and that a townsite was being built at the top of the hill to house the workers." Gerald gave us a what-else-is-new smile. "And that's how we found out."

Prior to Alcan's unannounced arrival, the Haisla lived off all the same creatures as the Heiltsuk and everyone else on the coast, plus one more: oolichan, a small, silver fish also known as "candlefish" because of the oil for which it was historically prized. A dried oolichan is so oily you can set fire to it with a match; boiled down, that oil becomes a pungent, nutrient-rich grease that keeps for months—a buttery fish paté. Just like salmon, oolichan live at sea but spawn in rivers, though the oolichan's range has always been smaller and limited to the northern rivers of what is now British Columbia. This made them a hugely valuable trading commodity; it was because of the oolichan that the ancient trading routes connecting the Pacific Northwest with the interior plains were known as Grease Trails.

One of the most prolific oolichan rivers was what is now called the Kitimat River, which empties into the head of Douglas Channel in a looping, multi-forked estuary that was taken over by industry in 1953. It should come as no surprise that this river's population of oolichan did not survive Uncle Al, who was soon joined by a pulp and paper mill that showed up on the Kitimat riverbanks ten years later. Within a generation, the two industries had created several thousand jobs, poisoned the river completely, and clearcut the entire watershed for good measure, thus delivering one of the quickest local-environment liquidations in British Columbia's history. The whole process took about four decades.

Then, along came Enbridge.

The Haisla were introduced to Enbridge in much the same way they met Uncle Al. In 2006, while canvassing for a suitable place to build the oil terminal, Enbridge cut down a number of sacred trees on Haisla territory. Needless to say, the Haisla joined the alliance of coastal First Nations firmly opposed to Northern Gateway. As the war of words gathered strength, few voices rang out louder than that of Gerald Amos; and when high-ranking members of the federal government began accusing First Nations and environmental groups of receiving foreign funding in the days leading up to the Joint Review Panel's debut in Kitimat, it was Gerald Amos who provided the most articulate response. It was published in the *Terrace Daily*, a local paper, on January 8, 2012, two days before the public hearings began in Kitamaat's public hall:

NO APOLOGY FORTHCOMING

Recently there has been a lot of criticism by supporters of the tar sands, and oil industry front groups, of Canadian non-profit organizations who have concerns regarding the proposed Enbridge Northern Gateway pipeline project, and the fact that they receive support from U.S. philanthropic foundations. ...

The insinuation that northern communities, and especially First Nations, can be bought by U.S. interests is paternalistic and insulting; if not some new iteration of hypocrisy that can only be characterized as soft core racism.

The Haisla have been fighting to protect this region from ill-conceived industrial developments for over thirty years, while at the same time showing leadership in developing projects that are safer and more sustainable, and that benefit all British Columbians. Our history in this regard is well known, be it our efforts to reform logging practices, pollution from industrial plants, or our successful efforts to protect the world's largest remaining intact coastal temperate rainforest, the Kitlope Valley. ...

We are not opposed to development. But we are opposed to stupidity and placing our homelands at terrible risk in order to satisfy the insatiable greed of the international oil industry. We do not accept the Prime Minister's claim that this project is in Canada's national interest, and it is certainly not nation building, but rather, planet destroying.

Haisla were the lead in developing the LNG project in Kitimat, the largest new industrial development in the north in thirty years. Natural gas is the cleanest hydrocarbon available, tar sands oil is the dirtiest. My community's decision to support natural gas development and oppose a tar sands pipeline is a considered and informed decision consistent with our ancestral responsibilities as First Nations who have never surrendered title to these lands. Yes, we need and want jobs. Long term, permanent, sustainable jobs we can be proud of, not six months of digging ditches for a tar sands pipe, or jobs cleaning up oil spills. ...

The Haisla reality is a growing list of ancestral foods which we no longer have access to. Oolichans were once the most important food resource of the Haisla. They are now all but extinct in the five rivers in our territory that once produced them in great abundance, such as a harvest of over 600 tons a year in the Kitamaat River alone. Abalone are also gone. Crabs, prawns and bottom fish in Douglas Channel are either gone or illegal for human consumption due to toxic pollution. Salmon habitat in the Kitimat River, once one of the jewels of the coast, is all but gone. Any semblance of salmon abundance is now reliant on a federal hatchery paid for by taxpayers, not the industries that destroyed the productivity of the river in the first place.

We have seen the magnificent forests of the Kitimat Valley, and other coastal watersheds, obliterated in an orgy of greed and destruction driven by short-term economic interests, instead of what we asked for; long-term sustainable and science-driven resource planning.

We are willing to share, but we will no longer be robbed.

Real protection of forest jobs comes from realistic and long-term forest planning, not blaming Enviros and First Nations for a decline in the forest industry that is the result of decades of over cutting and bad management by government and industry.

Now we face Enbridge and their proposal to bring dirty oil from the tar sands through our territory via a pipeline, and ship it through our waters via super tankers.

This is the largest and most insidious threat to our culture that has ever existed, with the possible exception of the Canadian government's violent imposition of the residential school system.

We have witnessed our Prime Minister and his Minister of Environment openly supporting this project, which makes a joke of the Joint Review Process. It is inconsistent with the

federal government's fiduciary responsibility to First Nations.
This government has abdicated any semblance of fairness or
balance in executing its responsibilities to our people, and in
fact to all Canadians. Why wouldn't we accept help in this
situation?

So, do not expect an apology any time soon for our will-
ingness to accept assistance from U.S. Foundations, or any-
one else of goodwill and principles. In fact, we will instead
use this as an opportunity to thank them for stepping up to
the plate and acting with charity, responsibility, integrity
and generosity in this time of rapid and uncertain change in
the world.

We can only hope our Prime Minister will consider their
example and truly come to an epiphany as to what really con-
stitutes nation building.

Of course it wasn't Kitamaat you heard about in the news
when the subject of Northern Gateway came up, but Kitimat,
and I had questions for them both. The town on the hill hadn't
got this much press since it was born. After a strong industrial start, Kitimat had settled into a steady decline that accelerated towards oblivion as the new millennium approached.
First the aluminum smelter downsized dramatically, then the
next two biggest employers—the pulp mill and a methane
plant—shut their doors completely. Then Enbridge came along
and promised to make Kitimat the nexus of the biggest nation-
building/planet-destroying project since the tar sands themselves. For the first time in half a century, the town was back in
the media's crosshairs.

I wondered how it felt. This was an industry town; was
Enbridge as welcome as anyone else? Did citizens and city
council feel they had a say in Northern Gateway's future, or

were they just so many leaves to be tossed whichever way the perfect storms of Big Oil and Globalization and Petropolitics blew? What did they think about the stink that Gerald Amos and the Haisla were making just down the road?

And so, over the two weeks that *Foxy* sheltered in Kitamaat's marina, Ilja and I hitchhiked into Kitimat just about every day.

One day I went in alone and after five minutes a red Camaro pulled over, a Haisla man in the driver's seat with long black hair just starting to grey. His limbs trembled with some kind of palsy, his hands shook on the wheel, and he wore a hearing aid. When I got in he looked at me and said, "Little too much sun, eh?"

"Guess so. Helluva summer it's been."

"Better buckle up."

But he didn't drive too fast. We cruised comfortably down the winding asphalt under trees with fat August leaves, and I asked what he did for a living.

"I work in the forests," he said.

"Logging?"

"That's right. Mostly down around Vancouver Island, but some up here as well."

"I guess it's all second or third growth by now, huh?"

"Nope. There's still lots of old growth left. We had a camp down in Surf Inlet"—on Princess Royal Island. "Big trees there, boy."

I paused a while, then asked, "You don't think it's a problem to log old-growth forests?"

"It's all work to me." A small silence. "Some old growth, eh, ought to be preserved. Can't cut it all down. But some of it's okay to cut. I love my job, I can tell you that. Except when I'm in hip deep snow!" He looked sideways at me and laughed.

I laughed, too. "I thought Kitamaat was Haisla for people of the snow," I said.

"Don't mean we like it." We were quiet again for a kilometre or two and then he spoke. "Now Enbridge wants to ship oil down Douglas Channel." I hadn't told him who I was or what I was doing here. I hadn't mentioned Enbridge at all. "That'll ruin everything. I'm against that. We all are. We'll never let it happen. Enbridge says they signed deals with a bunch of Indians from a bunch of tribes all along the pipeline route, but the people who signed stay secret. They don't have to say who they are." This was true. Enbridge claimed to have memorandums of understanding with twenty-six First Nations along the pipeline route (nobody was pretending they had any friends along the coastal tanker routes), but the company refused to name which tribes had come forward, or what the terms of their agreement was. And meanwhile not a single tribe would publicly admit to having signed anything with Enbridge's name on it. "Sounds pretty dubious to me," my ride said. "They first come here years ago to talk to us about the project, and they treated us like a bunch of simpletons. You know. Like we didn't know anything."

"So you think Enbridge won't get their pipeline, huh?"

"Oh. Eventually they will. Somebody will. If we shoot this one down, someone'll come along soon enough and try again. They've tried before, and they'll keep trying. Someone'll get it through."

We reached Kitimat's City Mall. He dropped me off at the parking lot with a quivering grin and a handshake. Once he had a grip, he held it firm. I thanked him and carried on to my next interview.

It was not, unfortunately, an interview with Joanne Monaghan, the mayor of Kitimat, because she refused to speak with me. Her assistant had emailed me earlier to say:

Mayor Monaghan asked me to thank you for your interest in our community. Mayor and Council have made a decision that they will not speak to the press or comment regarding the Northern Gateway Project at this time as they have taken a position of neutrality on the project.

Then the assistant emailed again to say Mayor Monaghan had changed her mind and I could call her. I did, expecting to set up a time for an interview, and she said in a curt voice that if I had any questions I might as well ask them now, but that I should know beforehand she refused to discuss anything related to Enbridge or Northern Gateway. The most obvious question was then why had she invited me to call her? But I wasn't feeling confrontational. Nor terribly original, I confess: I slipped into generic journalese and asked, "What is your top priority as mayor of Kitimat?" knowing the answer already because there is only one answer politicians in the western world may give to that question if they want to stay in office.

"Economic development," she said. But then she said something no one could have foreseen. "When I first took office I started up a monthly prayer group to pray for the economic well-being of Kitimat, and today we are booming."

To which I said thank you very much, and hung up.

I can report, however, that I did manage to infiltrate city hall, and therein, vis-à-vis Northern Gateway, discovered rumbles of dissent.

"I hate being neutral, because it means you're neutralized!" Phil Germuth, the only Kitimat city councillor who would speak with me on the record, was frustrated because Kitimat was the only town in northern British Columbia that hadn't issued a formal statement of opposition to Northern Gateway. They were officially neutral. It was an open secret that Mayor Monaghan was all for it, and that a majority of the town council sided with her, but public sentiments were sufficiently divided that they'd decided to play it safe. The mayor had told her councillors to follow her lead and avoid speaking to the press about it, but when I called Germuth he invited me straight away to come see him. "We've got more to lose than any other community here," he said. "No one else is at risk of both a pipeline and a tanker spill. Prince Rupert, Terrace, Smithers, Hazelton, they're all against it, and we're *neutral?*"

Germuth owned his own mechanic shop and was born and raised in Kitimat. He was forty-six years old, balding, with a chestnut goatee and hands like a coal miner's. He loved machines, loved industry, loved to work. "When I first heard about Enbridge and the Northern Gateway, I thought hey, great, jobs! Money! But when you educate yourself about it, you realize holy crap, this isn't such a good deal for fifty jobs." Fifty-two jobs, actually—the number Enbridge promised Kitimat, about the same as a single BC ferry employed.

"I pushed council to have a survey done so we could know where the citizens of Kitimat truly stand," Germuth told me, "but they shot the motion down. I'd estimate that this town is about 70/30 against the proposal. Most folks have caught on that we have everything to lose and nothing to gain. There's nothing Enbridge can tell me to make me think that when a supertanker collides with an island, we're not toast. Or when a pipeline ruptures into our river, we're not toast. That's where our drinking water comes from—how's Enbridge going to protect that if something goes wrong?" He shook his head. "Even if they promised us hundreds of jobs, I still wouldn't support them."

One other councillor was willing to meet with me, on condition of anonymity. I asked that person, what were the numbers that I wasn't seeing? Why did Mayor Monaghan and

Sockeye is prepared for smoking in Kitamaat.

others want to see Northern Gateway happen? After all, Kitimat's economy was resurgent, as the mayor herself had said. The aluminum smelter was expanding, several liquid natural gas projects were in the works, a new methanol plant was being built to replace the old one...there were jobs to be had and more coming, even without Enbridge's fifty-two positions.

"The numbers are 6.5 billion!" the councillor replied. "That's the kind of number Alcan threw around in the fifties, and it sustained this town for half a century. It produces a knee-jerk reaction, never mind that none of the money will actually go to Kitimat. There's a sort of abiding sense here that any industry, anything that creates any jobs at all, is good for Kitimat." As the councillor went on, it struck me that I was listening to a parable for all of Canada. "We're a conflicted town. This is an industrial town, but we love our clean water; we complain about the weather all the time, but we're surrounded by running water, by the river and by the ocean and the rain. It's a part of our fabric. Some time ago we coined a new slogan: *Kitimat, a marvel of nature and industry*. Well, it was just PR at the time, but after a while we realized, my god, it's true! That's what we are!"

But as Phil Germuth had said: "It probably doesn't make much difference what we say. First Nations are the only ones who can stop this thing now."

BACK IN KITAMAAT, a small log cabin across the street from the marina had a big sign warning intruders that it was surrounded by twenty-four-hour surveillance and night vision cameras. Intrigued, Ilja and I knocked on the door one day. It was an art shop containing half a million dollars' worth of yellow cedar carvings ornamented with abalone shells, along with silver and gold jewellery, all crafted by Gerald Amos' uncle, the eighty-year-old Sam Robinson, "chief of chiefs," native artist extraordinaire, story-telling dynamo.

"You're lucky," he said, the first time we walked in. "I just took two months off to rejuvenate my artistry and only got back to work couple days ago."

He was seated at his carving desk, glasses on, a block of wood in front of him and ten wisps of white hair left on his head. "I can tell a buyer from a looker at a glance," he told us. He spoke with a Haisla accent that sounded vaguely Polish; English was his second language. He stood, very slowly, then imitated the entrance for us: a *buyer* walks in and immediately looks closely at a piece, investigates it, then moves onto another, examining each work intently. A *looker* just wanders in and walks around, neither letting his gaze nor his steps linger in any one place. "You guys are lookers, but I don't mind. I've got all the money I need."

Sam had enough buyers these days. We hadn't been in his shop ten minutes before he opened a desk drawer and showed us a cheque for $150,000. "Gotta go to Hazelton to cash this one," he said, "people talk too much around here." He assured us this was nothing. He'd sold art pieces for way more than $150,000. On the wall was an exquisite paddle into which he'd carved a series of animals like a totem pole, using iridescent abalone shells wherever a creature's eyes peered out. "That'll be worth a million dollars," he said, "but not until after I'm dead. I'll take a hundred fifty thousand for it. Someone came in and offered me sixty thousand a while back. I said no way."

Sam wanted us to know he'd been on the cover of newspapers. He opened his desk drawer to show us, and there he was on the front page of the *Globe and Mail* in full regalia, a flowing black cape and a cedar crown sprinkled with fluffs of eagle down, talking stick in hand like Gandalf with his staff. "What'd I tell ya? Sammy Robinson, chief of chiefs!" The photo was taken on the first day of Northern Gateway public hearings, just down the road from here.

"We'll never let it happen," he said with a shrug, and put the newspaper away.

Sam had been wined and dined by Fidel Castro himself. The revolutionary invited him to his private villa two hours outside of Havana back in the eighties. He showed us the pictures, sat us down, and talked to us for an hour, telling story after story, and all we had to do was walk in, be polite—and buy twenty dollars worth of key chains before we left.

Sam Robinson may have been chief of chiefs, but since the title was hereditary any influence he had over the Haisla's development trajectory was of the soft-power persuasion. The people who signed the papers that made things happen or not were to be found in the band office, seat of the Haisla's elected leadership, plunked inside a trailer at the entrance to Kitamaat village. After a week of repeated requests, I was granted a brief audience with Ellis Ross, chief councillor of the Haisla Nation, quite possibly the busiest man in the Douglas Channel.

Ross was a dour man of forty-seven with greying hair clipped short around a balding dome, wearing jeans and a blue collared shirt the day I walked into his office. He couldn't talk about Northern Gateway, he said, not while the public hearings were underway. But I could ask him anything else.

A whiteboard in his office had a flow chart drawn in his neat hand, diagramming eleven industrial proposals the Haisla were considering, each at a different stage along the bifurcating paths towards acceptance or rejection.

"That's just a snapshot," he assured me. "We have reams of this stuff coming through. That board changes every week." In recent years, the Haisla had given up on land negotiations and started buying their territory back instead. With the commodity boom of the aughts, the rise of fracking in northern British Columbia and Alberta, and the maxing out of the only other deepwater port in northern British Columbia—Prince Rupert— the Haisla's waterfront property made them the most sought-after First Nation in the country. Royal Dutch Shell and China Investment Corp were among Ross's suitors; so was Natural Resources Minister Joe Oliver, who paid two personal visits to Ross shortly after my own.

The Haisla, in other words, were deluged, inundated, flooded and tsunami'd by the number of wealthy and powerful people who wanted to do things on their land—log it, mine it, dam it, but mostly ship energy through it. Hundreds of millions of dollars were being waved before them, and Ross recognized that as both a blessing and a curse.

"We have no capacity to deal with this stuff," he told me, shaking his head. "Council isn't elected because we're smart, or because we're educated. We're elected because we're popular. A lot of my colleagues haven't even graduated from high school." Ross himself made it through one year of college before quitting, and spent the next two decades beachcombing, logging, and driving small ferries for industry workers in Douglas Channel. He battled alcoholism throughout that time, but had been sober for the last decade. He had the air of a serious, intelligent man who knows he's in over his head.

The Haisla had a lot of say over what happened on or near their territory, but they couldn't oppose everything even if they'd wanted to, Ross told me. They were signing deals that would allow hundreds of liquid natural gas tankers a year to load up at a terminal built on Haisla territory. Natural gas would evaporate if spilled; it posed far less of a marine threat than bitumen. A 2006 deal that gave Apache Corp. the right to build a tanker terminal across the channel from where Enbridge wanted to build theirs had earned the Haisla $50 million, $12 million of which was instantly handed out in $8,000 cheques to every man, woman and child in the band. Similar deals with other gas companies were now on Ross's whiteboard. This infuriated the nations living downcoast, who worried about the effect hundreds of tankers would have on marine life and water quality even without a spill; it also raised pointed questions for environmental NGOs about the strategic wisdom of partnering with First Nations.

Blessed by geography and led by the blunt, pragmatic Mr. Ross, the Haisla were making money and enemies in equal measure.

"They ended up totally conflicted on this and they all decided: we're going to do this the dirtiest way possible and get all the money we can," was what Art Sterritt, executive director of the Coastal First Nations alliance, told reporters following a public dispute over the Haisla's embrace of LNG tankers.

"If I see any Haisla fishing in my territory I tell them to get the fuck out," a well-known Gitga'at leader said to me three weeks later. "They can take their LNG money and spend it at Safeway."

"If there's anyone that First Nations have a harder time getting along with than the Canadian government, it's ourselves," Ross told me. "If a white man comes into an Indian's community and says hey, I have a proposition for you, the Indian will say come in, let's talk about it. But if an Indian from a nearby tribe comes and says hey, I've got a proposition for you, the Indian will say go fuck yourself. Look at the Heiltsuk and the Owikeno. The first time I ever sat at a negotiating table with those two in the room, they wouldn't even look at each other. I thought, man, what happened that these guys hate each other so much? Then I learned that about seventy-five years ago, the Heiltsuk invited a group of Owikeno chiefs to a feast and beheaded every one of them. For them, it's like it happened yesterday.

"But it's not just those two, it's all of us. We were a warring community! We murdered and we pillaged and we took slaves. We were not a model society. That's the history people don't like to talk about. People talk about, you have to respect your elders; you have to pray to the great spirit. That's not our history. There was no great spirit in Haisla history. We have a lot of traditions, yes. We have culture, yes. And now, after being poor for a long time, the Haisla are on the verge of becoming a very rich nation. Great. So how are we going to balance that with our traditions? How are we going to hold on to our culture? What's going to happen to the environment? I have no idea.

"But the answer isn't going to come from blaming others for our problems or romanticizing the past. I'll tell you something else. My dad went through residential school and you know what he told me about it? He said it was the best thing that ever happened to him. He was a wild kid who didn't have anyone to raise him, and he said if he'd stayed on the reserve it would have been the end of him. Some people say I'm a victim of the residential schooling system because my father went through it. Bullshit. Everyone likes to blame the evil residential schools, evil prime minister, evil corporation. We have to stop blaming others and start taking responsibility for our own actions."

THERE WAS ONLY one other person in either Kitamaat or Kitimat who had as much to say as Ross. His name was Nate, and we found him at the Zoo.

The Zoo was a late night watering hole on the ground floor of the Kitimat Hotel, owned by a ruthless family of Chinese entrepreneurs whose youngest member, Luna, worked behind the bar. Luna had moved here from Shanghai nine months ago and was paying for a business degree with the money this summer job earned her. Pale and slender, a self-described traditional girl (her husband, the only man she'd ever been with, was still in Shanghai), Luna poured drinks for the neck-tattooed workers of Kitimat from midnight till four AM, laughing and flirting with them, sipping only Coca-Cola, surveying, between drink orders and jokes, the scene of human detritus strewn about the dark and uproarious chamber with the air of an Asian Mona Lisa.

It was Luna's job to call the agency and pick the stripper up from the airport, a new one every week. The one on stage that night was a tiny brunette from Vancouver with a terrific sense of humour, who turned her performance into more of a sexual taunt than a turn-on. She wrapped a strand of hair around each nipple and tugged her breasts playfully in opposite directions, laughing as she set the nostrils of her thick-browed audience aquiver. Then she clenched the handle of an empty beer jug between her naked butt cheeks and wiggled it so that the boys in the front row tossed their two-dollar coins in. We half expected her to queef at any moment, and maybe she did, but if so the music drowned it out.

It was halfway through that performance that we met Nate, the red-eyed engineer from Cameroon. Black and boisterous, Nate waved his white Russian in our faces, oblivious to the girl on stage. The only girl on his mind was in Toronto; he showed us her picture on his phone. She was beefing him, he said, because he hadn't been home to visit in so long. "But how'm I gonna visit her when I'm here makin money for her? She wants a $2,600 Louis Vuitton bag, ay!"

Nate was an optimist. He designed oil and gas facilities all over the world; the Persian Gulf, Nigeria, Cameroon, Kitimat. He was the most honest person on the coast.

"We've got thirty years to sell this oil before the world moves on. Gotta get it now! Sell it while you can! Everyone who knows anything knows that, everyone thinks that. What you think, man?"

"I think we're on opposite sides of the debate," I said.

"There's nothing to debate! We know how to build tankers, we know how to build pipelines, we know how to get the oil out of the ground. No problem! Gotta make that money!"

I clapped him on the back and clinked my glass to his. Our fingers matched up like piano keys. "I think oil is the addiction that will send us all to hell," I said, for the sake of conversation.

Nate threw his head back and laughed, exposing molars as white as my fingers. "What's the matter with you, man? You don't have any faith. We have the technology. Why don't you believe in science?"

"I do believe in science. Maybe we're talking to different scientists."

"This isn't the stone age, man! We know how to get that oil, and in thirty years it won't be worth anything. Sell it now or never. Everyone knows that! Why don't you believe in humanity?"

"Any thoughts on climate change?"

"Ay! Climate change! Fifty million years ago the climate was a hell of a lot warmer than it's going to be even in a hundred years. So we warm up the atmosphere a few degrees... who cares, man?"

"Ever seen an oil spill?"

"Have I ever seen an oil spill? Man, I have spilled *a lot* of oil in my life. I have *sinned*, man. You think I give a fuck about Douglas Channel?"

Ilja asked Nate if he would pose for a picture sometime, say this on the record. Suddenly Nate became shy and turned half away.

"No way, man," he said. "The tree huggers will come out and lynch me. Why you gotta be a tree hugger?"

"I'm not a tree hugger," Ilja said. "If everyone's thinking it, why won't anyone say it?"

"In Nigeria, man," Nate said, suddenly nostalgic, "if you want to build a pipeline, no problem. You just move two hundred thousand people and start digging, bam! Pipeline's built. No stupid reviews, no stupid government dragging its stupid ass with hearings, shit just gets *done*. Next project!"

Nate knew it was wrong to be greedy, to not give a fuck. And he didn't give a fuck, not at two in the morning with a white Russian in his hand and a girl waiting for her Louis Vuitton bag in Toronto. Nate had money, he spoke flawless French and English, he had an engineering degree and travelled the world and understood get-while-the-gettin's-good as only the peripatetic can. Make your money and move on.

Time for us to do the same. We thanked Nate for his candour and settled up with Luna, basking briefly in the sad wisdom of her goodbye smile, and caught a taxi back to *Foxy*.

SAM ROBINSON WAS in his shop again. The shapeless block of cedar on his desk was turning into a frog; yellow shavings were piling up around his feet. He didn't recognize me at first but welcomed me in, and when I nudged his memory it came back. He started right in on the slow stories.

"I never drank till I was forty-five," he said, "not till my kids grew up. My one son, he was a real good-looking guy, but all he did was party. I used to drive him to the beer parlour, pick him up from the beer parlour. Bought him a car when he was nineteen, he said he needed it. That same weekend, he crashed it! Killed two guys and ruined his own legs. I spent four years suffering for that, paying all those bills." People had been borrowing money from Sam his whole life, borrowing and not paying back. He went through several examples. "And it's not like I was rich," he exclaimed. "I was poor my whole life, until just a few years ago. Not that I'm rich now, but I'm comfortable."

The chief of chiefs scorned middlemen and sold all his own art personally. No galleries, no stores. There was a mask hanging on the wall that I liked with abalone tears running down the cheek, but it cost a thousand dollars, "or however much I feel like asking when someone tries to buy it. I can tell right away if someone's a buyer or a looker." He looked at me. "But I told you that already, didn't I." His memory was starting to go; he struggled for words and names, mixed up who was his cousin and who was his niece, which niece was which. "A lot of people are so focused on what's right in front of them, all they see is money. Money is the source of all evil, they say."

"I think a little money is good," I said, "but maybe too much money is bad. So they say." I was thinking how I hadn't paid my August rent yet, though it was more than halfway through the month; how my visa was overextended, as was my bank account; how I wasn't sure what our boat would cost to fix, how the advance a magazine promised me three months ago still hadn't come. The chief of chiefs nodded, stayed quiet, lost in his thoughts like I was in mine.

Outside the window, a group of young men were climbing the wooden posts by the dock and leaping into the bay between boats, while the girls watched and goaded them on.

"When I became hereditary chief, my mama said don't go into politics! Politics are the source of all evil, she said. But I couldn't help it, I always have to speak my mind. I was the first person to speak at the Northern Gateway hearings, did you know that?" And he pulled out again the *Globe and Mail* from January 11, 2012, with the picture of him in full regalia. Both the crown and the talking stick in the photo were resting casually in the corner of his shop. "I've got a birthday dinner to go to tonight," he said, after a small silence. "It's the mayor's birthday. Lobster."

I told him the story of my brief conversation with Joanne Monaghan. He listened with an indifferent smile.

"She's a real supporter of Enbridge," he said.

"But you two are friends, huh?"

"Oh yeah, she invites me to her birthday dinner every year. I always say I can stay friends with anyone, don't let politics get in the way. Except for my brother's kids." There was a rift from some time ago, he said, when his brother died and the kids wanted to become hereditary chiefs, and Sam refused to name them. "They don't know the history! You have to know the history if you want to become chief. The history that I talked about at the Enbridge hearings. I told that panel about all the names of all the places going up and down the Douglas Channel here, told them what they are called in our language; if you know that history, you can read the channel like a book. But I'm the only one left that knows it!" He said this proudly, not sadly. He was the chief of chiefs.

It was Sam Robinson who broke Ilja's dry spell, Art Project-wise, agreeing to pose in front of his studio in full regalia, standing still as a royal guard while mosquitos bit his face. Until then, the awkwardness of being a white guy waving a huge camera on the native reserve had held Ilja significantly back; that and the overwhelming task of keeping *Foxy* alive. But now *Foxy* was safely, happily docked, and Ilja had two months of photographic frustration to relieve. It wasn't just Art Project stuff that he shot. There were pictures of salmon as they started inching into the parched creeks; pictures of the smokeshacks in Kitamaat's backyards, with long rows of sockeye fillets hanging in the darkness, and pictures of the mothers who hung them; pictures of Haisla kids bouncing on trampolines; pictures of totem poles. A mailman from Kitimat named Murray Minchin, who had overcome a lifelong stutter to deliver a flawless testimony at the public hearings, posed with his wife and daughter for the sake of Art.

Another person Ilja shot was a man I'll call the Major. The Major was a Haisla man who had gotten wind that a pair of journalists were living aboard a sailboat in the marina, snooping around the reserve and talking politics, and he wanted to know why we hadn't come to talk to him. He was a big man who spoke loudly and exuded an angry menace. He found us early on in our stay, approaching us in the streets of Kitamaat at random intervals, until finally he accosted us at the dock one morning and demanded that we listen to what he had to say. Cornered, we agreed to join him at his house for a photo shoot and an interview.

The Major lived in a rundown house with an abandoned TV set planted in the front yard; the living room and kitchen looked like a kindergarten class had camped out here for a week. The Major was joined in the living room by two relatives, who, after posing in the yard for Ilja, sat quietly on the couch and let him do all the talking. I'd brought a bottle of wine and this cut the tension somewhat; once I'd poured a round into the plastic cups I found in the kitchen, the Major stood and cleared his throat, then delivered his address.

"We are the rightful chiefs of the Raven Clan," he began. "Let it be known that the institution of elected band council is an evil imposed upon us by the Indian Act, Section 74, and we repudiate this, just as we repudiate the Indian Act in its entirety." He paused for a sip and introduced the two men on the couch, who nodded politely and smiled.

"We must be careful about who we talk to," the Major said, "because there are agent provocateurs who have come amongst us. Their modus operandus includes tapping our phones and spying on us by satellite; they track our every move and they often seem to know what we are thinking before we do!" The two men on the couch nodded uneasily and looked out the window at the satellites orbiting invisibly on high.

"I caution you not to refer to Sam Robinson as the high chief of the Haisla Nation," the Major said next. "That is a contentious issue. You must be careful about what you publish because you could get into a lot of trouble." He looked at Ilja and me long and hard. I'd put my wine cup down on the grey carpet and was scribbling in my notebook as fast as I could, and this made him happy. He paused to make sure I was keeping pace, and didn't get going again until I looked up.

"I take issue with being called aboriginal," he went on, "because if you look at that word it means 'used to be original.' We are not *ab*original. We are original!

"I also take issue with being called First Nation. That expression has no legal standing. It crept into the lexicon somehow. Under the Indian Act, we are Indians. Let them say it!

"The apology of Stephen Harper for the residential school syndrome which we are suffering rings hollow in our ears, and it will continue to ring hollow until he revokes section 74 of the Indian Act, whose despotic contrivances operate to the direct detriment of our hereditary structures. The action of elected councils to deal with multinational corporations is illegal, and they have gleefully jumped, in my opinion, on the extinguishment bandwagon."

He paused, I scribbled. We both had a sip of wine and then he continued.

"And that's just the tip of the iceberg! I haven't gotten into water rights or land rights yet. It would take a book just to get into what has happened here in the last seven or eight years alone. I encourage you to come back here and write that book.

"Who gets to represent the nation: the elected council or the hereditary chiefs? It is my contention that the elected council has usurped our powers without due, prior, and informed consent. That is illegal, and we are pursuing the matter in court."

On this point he paused, and when I'd finished writing I looked up and saw him frowning at me.

"I would caution you not to publish anything that comes out of my mouth, in my name, because I have copyright to that. And also I could be arrested, because an injunction has been placed on us forbidding us from slandering the elected council."

His friends nodded solemnly. I wrote down that I shouldn't write down what he'd just told me not to write, then looked at Ilja, who was gazing deep into his empty cup. I poured another round and promised the Major I wouldn't use his name. Was it all right for me to keep writing? He insisted. I did so to the best of my abilities, but there was only so much I could catch and release of the Major's one hundred minutes of unflagging soliloquy, which leapt beyond tribal politics and delved into a rapid history of the new world order: the disastrous abandonment of the gold standard had ushered in a new era of usury crowned by the International Monetary Fund, which could only be defeated when the 99 per cent rose up under the leadership of the 350 million indigenous peoples of the earth. All we had to do was get rid of the thirteen families who controlled the world.

8

THE
 # KITLOPE

I**T WAS TIME** to leave Kitimat and Kitamaat and make our slow way home. Fall was fully upon us; the calm cloudless-ness of the shortening days was starting to seem like a trap from which a vicious storm would spring at any moment. But before we headed south, we were invited to bring *Foxy* a little farther east, into the mountains. There was a place called the Kitlope, Gerald Amos said, that we really oughtta see. Gerald was going there with his brother-in-conservationist-arms, a delightfully belligerent grandfather named Bruce Hill. The two of them were taking a group of American flyfishermen there; they'd be piling onto the *Suncrest*, aboard which it was a full day's journey, and since *Foxy* could only go half as fast at the best of times we left a day earlier.

Back into Douglas Channel under the iron sail, we made south until Devastation Channel opened an eastward vein that wound past mid-sized islands and forked repeatedly for fifteen nautical miles, when the final bifurcation came into sight, a fir-tipped Staniforth Point. The left fork led into Gardner Canal, a ninety-kilometre green snake undulating through high granite walls that devoured the horizon all the way to the canal's end, where the Kitlope began. With every curve and twist of the canal, the ramparts beside us erupted steeper and taller; 100, 150, 200 vertical metres. They plunged just as steeply below the surface, too; ten metres from the shore the water was a hundred metres deep, and as we cut a wake through the centre of that marine Amazon the submerged canyon bottom lay four hundred metres beneath *Foxy*'s hull. Glaciers gazed down from on high, slow-dripping curtains of water that shimmered over the rock and collected into channels carved out in a few short thousand years. The low hum of a hundred waterfalls pouring into the ocean drummed over Suzy's rumble like a summer-long piss of the titans, their effluent turning the ocean an opaque turquoise that reflected the mountains back into the sky.

Foxy's batteries started overcharging badly halfway up Gardner. The wire connecting the regulator to the alternator had melted. Fortunately we—Ilja—had packed a significant arsenal of spares. Wire replaced, engine fire averted, journey resumed.

We reached Chief Matthews Bay, a mammoth green canyon carved out of Gardner's walls by a glacier long ago. This was the last pullout before the Kitlope watershed, which now lay just around the corner. A log cabin had been built in the forest here, where we would meet the *Suncrest*. It was the best we'd timed anything all summer, pulling into the bay just as a smiling Gerald Amos, scowling Bruce Hill, and six Oregonians overtook us. Trailing behind them was a Lamborghini of a jetboat, tethered to the *Suncrest*'s stern and looking like she could have made the trip from Kitimat in twenty-five minutes flat.

They anchored ahead of us near the mouth of the bay, and soon the air filled with the jet boat's roar as they ferried their gear to the cabin. I had *Foxy*'s helm and was aiming to anchor thirty metres past the *Suncrest*, when suddenly our depth sounder went from bottomless to thirty feet, then twenty, then fifteen, none of which corresponded to the charts. The water was supposed to be deeper. *Foxy* was about to run aground. I said nothing and banked hard, drawing a sharp look from Ilja, and then Gerald appeared in the jet boat, calling unconcernedly, "Just raft up to us," and *Foxy* still hadn't touched bottom...Ilja came into the cockpit and took the wheel, pointed her towards the *Suncrest*. We tied on in forty glorious feet of water and jumped into Gerald's chariot.

"Gets shallower here every year with all the river runoff," he said as we motored to shore. Enormous stumps loomed beneath the water, their branches poking through the surface here and there. They were all that remained of ancient trees that had been flushed out of the forest above us by the storms that roiled through every year; the right combination of wind, rain and glacial runoff could topple timbers, launching them into the current of an engorged river along with many tons of topsoil. Each year, the river vomited another layer of silt and detritus into the mouth of the bay. "If you go by the charts," Gerald said, "pretty easy to anchor somewhere that looks deep enough, till low tide leaves you lying sideways in the mud."

Gerald showed us the safest route through the thicket of half-submerged stumps between our anchorage and the cabin. For the rest of the week, he and his crew would sleep in the cabin while Ilja and I slept aboard *Foxy* and took our inflatable back and forth to join them for meals and evening drinks.

That night, when we were all drinking our first glass of wine beneath the swallows darting over the cabin's broad

Gerald Amos fishes for salmon on a rainy day in the Kitlope.

patio, when the intrigues of Kitimat and Kitamaat had fallen away and the stress of *Foxy*'s next trial was still a week off, Gerald raised his glass and said, "Cheers! To everyone who gives a shit."

THE FIGHT TO save the Kitlope began in 1990, when Gerald was chief councillor of the Haisla Nation Council. At that time, an American NGO named Ecotrust, known for the work it had done to preserve tropical rainforests, had turned its gaze homeward to North America's temperate jungles.

Satellite images revealed that virtually all of the green fringe lining the coast from California to Alaska had been logged at least once. While the world's conservationists lamented Brazil's slash-and-burn policies, the United States liquidated its entire stock of ancient rainforest, saving but a few highway-side stands of cedar and hemlock for tourists to take snapshots of. Canada wasn't far behind, having logged over 80 per cent of our own coastal old growth. A number of untouched watersheds were scattered throughout what would soon become the Great Bear Rainforest, but all of them were smaller than 5,000 hectares and surrounded by clearcuts. On Vancouver Island, Clayoquot Sound represented a 200,000-hectare ray of hope that activists were already battling to protect. But farther north, Ecotrust discovered another watershed that was twice as big as Clayoquot.

The Kitlope was in fact the largest untouched stand of temperate rain forest left on the planet, a sprawling chain of rivers, lakes and valleys big enough to serve as its own evolutionary cabinet, home to moose and mountain goats and wolves and bears and falcons and bats and oolichan and five species of salmon and much, much more, all buffered from human development by the glaciated mountains that surrounded it like the walls of Troy. The system's only exit was through the Kitlope River, which emptied into the ninety-kilometre-long Gardner Canal and led, ultimately, to Douglas Channel.

None of this was news to Gerald and the Haisla, whose forebears had occupied permanent villages in the Kitlope for a few hundred generations before the population crash forced them to consolidate in Kitamaat, early in the twentieth century. The logging industry knew about the Kitlope, too; Eurocan, the same company that owned Kitimat's now-defunct pulp and paper mill, held the lease to all 400,000 hectares. As the 1990s gathered steam, so did the company's plans to start cutting.

Enter Bruce Hill, co-captain of the *Suncrest*, co-saviour of the Kitlope, sitting now beside Gerald like a foul-mouthed, smoking Santa.

Bruce Hill didn't speak, he exclaimed. Canadian by choice, American by birth, Bruce entered his twenties as an acid-dropping, jail-birding protagonist of the civil rights movement, and when that more or less succeeded he joined the anti-Vietnam war movement. By the time that ended he was burned out and wound up in the BC interior working as a "hippie logger" and a fishing guide. He quit logging, but not fishing; it was during a river-by-river search for good sockeye streams that he wound up in the Kitlope more than twenty years ago, around the same time that Ecotrust was studying it on a map and Gerald Amos was hatching battle plans against Eurocan.

Bruce told the story amidst feast preparations on the second night. The Americans had pulled several salmon out of the river that day and kept the two best for dinner; several crabs were boiling pinkly in a four-gallon pot, and there was a bucket of sausage-sized spot prawns that sparked a debate over whether they were better eaten raw or cooked in butter and garlic, so we were doing both. These things were happening while Bruce poured his third glass of wine and lit his fifteenth cigarette and scratched his beard and talked about the day he found the Kitlope.

"We finally got here and we see this barge at the rivermouth. So we take our boat up to it and there's all these engineers aboard. They're forestry guys, laying out the plans for roads and cutlines. They're getting ready to log the fucking Kitlope! We just said, man, you guys better watch out for the treehuggers. This place is awful pretty."

Pretty soon after that, Bruce found his way to Gerald's office together with Ecotrust's director. Bruce had by then already chartered a helicopter and hired a photographer to take aerial photographs of the area; now, tapping into Gerald's and Ecotrust's network, the three men set about distributing those pictures to potential donors in the hopes of enticing some to come see the place for themselves.

"All we had to do was bring people up here," Bruce exclaimed. "We brought about a hundred people in, and they coughed up millions."

And so, to condense the saga, began the four-year campaign that ended in total victory: In 1994, the entire Kitlope watershed was turned into a conservancy that no logger's blade would ever touch. In celebration, Ecotrust pitched in to build the cabin we were now filling with the scent of exquisitely fresh seafood, a cabin to which Gerald and Bruce were still taking wide-eyed outsiders.

"I hope you don't want a million dollars from us," I said to Bruce.

"Only if you got em," he said.

Gerald emerged from the cabin and sat down on the patio beside us. "Ten minutes to dinner," he said, and lit a cigar.

I asked, "Are there any Haisla left alive who were born up here?"

"One guy," Gerald said. "Cecil Paul."

Bruce nodded vigorously, "Cecil Paul, man. Guy's a legend. He is one of the most articulate Haisla elders alive—puts Gerald to shame." Gerald nodded and squinted at the embers of his cigar to see if it was burning evenly. "You should have heard him during the fight to save the Kitlope. Man. That guy led the charge. And what a story he's got. He's a reformed alcoholic, been sober for thirty... thirty-six years, Gerald?"

"Thirty-seven," Gerald said. I didn't ask why they were keeping track. "When he was younger he got lost for a long time in the downtown east side of Vancouver; he was a total wreck. In fact, my first job when I was sixteen was on a halibut trawler, and Cecil Paul was one of the crew boys. He was drunk all the time, even then. I don't know how many times I helped him back down to the dock when he couldn't walk. But he always looked out for me on the boat. Saved my life more than once."

"When Cecil was eighteen or so," Bruce said, "he got a job at the cannery in Butedale—"

"No, he got a job logging across the bay from Butedale, on the mainland," interrupted Gerald.

"Right. Well he fell in love with a girl who worked at the cannery. She was the cannery boss's daughter, and she fell in love back. Eventually Cecil approached her father and asked for his daughter's hand in marriage, and he told Cecil 'no daughter of mine is going to marry a fucking Indian!' It broke Cecil's heart, man! He quit his job, he went home once to see his mom and told her, mom, my heart is broken, I gotta get out of here and go travel for a while. So he did, he went south and travelled—"

"He drank, is what he did," Gerald said.

"Well he drank and he travelled," Bruce said, "and he was

gone for five years. Five years and he never checked home, not once in all that time. So he never found out that his lover in Butedale had written him a letter after he left, to tell him that she was pregnant with his baby. She carried it to term, but her dad told her 'there ain't gonna be no black babies in this family,' and he made her put the baby girl up for adoption." Bruce paused and refilled his glass, and looked out past the patio. The trees were being eaten by the fog, and it was impossible to say where the ocean ended and the mist began. "Gerald, you may have to jump in soon. I can never finish this story."

"Let's see how far you get this time," Gerald said.

"So five years go by," Bruce said after a slow sip. "Cecil doesn't even know he has a daughter. Eventually he gets home and reads the letter, but by then there was nothing he could do. He looked for the girl's mom, but she was none too happy to see him and wouldn't help him find their daughter." Cecil lost a few more years after that to the streets of east Van, but eventually he moved back to Kitamaat and pulled himself together. He became a respected community leader. By the time the campaign to save the Kitlope got underway, Cecil had become the Haisla's lead spokesperson on the issue. The Haisla's counterparts at the negotiating table were the logging executives and the provincial environment minister, a man named John Cashore.

"Cashore was very supportive to our cause," Gerald piped in, "and really one of the most vital players in the whole game; his alliance was crucial."

"Right," says Bruce, "he was the environment minister, and for a long time he'd lived in Port Simpson—"

"That's up near Prince Rupert, just north of here," Gerald explained, jutting his forehead northwards.

"Cashore had adopted three children while he was living there and raised them as his own," Bruce went on. "And one of them was Cecil's daughter. None of them had any way of knowing this at the time—Cecil and Cashore had been in close negotiations over the Kitlope for years, but neither of them suspected a thing. It wasn't like Cecil was going to ask the environment minister, hey man, you don't happen to have an adopted daughter who might be mine, do you?" Bruce stopped now and took his glasses off to rub one eye with a basketball-sized fist. "Gerald, I think you're going to have to take it from here."

"Well, if I can interject," Gerald said, "it also turned out that Cecil's sister had moved to Port Simpson some time ago, and she was quite friendly with Cashore's family; so much so that the little girl called her Aunty—without even realizing that this woman was, in fact, her biological aunt."

"But get this," Bruce blurted out, his voice quavering. "Guess what Cashore named Cecil's daughter. *Cecilia.* I mean, fuck, man!" and his voice cracked and Gerald took back the torch.

"When Cecilia got older and had a kid of her own, she approached Cashore and told him she wanted to find out who her biological parents were, was that all right with him? And he said sure, of course. They found out who the mom was and Cecilia called her up and said would it be all right if I visited you? And the mom agreed, and she was the one who told Cecilia that her dad was Cecil Paul."

"Goddammit," Bruce said, tears welling up in his eyes.

"So this stuff all came out near the very end of the campaign, just when all the negotiations were pretty much done and the papers ready to sign; but when that come out, all our critics tried to force Minister Cashore out of the process and have him replaced. They said it was a conflict of interests! Him having adopted a girl out of the goodness of his heart, with no idea until that final moment that she was the daughter of the

Haisla leader he'd been negotiating with. But I think it just
made them look bad to say so. How can you paint anything
bad out of that picture?"

At any rate, it hadn't stopped the deal from going through.
The Kitlope was saved. Gerald looked at Bruce's sniffling face
and smiled.

"Boy," he said, "we should write a book."

AND THEN IT started to rain. After five straight weeks of blue
sky, the clouds gathered and plunged to sea level, burying the
mountains in mist and unleashing a torrent that brought the
world to life. Each day the river beside our cabin rose higher,
and the salmon that had been gathering in the bay now started
running upstream in droves.

A friend of Bruce and Gerald's showed up in a jetboat of
his own. Now all of us could jet up to the Kitlope, which was
twenty kilometres up Gardner Canal from our cabin. The
advantage of a jetboat, aside from its speed, is that it can skim
over water less than a foot deep; with a jetboat you can pen-
etrate far up a river, so long as there aren't any rapids. We
decided the Americans would jump in with him, while Ilja
and I boarded Bruce and Gerald's jetboat. But Bruce was eye-
ing the clouds. He was sixty-five now and had had one heart
attack already; his back was so shot that he had to take breaks
while cooking to sit down, and he'd been to the Kitlope a hundred times already. Rather than stand in the driving rain on
an exposed aluminum deck for ten hours, he decided to stay
put, tend the wood stove, smoke and drink and read all day.

That meant it was Ilja and Gerald and me.

We sped off through a driving rain that hurt our eyeballs no
matter how hard we squinted. We were going eight times faster
than we'd moved all summer, and the exhilaration overcame

the discomfort. Gerald Amos shouted over the motor as we raced towards the Gardner Canal's terminus. Look, there, at the faded red hieroglyphics on that granite face, all square-ish lines and dots; no one knew how old they were. He pointed out old patches of flat forest that used to be reserves, places his uncle once canoed to all the way from Kitamaat, a journey of over a week. That waterfall there hit the rock in such a way that if the day was sunny and hot enough it sent a heated spray of water onto a flat shelf where you could shower just like at home; another waterfall obscured a crack in the rocks where seals raise their pups, because killer whales couldn't get in. That mountaintop was where the Haisla used to gather when they heard a raid was coming.

The ocean ended and became a shallow river that ran beside a meadow of tall sea grass. Gerald pointed to the spot where he'd once seen a bear chase a moose into the river; the moose was the stronger swimmer and powered against the current, while the grizzly got washed downstream. Farther on, he pointed out where a cougar almost ate him as a child. "I was playing outside a hunting cabin," he remembered, "and a blue jay started making a racket up in the trees. My aunt was in the smokehouse, and when she heard the blue jay she raced out and grabbed me and pulled me inside with her. Later we went back out and saw the fresh cougar tracks. You listen to those blue jays; they'll let you know if there's any big predator nearby. They'll shout every time."

There was a Guardian Watchmen's cabin a kilometer up the river with three motorboats tied to the bank. The Watchmen were a sort of First Nations ranger squad; each of the coastal First Nations had their own team of Watchmen who patrolled the ocean and forests in their territory, documenting wildlife and keeping an eye out for poachers. They didn't have the authority to arrest anyone, but you were extremely unlikely to keep doing what you were doing if a group of Watchmen wanted you to stop.

As Gerald approached their cabin, a young Haisla man appeared and waved hello. We pulled up to the shore and tied the boat to a tree and chatted with the Guardian, who on closer inspection must have still been a teenager. He looked nervous. Inside the post-and-beam, he told us, there was a team of three surveyors.

"Let's hear what they have to say," Gerald said. We walked under the dripping canopy to the front door, opened it and walked into a warm ball of dry heat. I hadn't realized till then that I was cold already. The three surveyors were in their long underwear, their clothes and jackets hung over a wood-burning stove to dry. Two were young, a man and a woman, with open, friendly faces; the third, clearly the boss, was middle-aged with a slight paunch and a sandy moustache and a standoffish air.

"Hi, I'm Gerald Amos," Gerald said, striding in like a man entering his own living room. The young man and woman shook his hand deferentially and said their names; the big-moustached man accepted Gerald's hand with a cautious air.

"Hello," he said.

"I hear you guys are surveying up here."

"Yes," said the boss. "We're doing the old reserve."

"Oh, really," Gerald said. "They already surveyed that, I thought. Long time ago."

"That's right," said the man. He went to his bunk and pulled out a weathered notebook, brought it to the table where Gerald had sprawled himself out. "These are the old surveys. They did them in 1891." We looked at faded black-and-white photographs of the meadows we'd just passed, overlaid with sketches of where a village existed until plague killed so many people that the remainder were too few to survive alone, and it became a place that people visited with great effort—by canoe—from their new home in Kitamaat. The surveyor's lines were unintelligible squiggles to my eye, but Gerald examined them with great interest.

"Of course the river's always shifting," Gerald said. "My uncle used to say that if you wanted the river to change course, you had to bury a sockeye in the ground where you wanted it to go." The old surveyor didn't know what to make of that and stayed quiet. Gerald looked at him and shrugged. "That's just how our people thought." Later, when we cruised farther upriver, Gerald would point at enormous trees stuck in the middle of the river or fallen against its banks, deadfalls that hadn't been here last summer, explaining how those obstacles affected the current, which in turn affected the river's course— a big enough tree would create an eddy that sucked in other driftwood, eventually creating a kind of breakwater that sent riverwater surging against another bank downstream and carving *it* out, a cascade of changes that got bigger all the way down the line. But now he just looked up at the surveyor. "Who sent you to do this, now?"

"It's for the Land Management Act," the man said. "Government wants all the reserves properly mapped out."

"That fast? The Act was only signed into law a few months ago."

"Well, they've sent us in to get it done."

The Land Management Act, Gerald said in answer to my query, had to do with government handing over control of ancestral reserve lands to the First Nations who claimed them. "But the fact that they're moving this fast on it tells me the government got whatever it was they wanted from the deal, and we shouldn't have signed so fast." He looked up at the man and gave what looked to me like a conspiratorial smile, but which the man clearly interpreted as hostile. "You'll have to forgive me for not trusting the government," Gerald said.

"We're not government," the man said, and put his notebook away.

"We've been trying for thirty years to get the government to compensate us for the land they took away with the Kemano power project," Gerald said, referring to the hydroelectric dam that powered Kitimat's aluminum smelter. "They keep finding one reason or other not to. Kitamaat village is 260 acres; much of that backs up the mountain, where you can't build houses, rather than the waterfront; the waterfront we do have isn't continuous, but broken up into chunks with sections of crown land on either side. Another old Haisla reserve that is farther up the Kitimat River was half washed away when that river changed course a few years back. You'd think we would get an equal amount of land on the other side of the river, or *somewhere*, but no, nothing changes and so half that reserve is now rushing water. So for thirty years we've been trying to get some of these issues resolved with the government, and we've made zero progress, and now this Land Management Act gets signed and *months* later surveyors show up, with no word to us, and start working. Something's up."

The old surveyor had gone back to his bunk by now and was studying his notes. Gerald looked around fondly at the cabin walls and said, "Anyway, I'm warm now. Let's get back to it."

The river opened into Kitlope Lake; three hundred sixty degrees of granite and ice loomed over us, melting into thin waterfalls that disappeared into thick forest before meeting the lake and feeding it; at a small pebbly beach next to a rockslide, dead sockeye floated belly up, their eggs freshly laid in the pebbles. Gerald spotted a flash of silver in the dark water and said, "There's a coho eating their eggs." (He could spot a running school of half a dozen fish from a hundred metres off and tell whether they were sockeye or coho, when all I saw was glimmer and shadow.) He casually pulled out his rod, flicked the spoon twenty metres from our boat, and hooked the coho. He reeled it in without changing his posture and pulled it into the boat, where we knocked it on the head and put it in a plastic bag and let it slide around the aluminum floor.

We drove up to the far side of the lake and then out the back end, up the Tezwa River. By the high mountain whose dribbling waters fed the Tezwa, Gerald told us, a Coca-Cola heiress had once been dropped off with a writer from an environmental magazine; they wanted to hike down to the lake from there, and Gerald had agreed to pick them up two days after their dropoff, but they'd taken a wrong turn in the thick bush and wound up huddling in the cold for days while Gerald flew over in a float plane looking for them. "When I finally found them," he laughed, "she told me that even when she was at her most miserable it felt amazing to walk through land that probably no human had ever walked through before. I told her she's right, our people knew better than ever to try walking through all that, for nothing."

Our gasoline started to run low. There was a waterfall farther up that he wanted to show us but we didn't have enough gas to get there, so we cut the engine and drifted back down with the current. In the silence, Gerald demonstrated his eagle call to us, a TV-Indian move if there ever was one.

"There are so few really wild places left in the world," he said. "That's what makes me happy about this one; that my grandchildren will be able to come here and spend time in a place that hasn't been logged out, that's still full of bears and eagles and fish living exactly as they did two thousand years ago." And then we fell silent, the silence turning so drowsy we all nodded off as we floated down the Tezwa for two kilometres, surrounded by true wilderness.

After dinner that night, Bruce played guitar and told us about the time he met Bo Didley at a party in Haight-Ashbury in the 1960s.

"Back in the Vietnam days," he said, "everyone was always playing music. Every time we got together, after rallies or before rallies or during rallies, someone would pull out a guitar and someone else a harmonica and then two people would start singing; the movement was made of music. You don't see that today." Then he grew morose. "I'm tired of this shit, man," Bruce said. "All I want to do is hang out with my granddaughter."

To change the subject I asked Gerald what his thoughts were on the whole how-should-we-as-non-natives-refer-to-native-inhabitants-of-the-land question; I apologized in advance for the stupidity of the question, but said I'd heard every title—native, Indian, native Indian, First Nation, aboriginal— denounced by various representatives of the people I wanted to describe, or at least refer to, without offending.

"I generally prefer to be called Haisla, but I know not everyone's heard of Haisla," Gerald said. "All I really ask is that whatever you call me, you say it with respect; it doesn't matter whether it's First Nation, or Indian, or aboriginal. Goes both ways. Sometime we'll say White Man. Often it comes across rough, but not always. You know, the term *gumshua* didn't originally mean 'white man.' That word in my language means to emerge from or come through a tight place. If you're trying to find a seat and the only space on the bench is between two people sitting close together, that's a *gumshua*. Well, the story goes that at first contact, our people saw what they thought was a huge log floating in from the ocean toward the shore; then all of a sudden all these people emerged from nowhere to stand on top of it—it was as though they'd climbed out of tiny holes in the wood. We'd never seen a European ship before! And so we called those people *gumshua*, and the name stuck."

Gerald talked about seeing the archives that recorded the Haisla's first formal contact with Europeans, when Captain Vancouver sailed into Douglas Channel and the chiefs paddled out to his boat in canoes to deliver a gift of two seventy-pound chinooks. "When I saw that," he said, "it really kicked in that our highest *nuyem*, our law, is and always has been to welcome strangers. The only difference between us is that I have ancestry in this land. Me and my people have lived here for ten thousand years. That's the only difference between me and you. Having said that, I welcome you here, for as long as you'd like to stay."

But it was time to go. Night had settled in. Bruce and Gerald and the Oregon Six lowered themselves into bed; Ilja and I drove the inflatable back to *Foxy* through a ghostly fog at low tide, our headlight illuminating the bony fingers of tree skeletons reaching through the water's surface. We eluded their grasp; slowly, carefully, we slid over a blackened sheet of glass toward a sailboat shrouded in mist, alone in an unfathomable world.

But not really. Even here we were connected to everyone we knew and didn't know by an artery of ocean that flowed to Douglas Channel and beyond, a conduit for salmon and orcas and humans and humpbacks, and yes, maybe oil slicks too. It didn't matter how tall the mountains were. Solitude was not an option.

WHALE POINT

WE WERE heading home now, I swear it. We only stopped in Hartley Bay to meet Helen Clifton. Eight hundred kilometres to go yet, and winter bearing down. But a serendipitous encounter on Hartley Bay's dock made one thing lead to another. You just don't turn down an invitation from Hermann the German.

Perhaps the best person to introduce the intrigue is another Herman with similar interests, the one who opened chapter 85 of *Moby Dick* with the following meditation:

That for six thousand years—and no one knows how many millions of ages before—the great whales should have been spouting all over the sea, and sprinkling and mistifying the gardens of the deep, as with so many sprinkling or mistifying pots; and that for some centuries back, thousands of hunters should have been close by the fountain of the whale, watching these sprinklings and spoutings—that all this should be, and yet, that down to this blessed minute (fifteen and a quarter minutes past one o'clock PM of this sixteenth day of December, A.D. 1851), it should still remain a problem, whether these spoutings are, after all, really water, or nothing but vapor—this is surely a noteworthy thing.

The mystery of the mists has since been resolved (nitrogen, mucous, seawater), but many whale-related mistifications remain; if you want to learn more about them, head to Hartley Bay and get in a southbound boat. When Douglas Channel opens into the wheel of Wright Sound, keep left and enter Whale Channel; wrap around Gil Island (do not follow the *Queen of the North*'s trajectory) until you reach a small finger of south-pointing land, a peninsula so slender you won't distinguish it from Gil Island's forested backdrop until you are almost upon it. That is Whale Point, and built into the trees on that peninsula is Cetacealab.

Cetacealab was born in 2002 after Hermann Meuter, aka Hermann the German, asked the Gitga'at for permission to build and operate a year-round whale research station in their territory.

"I remember when he came to us," Helen Clifton had said to us. "Here was this young German student who said he was in love with whales and he wanted to study them in our waters. We said, we're Killer Whale Clan, we know how important whales are. But first you'll have to give us a presentation about what you want to do. Well, he told us how each humpback whale's tail is like a fingerprint, and that's how you can tell them apart. And he made the women happy because he told us that killer whales are matrilineal, just like we are. Each pod is led by a matriarch and the men never leave her side for as long as she lives. Can you imagine, it took a German to come all the way across the world to show us this. But he said nobody knew much about the whales living this far north. No one knew how many there were, or how they travelled, or what their songs meant. Those were the kinds of things he wanted to study."

Permission granted. Helen's late husband, Johnny Clifton, showed Hermann where he thought the best place for a work/

live whale studio would be, and ten years later Hermann and his ex-wife (but still best friend and co-researcher—another story) Janie Wray were well ensconced as the sole human residents of Gil Island, living in a pair of driftwood cabins that overlooked some of the most prime cetacean habitat in the northern hemisphere. Seventeen pods of orcas chased salmon through their front yard, along with several chattering schools of dolphins and porpoises, the occasional stray minke, fin and grey whale, and a blossoming population of humpback whales who gathered here each summer to gorge on krill, herring, and other small fish.

Each cetacean species' particular set of clicks, moans, groans, wails, rumbles, squeals and screeches were captured by a network of ten underwater hydrophones that fed into a stereo whose speakers played twenty-four hours a day in Cetacealab. Whale Point was, above all, a recording studio with twenty-five square kilometres of surround sound, tracking every song sung between Douglas Channel and Caamaño Sound—the heart, by chance, of the coming tanker routes.

Hermann was a friendly giant of a man with startling blue eyes and an eccentric enthusiasm that gave him a Werner Herzogian air. Janie was a born conversationalist with a quick smile who shifted easily between the roles of graceful, relaxed host and brisk, aggressive whale-chaser.

"Our first summer here," Janie told us, "we counted forty-two humpbacks. That number's been growing constantly. This summer we counted over three hundred. Some of the increase comes from newborns whose mothers bring them here, some of it is because the old-timers are coming back."

"Whales live a long time," Hermann said. "Canadians hunted humpbacks here until the 1960s, so many of the whales who are alive today would remember that time and have been staying away. But word has obviously been spreading that it's safe again. No one is harpooning them anymore." The cold, nutrient-rich waters of the Great Bear Rainforest served a feast of krill, herring, mackerel, and other small fish that humpbacks gorged on for sixteen hours at a time, consuming up to fourteen hundred kilograms a day. "We also think they come here to practise their songs, because there is so little marine traffic," Hermann said. "The canyons here are deep and narrow and lined with rock. They make for great acoustics and create a perfect echo; sometimes we'll hear them sing a song and then pause for a few moments after it's finished. It seems that they are listening to their echo."

Hermann and Janie met while both were working at a killer whale research station called Orcalab, off northern Vancouver Island, in the 1990s. Janie had grown up on the island and held a marine biology degree from Malaspina college; Hermann had nothing but a scuba licence and a Germanic knack for gadgetry (it was Hermann who installed the solar panels and the micro-hydro plant that now powered the Cetacealab); he'd never seen nor heard a whale until he took a year off from university and went backpacking through Canada. During a kayak trip in Johnstone Strait, he saw a pod of orcas, and he recalled, "It hit me like a bag of bricks. I thought this is what I want to do with my life."

At the time, Orcalab was the northernmost point from which humans had studied North America's killer whale populations year-round. Hermann and Janie's initial motivation in setting up Cetacealab was to follow orcas into unfamiliar territory. They quickly identified a stable population of 220 to 230 individuals divided into 17 pods, and learned to recognize each pod by its musical signature. But the burgeoning humpback population, singing songs of much greater complexity, soon grabbed an equal share of their attention.

"Orcas call," Janie said, "humpbacks sing. If an orca's language is this big"—she held her hands close together, "then a humpback's language is *this* big," and she drew her arms wide. "Humpbacks do make short calls—feeding calls, social calls, presong calls, all kinds of signifiers. But when they *sing*, you know it. Each song lasts sixteen to eighteen minutes, and you can break it into very specific phrases that every single whale sings precisely the same way. Where the magic comes in is the song's evolution. Every year a few notes change from one summer to the next, and every single whale adopts the same changes."

After dinner Hermann and Janie took us to the beachfront cabin where she slept, and where the lab's stereo equipment was. They played us a few of the leviathan's groaning sonatas.

"So what does it all mean?"

"We have no idea!" Janie exclaimed, delighted by the mystery.

"All we really can say is that singing is a social behaviour," Hermann said. "For the first months of summer they are here to eat, and they are quiet, maybe making short calls but nothing more. But now the fall has come and it is time to migrate soon; their hormones are kicking in, and they are singing."

Every day, Herman and Janie alternated between staying in the lab and going out in Cetacealab's aluminum research boat. The person who stayed in the lab listened to the speakers for whale chatter, kept an eye out the window for cetacean passersby, chipped away at the endless data streams in need of organizing, and fielded calls from friendly boaters—mostly Gitga'at fishermen—who reported any whale sightings. Whenever a call like that came in, the lab rat relayed the whale's coordinates to the partner on the water.

The morning we tagged along, it was Janie's turn to take the boat out. It was cold and clear, not yet seven in the morning, and she was bundled in bright orange coveralls and a wool toque, an unconscious half-smile on her lips as she scanned the horizon for whale blows. There was a slight bump on the water from a ten-knot breeze coming in from the south and this made it harder to pick blemishes out of the horizon, but she still spotted three of them by the time I'd peeled an orange. Each blow was a few kilometres away; she could tell by their height that two of them belonged to fin whales.

"Fins almost never come into confined waters," she said, wistfully excited. "If it wasn't for this wind I'd go after them, but with the water so bumpy they'll be long gone by the time we get there."

Fin whales were remarkable for the distances over which they communicated, Janie said. Humpbacks could sing to one another from over twenty kilometres apart, but fins sang at a lower frequency, and their voices travelled thousands of kilometres. They could speak to one another from opposite sides of an ocean.

"Dolphins are the most talkative, though," Janie said as we carried on, looking for a whale close enough that we could catch up to it. "They're like the monkeys of the sea. They'll come into an area where humpbacks are lounging and surround them, chirping away at high frequency and wanting to play, and I swear the humpbacks start sounding and acting annoyed."

Two spurts of water rose to the west, near the shore of Campania Island, both lingering in the air despite the breeze. These were close and Janie steered us towards them.

"See how one blow's higher?" Janie said. "That's a mother and calf."

Ilja got his camera ready, struggling to keep a steady hand as we jounced along. I thought of Melville's mist-ery.

Cetacealab had a licence that allowed them to come right beside the whales; the closest you could legally approach a whale on a whale-watching vessel was a hundred metres away, but Janie could get close enough to touch. The water was too choppy for that today, so she slowed us down as we approached the mother and her calf until we fell in ten meters behind them. They appeared to give us no more thought—much less, in fact—than a human would a moth.

"Somehow they can feel your intention," Janie said. "When I first started doing this years ago, I was more anxious and the whales would scatter whenever I got close. Now I'm much more relaxed and they're all over the boat."

The mother was more than ten metres long, her calf perhaps a third that size; they swam slow and straight, slipping just beneath the waves and resurfacing every thirty seconds to blow. Their barnacled grey backs were all that showed; we couldn't see the long, armlike fins that are the humpback's distinguishing feature. Every so often the wind carried the stench of their breath to our noses, until both took one last breath and dove deep to feed, sending their tale flukes into the sky before disappearing under the waves.

Ilja's camera snapped, as did Janie's; both looked at their photos. "That's Sealion," Janie said, "with her first calf. We haven't named him yet." Janie could recognize over a hundred of the humpbacks by looking at their flukes.

Over the next three hours, we cruised from blow to blow, reaching and identifying a dozen humpbacks, Janie recording the name of each and where it was spotted, who it was with, how it was behaving. We were all hoping to see one breach, but none did.

"Why *do* whales breach?" Ilja asked.

"There's a few theories," Janie said. "One is, to knock off the barnacles that grow on their skin, sort of like scratching their backs. It's also reminiscent of a morning stretch; whales sleep for an hour or two at a time—they look like logs floating on the surface—and it's often right after they wake up that we see them breaching. Also it's a sign of health and vitality, so, like the songs, there's probably a display of sexual prowess thing going on. But it's hard to say because no one has actually documented humpback's mating behaviour. We don't know if they mate here, or in the tropics, or in mid-migration. There's so much we don't know it's almost embarrassing! Everything happens underwater, and we don't have submarines. All we have are microphones."

This lack of knowledge frustrated Hermann and Janie even as it motivated them to keep going. Their greatest hope was that their research would eventually yield enough data to prove that the waters around Gil Island provided critical habitat for humpback and orca populations alike; if they could prove that, then maybe they could get the region protected as a marine conservancy.

"Everything we're doing here is towards establishing habitat use," Janie said. "Where do they feed? Where do they mate? Are there hot spots where they congregate for particular reasons? We've noticed over the years that humpback whales form social groups in much the same way people do; they'll have certain groups they only feed with, other groups they only travel with, other groups they sing with. They're like us— the people you have over for dinner might not be the same people you'd want to go out with on a Friday night."

Even if Northern Gateway never went through, hundreds of natural gas-bearing tankers were likely to be plying these waters before the decade was out. "If all those proposals go through," Janie said, "I'm quite certain the whales will leave. What's the point of coming here if they can't hear each other sing?"

We were running low on gas and it was time to get back. *Foxy* was anchored across the channel from Whale Point, in a cove on the north end of Princess Royal Island. Janie dropped us off there and went back to Whale Point. Ilja and I took our dinghy to shore. Another estuary, another salmon stream, but Princess Royal's legendary population of spirit bears continued their boycott of our crosshairs. To compensate, Ilja shot several black bears from point blank range; they were so intent on the fish dashing about their ankles that they didn't mind the paparazzi any more than the humpbacks had.

We dropped in at Cetacealab the next afternoon to say goodbye, and while we were there a call came over the vhf.

Whale Point, Whale Point, Whale Point, this is Maple Leaf, *over.* The *Maple Leaf* was a hundred-foot, century-old wooden schooner, the oldest sailboat on the west coast. These days she was used for high-end ecotours, and just now she was in Caamaño Sound. Her guides had spotted a group of orcas on the south side of Ashdown Island and wanted Cetacealab to know. Janie's eyes grew wide.

"Really?" she cried into the microphone. "Oh that's marvellous!" She called Hermann on the handheld—he was in his own cabin—"Hermann, did you hear that?"

"No."

"Come over here, the *Maple Leaf* has spotted orcas."

Twenty seconds later Hermann was beside us in the lab with a tote bag under his arm. He leaned over the vhf.

"*Maple Leaf*, this is Whale Point," he called out. "Can you tell if they are transients or residents?"

"Yeah...looks like transients, over."

That was why we hadn't heard anything through the hydro-phones. Unlike resident orcas, who ate only fish and called as they hunted, transients ate seals and dolphins and occasion-ally other whales (though never other orcas); they hunted in silence, calling only after a kill. There were other differences, too. Residents kept to a defined range and lived in stable pods, and transients travelled in shifting groups that ranged from California to Alaska. The two groups hated one another and never interacted. They even sounded different. The call of a transient was richer, more sustained than a resident's call, like the difference between an oboe and a clarinet. Sea mammals didn't change their behaviour much if they heard a clarinet, but they panicked if they heard an oboe; Hermann and Janie had filmed dolphins beaching themselves at the sound.

"How can they tell on the *Maple Leaf* whether they're tran-sients or residents," I asked, "without a hydrophone?"

"Transients swim differently," Janie said. "They charge more aggressively through the water, take longer dives, gener-ally move more like hunters. You never see transients lollygag-ging around the way residents sometimes do."

It had been three weeks since any orcas at all had been spotted nearby, an African drought by Whale Point standards. Hermann radioed the *Maple Leaf* once more for their coordi-nates and all but ran out the door.

"How exciting," Janie said, gazing after Hermann like he was going skiing. We listened to the stereo a while longer in case the transients started calling, but the hunting must have been slow; all we heard were the aquarium sounds of bubbling water and shifting pebbles.

All three of us wished we could have joined Hermann, but there was too much else to do. September was almost over.

Ilja and I still had one more rendezvous to keep before we left Gitga'at territory—we were meeting Marven Robinson to look for spirit bears on Gribbell Island (they would elude us, the beasts—our only sighting all summer was of a white apparition, small in the distance, stepping gingerly along the rocky shore of Gribbell on our way to meet Marven; but by the time we turned *Foxy* around so that Ilja could shoot him the spirit fled back into the forest). After that we had many days of navigating through thick fog; we had half a dozen breakdowns to overcome; we had animals and people left to shoot, we had storms to hide from, we had elections to vote in and an oil company to thwart and a climate to stop from sliding at hyperspeed into the Jurassic. There wasn't enough time for any of it.

Yet none of those things mattered. It was two o'clock on a glorious afternoon, and there *was* time enough to get back to *Foxy* and head for Gribbell Island before the sun went down. Janie walked us down to the water where our tender was tied up, and she hugged us goodbye before heading up to the kitchen. She had to start cooking early today, she sighed. David Suzuki was coming for dinner.

THE STORY OF the Great Bear Rainforest is a hopeful one. The return of the humpbacks to the waters surrounding Whale Point was but one, albeit the most obvious, indication of a larger phenomenon: the resilience of nature. Here is living, breathing, splashing, roaring, flapping, biting proof that if you give an ecosystem the slightest of reprieves, it can and will bounce back. Had we visited this place before the 1990s, we would have beheld far more industrial traffic (primarily fishing- and logging-related) and far less wildlife. But over the past twenty years, industry has fallen quiet; that is partly because it extracted all the low-hanging fruit, partly because the price of things like softwood and salmon has plummeted on international markets, and partly because the Great Bear Rainforest Agreement placed the entire region under protection. For these and other reasons, there are a fraction as many fishing boats and logging barges as there once were in these waters— and as a result, the forest and ocean have staged a magnificent comeback. Kitimat has cleaned up its watershed and estuary; abalone are returning to Gitga'at territory; herring are staging a tentative but encouraging comeback in Heiltsuk waters. It is no exaggeration to say that, today, these are some of the richest fishing grounds on earth.

Resilience is built into human nature, too. The First Nations communities here, the Heiltsuk and the Gitga'at and the Haisla and also the ones we didn't have time to visit, the Kitasoo and Owikeno and the Haida and many more, hundreds of societies spread across the coast, the province, and the country, all of them have endured trials that can probably only be understood by the people who have lived them. How would it feel to have your entire country reduced to a few hundred people? How would it feel to be one of the last surviving speakers of English? But now, at least among the communities I met, it seems safe to say the worst is over. There are still troubles to overcome, disagreements to bridge, battles to fight. But if I had to give just one word to Bella Bella and Hartley Bay and Kitamaat, one word that sums up the collective mood, one word that stands above all the emotions competing for attention in those streets and boardwalks, it would be: *optimism*. I don't believe that was the case twenty years ago. With every day that passes, the future matters a little bit more, the past a little less.

It's precarious, of course. All of it. The two-decade window of calm granted to the Great Bear Rainforest is about to be cracked, possibly shattered, by the next wave of industrial development. Asia's markets are calling. Whatever happens to Northern Gateway, hundreds of liquefied natural gas tankers will soon be plying these waters, drowning the humpback's calls, wreaking nobody yet knows what kind of havoc on smaller species like the orca, salmon, and herring. Other industries eager to ship their own commodities will follow, because as we've been told since birth, Canada is a country rich in natural resources, and what choice do we have but to sell them to the highest bidder?

As the minister in charge of those resources said not long ago, "We are at a critical juncture because the global economy is now presenting Canada with an historic opportunity to take full advantage of our immense resources. But we must seize the moment. These opportunities won't last forever."

No, Mr. Joe Oliver, they won't. Opportunities never do. Already, it is looking like the chance to ram Northern Gateway down the Great Bear Rainforest's throat has come and gone. A month after we returned home from our journey, the good minister hinted for the very first time that there might be a problem with Ottawa's dearest pet project. "If we don't get people on side, we don't get the social licence," he said. "We could well get a positive regulatory conclusion from the joint panel that is looking at the Northern Gateway, but if the population is not on side, there is a big problem."

This was a startling, and welcome, rhetorical departure from the man who all but made *environmentalist* a dirty word. The admission that social licence matters should also serve as a beacon of hope for anyone wondering what options there are for change when the laws of the land seem set against them. Make noise. Make lots of noise. Make enough of it, sustain it long enough, and the powers that be will have to listen.

Of course, it would be nice if the noise we made did more than cause "a big problem." We'd also like it to inspire some big solutions.

But it's not like Enbridge or the Harper Administration are giving up on Northern Gateway. They're seeing this thing through. They're keen to show that they've been listening to the concerns of British Columbia's citizens, First Nations and otherwise, which is why in March of 2013 Joe Oliver flew to Vancouver for a special press conference. Standing on a platform in the Port of Vancouver, with a view to Burrard Inlet and the coast mountains behind them, Mr. Oliver announced that he was here to unveil a brand-new "world-class tanker safety system" full of "tanker safety measures" to be implemented via something called the "Safeguarding Canada's Seas and Skies Act."

"What we have to make sure is no pipeline proceeds unless it's safe for the environment and safe for Canadians," Oliver said. "I'm sure British Columbians will absolutely respond to the science and the facts going forward."

The fact was, the only new measure the Act brought forward was to bring Canada's Marine Liability Act into compliance with the 2010 International Convention on Liability and Compensation for Damage. This would do absolutely nothing to help prevent an oil spill, though it would add some money to the kitty when time came to clean one up. Everything else in Oliver's "new" plan, from double-hulled tankers to aerial monitoring systems, had in fact been part of the original plan, the one whose science and facts so many British Columbians were worried about in the first place.

Another thing that didn't change under Oliver's celebrated Act? Vancouver's coast guard station, its marine traffic control centre, and its oil spill response units would all remain closed, as per Bill c-38.

Too bad. They were nearly needed on that sunny March day. In order to bolster the press conference with the proper optics, Oliver had called for the *Burrard Cleaner 9*, Canada's largest oil-spill response vessel, to come in from Victoria and float in the harbour behind him, where it would provide a suitable backdrop. Unfortunately, the *Burrard Cleaner 9* arrived several hours late for its appointment. It got hung up on a sandbar along the way, and almost hit a ferry.

TOP *The author at the helm.*

ABOVE *Ilja Herb awaiting his prey.*

FACING Foxy *and the* Suncrest, *at anchor in Chief Matthews Bay, near the Kitlope.*

ABOVE *A seabus isn't the only way to get from Bella Bella to Shearwater.*

A school of spawning pink salmon near the end of their life's migration.

A mother grizzly with her cubs in the Koeye watershed.

FACING *The Church in Hartley Bay.*

TOP *Teenagers fish from the breakwater protecting Hartley Bay's marina, at the mouth of Douglas Channel.*

ABOVE *Wally Bolton, a Gitga'at fisherman, checks his halibut line at dawn in Douglas Channel.*

TOP *Jessie Housty digging up hellebore roots in the Koeye watershed.*

ABOVE *Strips of sockeye fill a smoke shack in one of Kitamaat's back yards.*

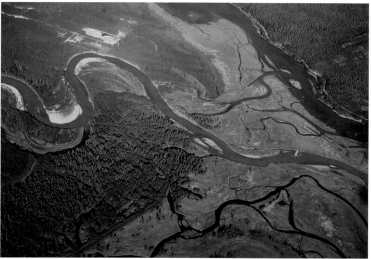

TOP *Three humpback whales splashing and feeding in Bishop Bay, not far from Hartley Bay.*

ABOVE *The Kitimat estuary, at the head of Douglas Channel, is slowly recovering from decades of industrial abuse.*

Contrary to Enbridge's cartoon, islands do exist along the Northern Gateway tanker route.

The entrance to Gardner Canal, where glacial runoff turns the ocean green.

Hereditary Haisla chief and legendary carver Sam Robinson, posing in full regalia for a double exposure. An aerial view of Haisla territory provides the backdrop.

POSTSCRIPT

A<small>T</small> 1:14 in the morning of July 6, 2013, a seventy-two-car train carrying heavy crude from North Dakota exploded into history in the middle of a southern Quebec town called Lac-Mégantic. Operated by Montreal, Maine and Atlantic Railway, a U.S.-based company, the train was bound for a refinery at Saint John, New Brunswick. It had been parked for the night on a hill above town, and left there unattended; shortly after midnight, the brakes holding it in place failed and 45,000 barrels of oil began rolling downhill—slowly at first, but picking up speed and surpassing 100 kilometers per hour by the time it reached the town center, where all but 9 of the train cars flew off the decrepit track, sparked into flame, and turned downtown Lac-Mégantic into a lake of burning oil. Over 30 buildings were incinerated, along with 47 people, many of whom had to be presumed dead because they were vaporized, leaving no remains. It was Canada's deadliest train accident in 150 years.

The tragedy could have been avoided, but its interpretation as proof of North America's need for more pipelines was probably inevitable. Never mind that oil pipelines have caused even deadlier explosions on other continents in recent years;

on ours they have not, and for many people that is the only evidence that matters.

In the immediate aftermath, proponents of the railway and pipeline industries each offered statistics claiming their industry has the better track record. TransCanada, the company behind Keystone XL (which, if built, would likely have piped the oil that exploded in Lac-Mégantic to refineries on the Gulf Coast instead), stated that rail transport is ten times more accident prone than pipelines. Meanwhile, the Association of American Railroads, which keeps tabs on continental shipments, said exactly the opposite was true—according to them, it is rail that is ten times safer than pipelines. Michael Bourqe, President and CEO of the Railway Association of Canada, aimed for middle ground, releasing a public statement in which he allowed that "railways have a higher (albeit very low) chance of an incident but a lower magnitude of release than pipelines."

The discrepancy between the competing statistics is simply a reflection of which years were selected for analysis. Compiling statistics that favour pipelines over trains, or vice versa, is simply a matter of choosing the right time period. Overall, it appears that pipelines do have a better safety record, though the difference is slight in the extreme—each industry boasts a safe-delivery rate of more than 99 per cent.

Still, on a continent that moves over twenty million barrels of oil each day (not to mention natural gas, which is far more explosive), even a 0.001 per cent greater chance of an accident is well worth factoring in. Just ask the residents of Lac-Mégantic. So if our primary goal in transporting energy is to avoid blowing up small towns, then yes, it might be wise to start replacing oil-bearing trains with pipelines. Only let's keep in mind that it was a ruptured pipeline, not a train wreck, that caused some 7000 barrels of oil to flow through the residential streets of another small town called Mayflower, Arkansas, three months before Quebec's disaster. Or that in 2007, an excavator struck Kinder Morgan's pipeline in Burnaby, BC, and sprayed 1500 barrels of crude all over the neighbourhood. No one was hurt in those accidents, but we now have an idea what might have happened had either of those spills caught fire.

The immediate lesson to be drawn from Lac-Mégantic, in other words, is not that we should seek an alternative means of transporting oil. "All modes for transporting oil to markets are inherently dangerous, as the derailment in Lac-Mégantic tragically illustrates," wrote the Communications, Energy, and Paperworkers Union of Canada (which represents 35,000 workers in oil extraction, transport and refining) in testimony submitted to Canada's National Energy Board. "The answer is more stringent regulation, rigorous oversight, and full transparency—whatever the mode of delivery."

Montreal, Maine, and Atlantic Railway was far from the only company operating in a regulatory vacuum. Two weeks after Lac-Mégantic, Transport Canada acknowledged as much when it belatedly issued new rules forbidding trains bearing dangerous goods from being left unwatched on a main track, and requiring at least two crew members to be aboard during operation (Lac-Mégantic's fatal train only had one). Hopefully those rules are followed up with others to ensure that train cars filled with oil are built strong enough not to spill it, and that the tracks they run over aren't falling apart.

At least that would be a good place to start. But there is a deeper point to be made here than the need for better regulations. The rules that would have prevented Lac-Mégantic's conflagration were all brought to Transport Canada's attention long before July 6, 2013. Those recommendations were ignored, just as they've been ignored or abandoned elsewhere in the energy sector—and, increasingly, across the industrial board—because no one in a position to act on them dared to hamper economic growth. The anguish of Lac-Mégantic's survivors will undoubtedly be compounded by the knowledge of how easily the derailment could have been prevented, if only we'd taken the time to manage that growth more carefully.

The point, then—or rather, the question—has to do with growth itself. Namely: at what point do the costs of growing our economy outweigh the benefits? With a handful of notable exceptions, no politician or influential economist is willing to take this question seriously. Seeing as we live on a demonstrably finite planet, the pursuit of endless economic growth seems like a risky paradigm to follow. And yet we pursue it more doggedly today than ever, fuelling it with oil every step of the way. North Americans have the good fortune to occupy one of the least crowded corners of this increasingly populated planet, but even here, with all this space and in the midst of an unexpected oil glut, the dangers of reckless growth rear their head from time to time. With that in mind, it's worth looking beyond the obvious rules that could have saved Lac-Mégantic, and focusing on why they weren't there in the first place.

It's no secret that improved technology and quadrupled oil prices have delivered a twenty-first-century boom to North American oil producers. In Canada, the boom is concentrated in the tar sands; our American analogue lies in North Dakota's Bakken field—the source of Lac-Mégantic's forty-eight-hour blaze—where the oil is trapped in shale instead of sand. Until recently, there was no cost-effective way to suck oil from rock. Now, the United States Geological Survey estimates that 7.4 billion barrels of oil are recoverable from the Bakken field. And just like in Alberta, nobody's waiting for pipelines to be approved before they get the process started. Not when there are other ways to bring the oil to market.

In 2009, Canada's train network moved 500 carloads of oil; by 2013 that figure had risen to 140,000 carloads. The U.S. has followed a similar trajectory, jumping from 9,500 carloads in 2008 to almost 400,000 in 2013. Anyone who paid attention to the situation was aware that both the rail networks and the train cars rolling over them were ageing and dangerously unsupervised. In fact, that was the pipeline industry's argument all along: reject our pipeline applications, they said, and the oil will just be moved by rail instead. It's already happening. The U.S. State Department said much the same thing in a March 2013 report on Keystone XL, in which it concluded: "Limitations on pipeline transport would force more crude oil to be transported via other modes of transportation, such as rail."

Levelling off our oil production—not stopping it, not slowing it down, but simply preventing it from accelerating—seems not to be a policy option on either side of the border. When Canada's Natural Resources Minister said "I don't think anybody feels that [trains] could be a substitute for pipelines," in response to the State Department's Keystone report, he wasn't arguing for stabilized growth or improved train regulations or any other radical alternatives; he was saying new pipelines are the only option. And he was saying so not because pipelines are safer, but because they're cheaper. Apparently, it is inevitable that so long as demand exists, oil producers will pull oil from the ground as fast as technologically possible, and there is nothing the people who write our laws can do to stop them. Until forty-seven innocents lost their lives, they couldn't even make rail operators hire a single person to keep an eye on their parked trains.

It's easy, of course, to blame governments and corporations whose executives we'll never meet, and whose competing priorities we'll never fully grasp. Private oil production is a function of public demand—we all share responsibility for Lac-Mégantic, just as *Exxon Valdez*, Deepwater Horizon, and Enbridge's Kalamazoo spill were to some extent collective mistakes. Who couldn't carpool more often, or write their member of parliament every once in a while to let them know that, say, public transit matters? The truth is we're all involved in this. Even when we think all we're doing is nothing, what we're actually doing is voting for business as usual. And that vote is another big part of the problem; any politician who tries to increase our energy costs or decrease the hyper-convenience of modernity runs the risk of losing the next election.

But the fact remains that there are people and institutions whose job it is to keep an eye on things the rest of us lack the time and training to monitor. The state of a train track, the integrity of a pipeline, the viability of a tanker route—those things, yes, but also, perhaps especially, bigger picture stuff like the impact of our collective behaviour on the ecosystems that sustain us. Like how we're going to power our cities when the current boom busts and fossil fuels run low. Like how we might at least *start* to rethink growth and, ultimately, retool our economies to service a higher goal than consuming more of everything. That may have worked for the last century or two, but it's hard to see it working for the next.

Lac-Mégantic offers a chilling parable for human civilization's current path. But not all runaway trains have to end in flames. If we abandon the illusion that someone wise is at the helm, if we jump aboard ourselves and put the right people in charge, we might find that it's not too late to switch lines and avoid catastrophe. What better way is there to honour the dead?

ACKNOWLEDGEMENTS

A FEW DAYS before this book went to press, a late-night blaze broke out in Bella Bella that destroyed the most familiar building in town. One day, the Heiltsuk had a grocery store, post office, liquor store and library; the next, they didn't. The legendary Koeye Café, where I spent many hours chatting with fascinating people, reading great books, poaching Internet, drinking coffee and generally testing the limits of my hosts' hospitality, was reduced to ash. Qqs headquarters and all their records went with it.

There was no malicious intent behind the fire—it resulted from an accident, not arson—and nobody was hurt. No doubt all will be rebuilt in time. But in a community as small and isolated as Bella Bella, this was no small disaster. It offered a harshly literal reminder that this part of the world has plenty of fires in need of dousing. The Heiltsuk need no such reminders, but sometimes, I think, us outsiders do.

Thanks, Bella Bella, and all of you who live there, for being so good to Ilja and me when you had so many other demands on your time. Same thanks to Hartley Bay and Kitamaat. Thanks for putting up with us and occasionally putting us up, for letting two strangers hang around for days and weeks and pester you with questions and cameras, for welcoming us into your homes and wild spaces and letting us try to relate a few stories that are rightfully yours to tell.

Thank you, Chris Filardi, for making the introduction that got this whole project rolling, and for helping us believe in ourselves after it was well underway. Thanks, Larry Jorgenson and the Housty family and your extended clan at Qqs and Koeye, for letting us explore your world. Thank you, Chief Harvey Humchitt, for giving us the nod and teaching me how to cook and eat crab. Thank you, Michael Reid and Sarah Stoner for rafting up with us in a tight spot, and introducing us to many great people, and telling stories late into the night. Thanks Bruce Hill and Gerald Amos for showing us the place you helped save. Thanks Janie and Hermann for sharing your magic with us. And thanks, Marven Robinson, for that time at Riorden Creek.

In Kitimat, Kelly Marsh and his family were great friends to have. Thanks for your insight and time, Kelly; thanks also to Murray Minchin, John Chapman, and Bracket Bob, for your various invaluable efforts. Thanks Garry Appelt for coming all that way just so we could see our subject from above.

Thanks to the many people and institutions who have devoted much of their lives to the cause of the Great Bear Rainforest. At Raincoast, Chris Darimont and Brian Falconer were helpful allies. At Sierra Club BC, Caitlyn Vernon shared a library's worth of information and contacts. Huge thanks also to everyone at the Dogwood Initiative, Living Oceans Society, Pacific Wild, and Douglas Channel Watch. Thanks to Eric Peterson, Christina Munck, and the Hakai Beach Institute for offering such lovely safe harbour.

And of course, none of this would have happened without our friends, family, and wide community of well-wishers who believed in our improbable notion from the start, and pitched in so that we could buy survival suits and new sails and food and a hundred other things. That outpouring of love and encouragement and material support blew my mind, and Ilja's too. Special thanks to Shawn Morris and April Trigg for bringing our fundraisers to life.

Big thanks to Pato, who donated many precious hours of time and expertise to help us get *Foxy* shipshape before departure. Thank you Elke Herb, for letting us turn your house into a chaotic headquarters, and for feeding us so often and so well in those final hectic weeks.

Thank you Carmine Starnino, my editor at *Reader's Digest*, for signing on early, fighting on our behalf, and working so hard with me on the first piece of writing to come out of our trip. Thank you Trena White, my book editor, for instantly saying yes, and later for taking time out of early motherhood to help me bring this book to life.

Lastly, thanks to the team at Harbour Publishing, who swept in to lift Douglas & McIntyre from the ashes and ensured that many more books than just this one will see the light of day. I don't think any of you have slept in half a year. I know I'm not alone in feeling immensely grateful for your efforts.

INDEX